Streams of Experience

Streams of Experience

REFLECTIONS ON THE HISTORY AND PHILOSOPHY OF AMERICAN CULTURE

JOHN J. MC DERMOTT

Foreword by Norman Grabo

THE UNIVERSITY OF MASSACHUSETTS PRESS

AMHERST

Copyright © 1986 by The University of Massachusetts Press
All rights reserved
Printed in the United States of America
First paperback edition, 1987
Designed by Barbara Werden
Set in Linoterm Sabon at University of Massachusetts Press
Printed by Cushing-Malloy, Inc. and bound by John H. Dekker & Sons

Library of Congress Cataloging-in-Publication Data
McDermott, John J. (John Joseph), 1932–
Streams of experience.
Bibliography: p.
Includes index.
1. United States—Civilization. 2. United States—
Civilization—Philosophy. I. Title.
E169.1.M4973   1986   191   85–16494
ISBN 0–87023–496–X (alk. paper)
ISBN 0–87023–597–4 (pbk.)

For

TARA MC DERMOTT

1961–

Our Fifth Born

Generous Spirit, Elegant Dreamer,

and Creative Designer

CONTENTS

FOREWORD

The fifteen essays and addresses before you were composed at different times, for varying occasions. A mere glance at their titles suggests what?—range? diversity? eccentricity? They are certainly not systematic, as philosophy is sometimes said to be systematic: cultural immortality, the child in the twenty-first century, the importance of Emerson, death, transiency, loneliness, urban aesthetics, the handicapped, cultural literacy, classical American philosophy. Of course they gather into an order, a movement, and thereby something of a direction—foundations permit journeys and quests, explorations that eventuate in appraisals, assays of the heft and beauty of experience. That much is clear from the table of contents. What quickly becomes clearer from the essays themselves is another order of conceptual integrity, a coherence both of subject and function in this very reflective and reflexive book.

Reflections, of course, both dazzle and disturb. As deep thought, rumination, inward pursuit, the pause that confesses—more or less as John McDermott calls this collection "reflections"—there is often the dazzling detail, arresting expression, the lightning perception of connectedness that one sensed before, perhaps, but never saw quite so clearly. As McDermott bounces his light off the objects we know around us, the experiences we have shared with varying degrees of alertness, the effect is like sunshine bouncing off a mirror, or off an approaching windshield on a highway. If reflections imply philosophical musing, they also denote a visual and optical property, a mode of perception as physical as it is rational.

Consider the Vietnam War Veterans' Memorial with its reflective surface in which the viewers find themselves embedded in the same rock that names the American victims of that war. Or Edmund Wilson in his *Upstate* journals, writing of his past, looking up at "the old framed map on the opposite wall. The glass reflects and just contains the window behind me now—the white curtains, the June green of the lilac bushes, with myself, head and shoulders, at the bottom, dim but rather darkly ruddy, the line of the mat going through my chest." A figured mirror reflecting a window that itself reflects as it opens onto the world, a darkly ruddy self in between. Like Wilson's friend Vladimir Nabokov—especially in the patterned reflections of *Pnin*—John McDermott erects reflections as shiny and aspiring as the high-rise structures of modern Houston, structures that glare and dazzle, containing what they face and throwing it back. As apparently the case with much glass-wall architecture, intentionality signifies less than effect. These essays constitute what Julia Bader calls in her exquisite study of Nabokov, a crystal land—a multifaceted reflector, a kind of house of mirrors defining identity by patterned indirection.

"Being in the world is not a cakewalk," says McDermott in chapter 9, but what it means to be in the world is nonetheless the central subject of these essays. Who is that self between the figured map of the past and the transparent and fragile but nonetheless clearly demarked future? In an obvious sense, of course, that self is McDermott, I, you yourself. But between the past that reflects us and no longer exists, and the future that reflects us equally but does not yet exist, what then are you and I but figments between two nonbeings? a kind of mental hologram whose "being" is merely a function of perception, of consciousness? William Faulkner caught the frustration, perhaps the insanity, of that perspective in *As I Lay Dying* in 1930. Darl Bundren, who will end up in a state institution at Jackson, worries the perplexity in the fact of his mother's death:

> In a strange room you must empty yourself for sleep. And before you are emptied for sleep, what are you. And when you are emptied for sleep you are not. And when you are filled with sleep you never were. I dont know what I am. I dont know if I am or not. . . . As since sleep is is-not and rain and wind are *was*, [a wagon] is not. Yet the wagon *is*, because when the wagon is *was*, Addie Bundren will not be. And Jewel *is*, so Addie Bundren must be. And then I must be, or I could not empty myself for sleep in a strange room. And so if I am not emptied yet, I am *is*.

Of course McDermott's Self in these essays is awake and full, more robust and Promethean than the fragile Darl, a ruddier and less tenebrous *is*.

For that being in the world is the energetic and vital bridge between past and future as well as the convergence of their reflections. McDermott remarks early on the pervasive homelessness of the American experience, a characteristic perceived by Tocqueville as a kind of unrooted restlessness. No doubt the American Self is unrooted and restless, but the result has not been aimless wandering so much as a directed journey westward, what McDermott calls an odyssey. For Homer that odyssey was both a movement out and a movement back, a great circle in the mind whose end is its beginning. With greater geographical scope, the American odyssey, too, by going in one direction suffers a return, executes a rondure of the mind, and settles finally where civilization began. Walt Whitman celebrated and sang that odyssey in his "Passage to India" in 1871. Whitman hymns modern technology—the Suez Canal, the Transatlantic Cable, and finally the Transcontinental Railroad that brought East to West, not to a terminus, however, but once again to the Pacific Ocean with its direct access to India. America in this poem is a bridge, a passage to more than India; it is, this latest technological marvel,

> Passage indeed O soul to primal thought,
> Not lands and seas alone, thy own clear freshness,
> The young maturity of brood and bloom,
> To realms of budding bibles.
>
> O soul, repressless, I with thee and thou with me,
> Thy circumnavigation of the world begin,
> Of man, the voyage of his mind's return,
> To reason's early paradise,
> Back, back to wisdom's birth, to innocent intuitions,
> Again with fair creation.

Like Whitman's, McDermott's American odyssey brings us back to clear freshness and budding bibles. Past and future conjoin, not in Emerson's transparent eyeball but in Wilson's—and McDermott's—"dim but rather darkly ruddy" presence.

A weakness in that ruddy bridge, that Golden Gate "to reason's early paradise," is that, so curved upon itself, its end in its beginnings, it becomes a conceptual equivalent to the wonderful engineering feat exposed by the Illinois engineer George W. G. Ferris at the World's Columbian Exposition in Chicago in 1891, potent with implication but fit mainly for amusement. It implies a solipsism and political paralysis. McDermott begins this book, therefore, with a discussion of the archetypal Ferris wheel—Plato's allegory of the cave—yet another odyssey of the soul out and up to truth, and then back down and in to the world of shadows. Out goes the philosopher; down comes the poet—dazzled in both directions by light and darkness. Whitman, who died the year after Ferris's wheel began turning would not, I think, have accepted Plato's image of the poet as the self descending from a view of ultimate truth, goodness, and beauty. Certainly Emerson, who set Whitman to boiling back in the 1850s did not, and it is to Emerson that McDermott turns next. Lecturing on "The Poet" in 1844, Emerson drew a distinction (in that highly Platonic essay) between poets and mystics. "Here is the difference," he wrote, "betwixt the poet and the mystic, that the last nails a symbol to one sense, which was a true sense for a moment, but soon becomes old and false. For all symbols are fluxional; all language is vehicular and transitive, and is good, as ferries and horses are, for conveyance, not as farms and houses are, for homestead. Mysticism consists in the mistake of an accidental and individual symbol for an universal one." Perhaps not every voyager who avoids the mystic's mistake deserves to be called Poet, but it seems that something like Emerson's faith in flux and the brave willingness of all the American scholars McDermott so much admires—particularly William James, Josiah Royce, and John Dewey—to face the condition of a fluxional nature are the ways out of Plato's poential solipsism, and the grounds for social action. Ideologies, like mysticism, err by investing momentary symbols with absolute value. McDermott refuses to make that error, and is willing to take the risks involved.

The United States is at present undergoing a fit of educational complaining, pulse taking, and prescribing for the future. One former secretary of education tells us we are *A Nation at Risk* and establishes an "Imperative for Educational Reform" at the elementary and high-school level. A new secretary of education laments the loss of a sense of Western cultural continuity and prescribes a program *To Reclaim a Legacy* by a return to the study of great works of the past at the secondary and college level. And a committee of the Association of American Colleges declares American college majors to be essentially moribund, putting the blame on an irresponsible professoriate, and arguing in part that the "spirit of freedom and individual enterprise has supported non-accountability and underwritten a great deal of irresponsibility" (*Chronicle of Higher Education*, Feb. 13, 1985, p. 28). To each of these there are angry rebuttals on varieties of grounds—economic, social, political, and idealistic. One remembers that the Harvard class of 1671 simply hung its senior class tutor by his collar from a nail in the closet and ran away because he refused to teach the "right" books. The argument about being rightly in the American world is a very old one, and perhaps being at risk is the right way to be.

The essays that follow do speak, sometimes explicitly, mostly by implication, to many of the current educational concerns. Sometimes, as in the plea for "Cultural Literacy," they verge toward the programmatic, but on the whole they avoid the tendency of much recent and undoubtedly influential educational thought to concentrate on particular programs, courses, and sequences of study—the kind of thought that produced the time/motion efficiencies of discipline Michel Foucault reminds us of in *Discipline and Punish*. The problem of Emerson's American Scholar—his Man Thinking—is essentially McDermott's problem, how to use the past without becoming entrapped in it, how to make culture a tool for amelioration and improvement. If man enlightened does indeed eventually have to descend back into Plato's cave, McDermott prefers to emphasize the upward thrust, the breaking of chains, letting go, escaping the idols of Baconian invention, and Bacon with them. Everywhere in these essays there is casting off—casting off of time, of the chains of thought, of physical and spiritual handicaps, of habit, even of life. Founded on the vital pluralism of James and Dewey, McDermott's past reflects a future as vivid in its ameliorating possibilities as Shelley's "dome of many-colored glass." But this is a dome inside of which we sit, watching the play of reflections—Nietzsche's "live dangerously" glances at Auschwitz and Hiroshima, Walter Mitty flirts with A. R. Luria's Soldier Zasetsky, Marcus Aurelius beams upon Willy Loman, Martin Luther and Susan Sontag shutter at one another, John Winthrop faces, indirectly, the Great Sleeping Sickness of 1916–27, Biafra glowers at Karl Marx, and Chaucer peers at the great glass fronts of Houston and the West. Maria Montessori glares at Camus, and Dylan Thomas sparkles before B. F. Skinner. Lots of dazzle, lots of glare.

The surprise of these essays is partly what one must find charming in them, agree or not with their propositions. That is why their final movement toward questions of aesthetics and the experience of the world around us is so right. Edgar Allan Poe, with his infamous prescience, had Nabokov's crystal land dead right. One could argue, as Poe did himself most strongly, that the experience of beauty has with intellect or conscience "only collateral relations. It has no dependence, unless incidentally, upon either Duty or *Truth*." At base, of course, Poe believed no such thing, and in "The Rationale of Verse" (1843) he tried, as Jonathan

Edwards had a full century earlier, to express his real thought upon the subject, laying it (again like Edwards) on the back of Francis Hutcheson's famous principle of Unity in Variety. "It is sufficient," says Poe, "that man derives enjoyment from his perception of equality. Let us examine a crystal. We are at once interested by the equality between the sides and between the angles of one of its faces; the equality of the sides pleases us, that of the angles doubles the pleasure." As he proceeds, it is clear that Poe's mathematical equalities have their moral and ethical implications as well. For what are reflections but optical equalities, duplications of images and originals, multiplied identities? McDermott reflects like the equal sign of an equation. The figures to either side of that equal sign may differ in outward shape, but they are identical in value and function. In the mirror of McDermott's mind, the incidental and the trivial have as much use as the great and established, which is what gives that mind and its thought such vitality.

Being in the world may not be a cakewalk, but these essays do make it dance. McDermott calls them "an effort to wander reflectively over our experience." Like Whitman he ties the architects of the mind to the budding bibles in our own, a perpetual renewal and celebration as well as an advance upon the future. At the beginning of the eighteenth century, William Byrd of Westover duly recorded in his diary, "Because I could not walk, I danced." He meant merely that rain confined him to indoor calisthenics instead of his usual stroll. But there is poetry in the play of those words and dance in the play of McDermott's ideas. We need not, like Whitman's follower William Carlos Williams in "Danse Russe"

> dance naked, grotesquely
> before my mirror
> waving my shirt round my head
> and singing softly to myself.

Perhaps it is enough for our dance to witness the reflections of these essays bouncing between the framed and mapped past and the window of the future, finding ourselves made darker, ruddier, and more distinct by them.

NORMAN S. GRABO
Chapman Professor of English
University of Tulsa

PREFACE

Reflection is native and constant.
JOHN DEWEY, "The Need for a Recovery of Philosophy"

Ralph Waldo Emerson was a profoundly reflective person, but he took it as a personal responsibility to share those reflections in a public way by virtue of addresses, lectures, and a series of published essays. I believe that philosophers should more often emulate the activities of Emerson. This is not to bypass and certainly not to denigrate the need and importance of technical philosophy, the results of which are circulated almost exclusively among one's philosophical peers. To the contrary, I hold that such inquiry at the ground of philosophical thought is salutary in itself. Nonetheless, occasionally we should attempt to draw out the implications of our philosophical work as directed toward a wider and more varied audience. It is in that sense that I wish to work in the tradition of Emerson.

The present volume is a second effort of this kind. The first, *The Culture of Experience: Philosophical Essays in the American Grain*, appeared ten years ago. The intervening time has brought us within short reach of the penultimate decade of both a century and a millennium. The year 2000 has become a watchword, a slogan, and a reason to invoke prospective planning programs on all fronts. We have been saturated with talk of the future in both its foreboding and promissory sense. The future, however, does not exist as such. Only the present exists, laden and laced with the accrued wisdom, foibles, and disasters of the past. Any sense of experience of the present which does not embrace the lessons and learning of the past is foolhardy and dangerous to human survival. Yet the present has a forward reach, an awareness that more is to come, however vague it may be in our imagination. We are at our best when we both embrace the past and live on the edge of our experiences, tilted toward a new day and new possibilities.

It is not easy for us to sustain this double-barreled sensitivity on the one hand to the history of our experience, personal and collective, and on the other to the potentiality of experience in the future. William James once cited Kierkegaard "to the effect that we live forwards, but we understand backwards."[1] A major question confronting us is whether our understanding of the past can be more than mere retrospection. Can this understanding be carried with us as a living dimension in the way in which we build ourselves into the future? The first three chapters of this book, in Section I, have that intention precisely in mind. I scour both the European and American pasts for selected figures whose thought constitutes a paradigmatic shift in our consciousness. These thinkers, by no means exhaustive of the possible roster, force us to confront our own experience in a more reflective and less naive way. I read them as dramatic samples of the power of written philosophical wisdom to effect a salutary change in our awareness of the human condition.

The alternating wisdom of the past and the sense of obligation to the future is the gathering locus of the four essays in Section II. The cultural touchstone here is America, its journey from the seventeenth century to the present and its controversial role in our global future. I attempt to sort out the richer contentions in American culture from its often seamy and self-preening pose on the world stage. In my view, the bequest of America is crucial to the next century, assuming it takes the form of an articulation and institutionalization of our wisest positions, that is, meliorism, pluralism, positive provincialism, the avoidance of closure, and a commitment to the affairs of time as sacred. The history of America is an accurate cameo version, both actually and symbolically, of the forthcoming make-up of global culture. It is an obvious historical fact that America has not always been loyal to its own most profound traditions. It is also true, however, that the history of America and the history of American thought have frequently displayed an awareness of the cultural and political characteristics most congenial to the development of a creatively human future, globally experienced. I attempt to sort out the considerable resource of American insight from its frequent ineptness and violation of its own wisdom.

In Section III, I seek to show that philosophical generalizations, if rooted in experience, can withstand the test of applicability to concrete personal, social, and institutional settings. To this end I focus on events, things, and beliefs which make up the way that we live our lives. Despite the thickness and complexity, for good or ill, of our daily living by virtue of media, sound, shape, texture, sight, color, and situation, it is still possible for us to weave a continuous reflective thread throughout this maze of perceptions, affections, and experiences.

The flow of human experience alternates between the habitual and the personal. Most often our experiences seem vague, even inchoate. It is as if we were carried by a stream, sometimes being jetsam, seemingly discarded by the rush of events, whereas other times we are but flotsam, floating disconnected from our roots, our home, and our thoughts.

Yet, periodically our experiences force themselves upon us and demand awareness, retrospection, and evaluation. Such personal response is not learned by rote, for it assumes the capacity to diagnose the potential richness in all of our experience. This book has as its intention to assist the reader in his or her effort to plumb the streams of experience as they convulse us in a distinctively American way, our way, for better or for worse. The inspiration here then, is Emerson, for whom not the literal but the symbolical character of life is the source of our humanity. In a paraphrase of Immanuel Kant, I focus here on not only what should we know but also on what should we do?

The writings gathered in this book are reflective steps along the way, loci of concern which point to possibilities, dangers, and the fabric of the world in which we find ourselves. None of these pieces is final in any scientific or methodological sense of that word. In this, I follow William James, who cites the unsung American thinker Benjamin Blood as saying, "There is no conclusion. What has been concluded, that we might conclude in regard to it?"[2] Consequently, I regard all of these pieces as tentative, reaching, and the results of philosophical reflection upon experiences undergone or empirically informed hunches. In spite of this tentativeness, all of them confront data, hard data—the experience of the author, of others who tell tales and of human beings in the world who communicate in a variety of ways. The purposeful hope of these writings is to challenge, enrich, question, and dignify the human odyssey.

If one were to say, "What is happening?"—a contemporary version of *Quo vadis?*—the response would most likely be as follows: the bomb, population, cities, pollution, schools, children, the handicapped, community, violence, the end of the century, America, death, always death. These writings talk about such things. Perhaps they can help others when they talk about such things.

JOHN J. MC DERMOTT
College Station, Texas
January 1985

ACKNOWLEDGMENTS

Many of these essays were first read as public lectures to audiences here in the United States and in Europe. Frequently the response of the audience was very helpful in both a critical and a suggestive way. I thank those many people who have assisted me in my work. I am grateful also to the original publishers of some of these essays for permission to include them in this book, and to my anonymous prepublication readers for the University of Massachusetts Press.

I have benefited from the perceptive criticism of these essays by Peter Manicas, Alan Rosenberg, Gary Brodsky, John Lachs, Roger Asselineau, Richard Pruitt, Robert Solomon, Raymond McDermott, Manuel Davenport, Marise McDermott, Gérard Deledalle, and Thelma Lavine. Encouragement and advice on the publication of this book was provided by Donald McQuade and Robert McDermott, both of whom offered sage advice on the choice of title. Careful and creative editorial assistance came from Alden Turner, Greg Moses, Gerald Galgan, and especially Giles Gunn, each of whom devoted considerable time and skill to improving the manuscript. James Campbell prepared a detailed, critical copyediting of the manuscript and submitted countless creative suggestions, some of which corrected my errors. I am grateful to my editor, Richard Martin, and to the project editor, Pam Campbell, for their support and care in shepherding this book to publication.

I am grateful to the Association of Former Students at Texas A & M University for awarding me a Faculty Development leave and to Dean Clinton Phillips for his indefatigable concern for scholarship and for providing the impetus so that faculty have time to reflect and to write.

The preparation of this manuscript from my end was the work of Pat Bond, my research assistant. Loyal to a fault, she is both flawless and genial in her management of the details necessary to achieve the highest quality in the submission of a book-length manuscript. I am especially grateful to her for final copyediting, textual research, proofreading, and for preparing the index.

As in all of my work, the most creative support comes from my wife, Virginia Picarelli McDermott. She is critical without carping and provides the human touchstone by which I attempt to measure the integrity of my judgments about the nectar of experience. I am extremely fortunate and grateful to have such an affectionate companion of some thirty-five years as is Virginia, who shares my life and my work.

*

I am grateful to the original publishers for permission to reprint the following essays:

Columbia University Press, for "Spires of Influence: The Importance of Emerson for Classical American Philosophy," in *History, Religion and Spiritual Democracy: Essays in Honor of Joseph L. Blau*, ed. Maurice Wohlgelernter, © 1980, Columbia University Press.

Rice Studies for "The Promethean Self and Community in the Philosophy of William James" and "Transiency and Amelioration: An American Bequest for the New Millennium" (Fall 1980). By permission of Rice University Studies.

Teachers College Record for "America: The Loneliness of the Quest" (Winter 1983).

Journal of Philosophy for "Classical American Philosophy: A Reflective Bequest to the Twenty-First Century" (November 1984).

Texas Humanist for "The Inevitability of Our Own Death: The Celebration of Time as a Prelude to Disaster" (April 1981) and "Glass Without Feet: Dimensions of Urban Aesthetics" (January/February 1984).

American Montessori Society Bulletin for "Do Not Bequeath a Shamble: The Child in the Twenty-First Century," 1980. Paper presented at the AMS 20th Anniversary Seminar, AMS, 150 Fifth Avenue, New York City, New York 10011.

National Society for the Study of Education for "Cultural Literacy: A Time for a New Curriculum," *The Humanities in Pre-Collegiate Educa-*

tion, pt. 2 of the Eighty-third Yearbook of the National Society for the Study of Education, ed. Benjamin Ladner (Chicago: University of Chicago Press, 1984).

California State College at Bakersfield for "Isolation as Starvation: John Dewey and a Philosophy of the Handicapped," from *A New Challenge to the Educational Dream: The Handicapped,* 1981.

American Studies International for "The Renascence of Classical American Philosophy," 1982.

I am also grateful to Michael Cole and Basic Books for permission to reprint from A. R. Luria, *The Man with a Shattered World* (New York: Basic Books, 1972), pp. 46–49.

EDITORIAL NOTES ON THE TEXT

Where citations or texts have been occasionally repeated, I have cross-referenced the material in question to other chapters in this book. I have made every effort to keep such repetitions to a bare minimum, and the few which remain I have regarded as essential to the flow of the chapter in question. For references to the writings of James, Royce, and Dewey, I have used either my own editions, published by The University of Chicago Press, or where appropriate, the critical edition of James's work published by Harvard University Press and the critical edition of Dewey's work published by Southern Illinois University Press. Again, where I found it significant, I have placed in the text the dates of the original publication of many of the works cited. Readers who seek out either my editions or those of Harvard and Southern Illinois will find all of the original publication information.

I have made every effort to avoid any male chauvinist language in my own writing. Most of the texts cited are old-fashioned on this matter. I apologize for the constant sexist appellations in those texts, but they cannot be reconstructed. Let us assume that when "man" is used, I, at least, have in mind men and women, equally.

One

SOME PHILOSOPHICAL FOUNDATIONS

The consciousness of each person has a studied obviousness to its makeup. Costume, song, cuisine, ritual, liturgy, and social and political mores constitute the way in which we think, behave, believe, and hope. For some of us, the historical roots of this apparent obviousness have a tantalizing hold on our imagination. How did we come to be this way or that way? Each of the major modern civilizations can trace its lineage far back into the storied past of prehistory, history, and the events subsequent to the beginning of global consciousness. Civilizations are not so much superior, one to the other, as they are distinctive, different, and an embodiment of one or more of the many divergent strategies for becoming and being human.

The essays in this section focus on the master paradigmatic figures of Western philosophy and their contributions to the shifts in collective consciousness which occur epochally in the history of any great civilization. The European strand precedes that of the American and so we discuss Plato, Augustine, Descartes, Kant, Nietzsche, and James before we concentrate on the role of Emerson and James, once more, as partial founders of our contemporary consciousness.

Strictly speaking, all of the thinkers of the past should be included in an assessment of how we have come to be the way we are. One could argue for the inclusion of John Locke and Jean Jacques Rousseau as rich deposits of our national consciousness. To be truthful, I have chosen those thinkers who have stung me or who have forced me to move the fixed furniture of my domesticated mind, sometimes liberating me from the tired excrescence of habituation and routine. For me, these historical cameos are gateways to a richer understanding of my American past, that is, my human past. These historical sorties, of course, are but a beginning.

1 The Cultural Immortality of Philosophy as Human Drama

For it is owing to their wonder that men both now begin and at first began to philosophize; they wondered originally at the obvious difficulties, then advanced little by little and stated difficulties about the great matters, e.g. about the phenomena of the moon and those of the sun and of the stars, and about the genesis of the universe. And a man who is puzzled and wonders thinks himself ignorant (whence even the lover of myth is in a sense a lover of Wisdom, for the myth is composed of wonders); therefore since they philosophized in order to escape from ignorance, evidently they were pursuing science in order to know, and not for any utilitarian end. And this is confirmed by the facts; for it was when almost all the necessities of life and the things that make for comfort and recreation had been secured, that such knowledge began to be sought. Evidently then we do not seek it for the sake of any other advantage; but as the man is free, we say, who exists for his own sake and not for another's, so we pursue this as the only free science, for it alone exists for its own sake.

ARISTOTLE, "Metaphysics"

I. INTRODUCTION

The history of philosophy in Western civilization is a vast intellectual map characterized by periods of speculative explosions followed by larger periods of absorption and redress. If we accept the common wisdom that Western civilization began with the Greeks, then the paramount role of philosophy is obvious, for philosophical speculation was the formative dimension of Greek civilization. Philosophy is the mother of most of the intellectual and academic disciplines as we now know them. Rhetoric, logic, the sciences, the social sciences, economics, and politics all trace their lineage to philosophy. And Western theology would be bare bones if it were not for philosophical ideas. Indeed, as late as the eighteenth century, scientists were actually philosophers. Mathematics and physics were brought into being by philosophers—as witness the invention of the calculus, an attempted philosophical resolution of the problem of infinity. If, in the twentieth century, the sciences contend that they are independent of philosophical ideas, we can still point to the work of Niels Bohr and Werner Heisenberg, who were profoundly influenced by philosophy and wrote philosophical treatises. Quantum mechanics is as much a philosophical hypothesis as a scientific one, as is the biology which points to the molecular structure of beings.

The influence of philosophers throughout the centuries is dazzling and way out of proportion to the number of philosophers recognized in the canon of important thinkers. We note Aristotle's organization of the intellectual disciplines and his pioneering work in biology and astronomy. Of significance also is Francis Bacon's stress on the inductive method and Descartes's invention of analytic geometry. The doctrine of toleration, so central to our democratic form of government, traces to Locke, whereas Western civilization owes much to the defense of liberty by John Stuart Mill. Virtually the only interesting theories of education trace to philosophers: Plato, Rousseau, Herbart, Montessori and, above all, John Dewey. The major reason why contemporary educational theory is so utterly boring is precisely because it has been shorn of philosophical imagination. Finally, we should not forget that Karl Marx, perhaps the single most influential thinker in human history, was a philosopher.

I could continue this pantheon of influential philosophers indefinitely, but suffice it to say that to be ignorant of the history of philosophy while pursuing a study of the meaning of human life is akin to studying the human body while remaining ignorant of the brain and the liver. Socrates once said that the unexamined life is not worth living, and for William James philosophy was the habit of always seeing an alternative. For me, the importance of philosophy proceeds from the fact that it is not afraid of anything. No idea is too daring to be pursued to its realization. Please notice that I did not say "afraid of nothing," for "nothing" is a serious problem in philosophy. In fact, the most important philosophical question, still with us, reads, Why is there something rather than nothing? To this question there is neither a perceivable nor a conceivable answer; yet having asked it over 2,000 years ago, we are burdened with re-asking it and probing its significance. In effect, philosophy does not become tired and does not jettison its old questions; rather it adds new ones. It is in this way that we can speak of philosophy as culturally immortal, for so long as life exists, questions as to its origin, meaning, and future are of paramount concern.

On occasion, the responses to these perennial questions take on a dramatic and novel formulation, so much so that they become permanent deposits in our cultural history and in our collective consciousness, even if not so acknowledged by those who have had the deep misfortune not to have studied philosophy. I turn now to a presentation of several of these paradigmatic moments in the history of Western thought.

II. PLATO'S CAVE AND THE SEARCH FOR LIGHT

In Book VII of the *Republic*,[1] Plato (427–347 BC) introduces an allegory to describe what he takes to be our fundamental situation. We are imprisoned in a cave, fettered by the neck and the legs so that we can only look forward to a wall in front of us. On the wall are cast shadows of human figures with baskets of food on their heads and of animals carried by bearers. The shadows are projected by the light of a fire in back of a parapet (behind us) on which pass the figures. A slight diffusion of daylight breaks in from the entrance to the cave, high above and to the side of the parapet. Because, as prisoners, we see only shadows, we take these images to be real. For reasons not given in the allegory, one of the prisoners is compelled to leave his chains and make his way to the upper world. After a period of adjustment to the emergence of light, the former prisoner stands in the glare of the sun. Returning to the cave, he attempts to instruct his fellow prisoners that they see only shadows and that he brings to them the knowledge of the real, sensible world. The prisoners threaten to kill him if he persists in this attempt to unmask their view of the world—a clear reference to the trial and death of Socrates for comparable activities in classical Athens.

In order to explicate this deceptively simple allegory by Plato, I have to introduce at least one more theme, this one from Plato's dialogue "Meno."[2] Socrates asks Meno to tell him the nature of virtue. Meno responds with a series of definitions which Socrates rejects as instances of virtue but not equivalent to its nature, that is, its *eidos* or form. Meno becomes irritated at Socrates for constantly confusing him and strikes back with two devastating questions. First, if you do not know what you seek, how do you know that it exists? Second, should you find it, how would you know that it is what you have been seeking?[3] To these questions,

Socrates, representing Plato, introduces a myth, the upshot of which is that before our present embodiment, our souls had access to another world wherein we knew the true forms of reality. Our task now is to recall these forms and to shed ourselves of the material world which blocks our vision. True pedagogy moves us from the world of shadows, through the world of material things, and then through the mathematical forms until we have access to the forms themselves, especially of truth, beauty, and the good.

The paradox of Plato's position can be stated as follows: we know more than we should but less than we can. As human beings, we sense the world one thing at a time: a chair, a book, a person. Yet, we can speak of book, chair, and person to include endless individual instances. Our percepts are singular but our concepts are general. How is this possible? The history of philosophy is faced with a variety of responses to this basic and puzzling question. It is not Plato's response so much as the question itself which is intriguing. More than 2,000 years before Freud, Plato informs us that the world is not what it seems to be. Further, he tells us that we can be in touch with powers beyond our immediate ken. Physics is only a local discipline, for our minds can penetrate the physical world and reach to the forms of things, independent of their singular, sensate characteristics.

Now, if we return to the cave, we find our situation deepened considerably. The cave is a description of our life, our neighborhood, our region, our university, our state, our career, our family, our religion, and our politics. Where we are at any given time is in one cave or another. The task is to know that, a task more subtle and more arduous than at first glance. The height of self-deception is to think that where we are, what we do, and what we believe is where others are, do, and believe. Worse, we think that this is what others *should* do and believe. The crucial question pertaining to Plato's cave has to do with the person leaving. How did that happen? Was there a fight in the cave, such that some helped one to escape?[4] If so, who informed him of the self-deception in which he was mired? And why did they not respond positively when he returned? Or is it that the escaped prisoner was in touch with powers which transcended the cave, powers given only to the few? Or still further, perhaps the fetters are self-inflicted and can be dropped by an act of the will, if we but had the will.[5]

As I see our situation, there are three possible positions of people regarding the cave. First, there are those who have broken out and are proceeding toward the light. I have not met any such persons and am dubious about reports that they exist, although my reading tells me of occasional instances. Second, there are those of us who are in the cave but are aware of its self-deception. We are restless and of good will, yet we lack either the energy, the courage, or the originality to escape. Finally, there are opponents: those who are in the cave and refuse to admit to their situation. They become hostile to any effort which is directed toward enlightening them as to their actual plight. The more we insist on the existence of the cave, the more stubborn they become as to the righteousness of their way, their cause and, above all, their blindness. The Greeks had a word for this attitude. They called it *hubris*, roughly translated as stubborn pride in an unworthy, unworkable, inelegant, and self-deceiving cause. For Plato, the dissolving, unmasking, or disarming of this attitude was the key issue in pedagogy. And that is why, for Plato, philosophy is *therapeia*, an attempted healing of our wounded and encapsulated psyche. Thus, Shakespeare was a Platonist when he wrote, "There are more things in heaven and earth, Horatio, than are dreamt of in your philosophy."[6] Plato's dreams may not be yours or mine, but his philosophy makes it clear that we should dream of things unseen and unknown.

III. THE AUGUSTINIAN SELF AS DIVINE IMAGE

I turn now to a second paradigmatic event in the history of Western consciousness, that of the doctrine of the Trinity as promulgated by Augustine (354–430). Those unfamiliar with philosophy may be unaware that Christianity would have been an empty shell were it not for its marriage to Greek philosophy, especially of the Neoplatonic variety. Augustine, of course, is not the founder of the doctrine of the Trinity. Indeed, the currents and crosscurrents of Greek philosophy, pagan ritual, Jewish ethics, and Christian belief constitute a dazzling intellectual enterprise of the first 400 years after the death of Christ. Nonetheless, Augustine was the most original spokesman for the doctrine of the Trinity as well as being the most explicitly philosophical of the Fathers of the early Church. It is precisely the philosophical fallout from Augustine's doctrine of the Trinity which interests philosophers, for it continues Plato's view of the world and casts a spell over the intellectual life of Europe for 1,000 years, until it is replaced by the secular Platonism of Descartes.

The doctrine of the Trinity is a brilliant intellectual construction of one of the most implausible contentions in the history of religion, namely, that one God is three persons, each exactly and equivalently God. Augustine puts the quandary clearly.

> Some persons, however, find a difficulty in this faith; when they hear that the Father is God, and the Son God, and the Holy Spirit God, and yet that this Trinity is not three Gods, but one God; and they ask how they are to understand this: especially when it is said that the Trinity works indivisibly in everything that God works, and yet that a certain voice of the Father spoke, which is not the voice of the Son; and that none except the Son was born in the flesh, and suffered, and rose again, and ascended into heaven; and that none except the Holy Spirit came in the form of a dove. They wish to understand how the Trinity uttered that voice which was only of the Father; and how the same Trinity created that flesh in which the Son only was born of the Virgin; and how the very same Trinity itself wrought that form of a dove, in which the Holy Spirit only appeared. Yet, otherwise, the Trinity does not work indivisibly, but the Father does some things, the Son other things, and the Holy Spirit yet others: or else, if they do some things together, some severally, then the Trinity is not indivisible. It is a difficulty, too to them, in what manner the Holy Spirit is in the Trinity, whom neither the Father nor the Son, nor both, have begotten, although He is the Spirit both of the Father and of the Son. Since, then, men weary us with asking such questions, let us unfold to them, as we are able, whatever wisdom God's gift has bestowed upon our weakness on this subject . . .[7]

The rudiments of the doctrine itself are quite simple. God is infinite and therefore has infinite knowledge. Further, in that God knows all, he knows himself. Infinite knowledge of himself is equivalent to an infinite person, the Son. Where there are two there is a relationship, in this case an infinite relationship, equivalent to the Spirit, the third person of the Trinity. The entire argument hinges on the philosophical proposition that what is infinite must exist, for if it were only conceptual, then any existing thing would be superior, thereby denying the infinite.

There is no question that philosophical difficulties abound in this formulation. Aside from the obvious one that we have no rational verification that the infinite God exists in the first place, we have to ask also, why do these infinite relationships stop at three? Should it not follow that the Son and the Spirit have such a relationship and, likewise, the Spirit and the Father? Fortunately, these problems are not at the center of the present discussion. Rather, we focus on the nature of the Son and the remarkable contention that in the person of Christ, God became human. Our concern here is not with the religious claim but rather with its import for epistemology, that is, for what and how we know.

Et verbum caro factum est is the message of the Christian scriptures, namely, and the Word was made flesh.[8] In the original Greek of St. John, the word for the Word, for the Christ, was *logos*. For 500 years of Greek philosophy, beginning with Heraclitus, *logos* was the term used to describe the deepest manifestation of *phusus*, of nature, of all that was or could be. John writes: In the beginning was the *logos*.[9] This was not new to the Greeks. That God the Son was an idea, an *eidos*, would not have been new to Plato. But what was new, staggeringly new, was that the *logos* chose flesh, matter, to appear to the world. The appearance of God, the theophany, in early Christian thought uses the Platonic tradition yet makes a radical break with its most cherished assumption. The Platonists believed that the material world was an obfuscation which had to be transcended if one were to reach for the *eidai*, the ultimate forms. Augustine, however, was influenced not only by the Platonists but also by the Greek and Roman stoics. They taught him that the human world was penetrated by the *eidai*, known as, significantly, *logoi spermatikoi*, or in the Latin of Augustine, *rationes seminales*. These seeded reasons or ideas were open to us if we practiced the doctrine of *apatheia*, that is, allowed nature to take an unhindered course within the very fabric of our being. The task, then, is for each of us, as a microcosm, to become continuous with nature as a macrocosm and, in so doing, we shall be consumed in the fire of an ultimate harmony. Despite the power of this position, we face a serious difficulty in accepting it. If Plato's world of forms is unreachable, the stoic doctrine of consummation in nature obliviates our personal lives. Nowhere is this more graphically stated than by Marcus Aurelius, Roman emperor and stoic philosopher.

> Of human life the time is a point, and the substance is in a flux, and the perception dull, and the composition of the whole body subject to putrefaction, and the soul a whirl, and fortune hard to divine, and fame a thing devoid of judgement. And, to say all in a word, everything which belongs to the body is a stream, and what belongs to the soul is a dream and vapour, and life is a warfare and a stranger's sojourn, and afterfame is oblivion.[10]

Despite the philosophical problems with Plato's world of ideas and the stoics' doctrine of *apatheia*, if we merge them, as Augustine does, they provide an excellent explanatory framework for the person of Christ in relation to the problems of knowledge. Christ is the supreme *eidos*, the idea that God has of himself. He is also the *logos*, the way in which God appears to the world. And it is extremely noteworthy that the "way" of the Christ is to be the true light that enlightens every man who comes into the world.[11] Following Plato and the Jewish-Christian teaching of original sin, we are born prisoners in the cave of our own making. Following the doctrine of the Trinity, Christ, the *logos*, is the light which appears to us in the cave and summons us to liberation. Augustinean epistemology holds that to be a Christian is to be in a world which is bathed with light, and to be able to behold the seeded reasons of the stoics as alive and obvious. For Augustine, the world is laced with *vestigia dei*, the traces and shadows of God. Yet, this scenario is definitely that of Plato, for both the world of ideas and the cave are central themes in early Christian teaching. The radical difference is that by virtue of the Incarnation, Christian thinkers, especially Augustine, find a way for the supreme idea, the *logos*, to be both supreme and to penetrate the cave.

Plato is vague about how and why the one prisoner escapes. Augustine is not vague. We have it within our power, if called, to convert toward the light. In the Jewish sense of a *teshuvah*, we must turn our whole body, not just our mind, if we are to truly seek and find the light. In the words of Baruch Spinoza, the great Jewish philosopher of the seventeenth century, we must be prepared for a "De Emendatione Intellectus," a moral healing of the understanding, if we are to know at all.[12] And still later, in the nineteenth century, William James can say that belief helps to create its own verification.[13] It was Augustine who gave decisive impetus to a moral epistemology. His person and his thought dominated medieval culture. He is a key figure in the powerful doctrines of conversion as found in Luther and Calvin. And long after Christianity ceased to be at the center of European intellectual life, Augustine's stress on a change of heart, if we are to see and to know, remains with us an abiding remembrance of the omnipresence of Plato's cave and of mine and of yours.

IV. THE CARTESIAN SELF AS INFINITE

Despite the bold, speculative character of the Western revealed religions, Judaism, Christianity, and Islam, each of them accepted the finite cosmology of the Greeks, especially as promulgated by Aristotle. Although this commitment can be understood historically and aesthetically, it was unfortunate from a theological vantage point. How, for example, can one believe that God is infinite and still accept a version of nature as closed, fixed, and intelligible? The commitment to Aristotle's cosmology is especially strange for Christianity, for as we have seen in the Trinitarianism of Augustine, Christians believe in a material continuity between the earth, human life, and the infinite God. Aristotle, brilliant philosopher and scientist, was no match for the extraordinary vision of nature which was implicit in Christian theology. Indeed, only post-Copernican quantum cosmology can fulfill the intentions of Augustine. (The naivete of Christianity with regard to the physical world has reappeared in our time under the nostrum of creationism. This is not only nonsense from the side of science, it is also heterodox Christianity, for it traps the infinite God into an unimaginative one-shot creation and, more seriously, denies the Christian claim that human history is a cocreator in the evolution of nature such that we culminate in the richness of a freely wrought realization of the intentions of a nondeterministic God.)

Returning to the center of our discussion, the medieval Christian cosmological, theological, and cartographical assumptions come apart at the seams in the tumultuous sixteenth century. In 1507, the Waldseemüller map, for the first time, presented the world in two distinct hemispheres. To Europe, Asia, and Africa, there was added the fourth part of America. The medieval assumption of a single continent, as protected by God from the violence of the oceans, was shattered. In 1517, Luther posted his theses on the castle door at Wittenberg and the Reformation began. The unity of medieval Christendom was soon to be in disarray. In 1543, the Polish astronomer Nicolaus Copernicus published his *De Revolutionibus Orbium Coelestium Libri IV*, a work which was to spell the end of the Aristotelian-Ptolemaic geocentric cosmology. The controversy surrounding the heliocentric theory of Copernicus was to become one of the most fascinating and complex in European intellectual history, and in time would involve the Roman Catholic Church, the Inquisition, and the persons of Galileo, Cusanus, Melancthon, Bruno, and finally Newton. In the midst of the ferment, the most intriguing thinker is René Descartes (1596–1650), for it is he who most directly responds to the implications of the Copernican revolution.

One of the casualties of Copernicanism was the Aristotelian doctrine of natural place, whereby everything that exists, celestial or terrestrial, had its proper place in the rational scheme. The most important implication of this doctrine was that the earth was the center of the universe and concomitantly that human life, as the center of the earth, was thereby central to cosmic life. Copernicanism rendered the earth as but a satellite, moving both around the sun and on its own axis. The crisis was clear. If stability and physical centrality were essential for metaphysical importance, the post-Copernican version of human life rendered us dwarfed and inconsequential. The English poet John Donne says it best in his "Anatomy of the World."

> And new Philosophy calls all in doubt,
> The Element of fire is quite put out;
> The Sun is lost, and the earth, and no man's wit
> Can well direct him where to look for it.
> And freely men confess that this world's spent,
> When in the Planets, and the Firmament
> They seek so many new; then see that this
> Is crumbled out again to his Atomies.
> 'Til all in pieces, all coherence gone;
> All just supply, and all Relation:
> Prince, Subject, Father, Son, are things forgot,
> For every man alone thinks he hath got
> To be a Phenix, and that then can be
> None of that kind, of which he is, but he.[14]

Or perhaps you prefer the plaintive remark of Pascal: "The eternal silence of these infinite spaces frightens me."[15] Whether it be Donne or Pascal, among others, a crisis in the meaning of the human self had erupted in the late sixteenth century. With Copernicanism came a new doctrine of place. In Aristotelianism everything had a natural place, and the human organism was not an exception. Copernicanism dealt a devastating blow to this living-room version of the cosmos by casting deep doubt on the fixed character of the planets. In Aristotelian perspective, the importance of human life was inextricably tied to the importance of the planet earth as nothing less than the physical center of the cosmos. Copernicanism eradicated that centrality and forebade a deep disquiet about the ontological status of human life. The intervening centuries between Copernicanism and the twentieth century witnessed an effort at temporary repair by Newtonian physics. But the remedy could not hold and the full implications of Copernicanism finally arrived in our century, sustained by quantum mechanics, a new cosmology, and the social collapse of religious, political, and ideological eschatologies. The deepest contemporary ontological problem is that of homelessness. The vast, limitless, perhaps infinite universe does not award us a place. The planet earth is a node in the midst of cosmic unintelligibility. According to Aristotle, who we are is where we are. And where anything is, is a function of where everything is, in relation to a center and a periphery. If that is so, we are now no one, for we are nowhere, in that we do not know the extension of the cosmos or, for that matter, whether it has any periphery at all.

It is in the context of this dramatic situation that we consider one aspect of the philosophy of Descartes. He was clearly sympathetic with Copernicanism, as we see in his early work *Le Monde* (1634), which he had to suppress after the condemnation of Galileo. The implications of Copernicanism acted as a specter behind all of the works of Descartes. If heliocentrism is true, then the Aristotelian doctrine of natural place is wrecked. Further, if the earth is not the center of the universe, then human life cannot count on physical centrality for the source of its epistemic certitude. In a series of bold and ingenious methodological and philosophical moves, Descartes sets out to reanchor the possibility of human certitude. He proceeds in the following way. It is conceivable that God does not exist. In that God is the guarantor of our sense experience, it is also conceivable that I am deluded as to the existence of the physical world, including my body. What is not conceivable, however, is that I, as a thinking being, do not exist, for, in one of the most famous of all philosophical phrases, *Cogito ergo sum*: in that I think, I exist. In the *Discourse Concerning Method*, Descartes writes:

> But immediately afterward I noticed that, while I thus wished to think that everything was false, it was necessary that I who was thinking be something. And noting that this truth, I think, therefore I am, was so firm and so assured that all the most extravagant suppositions of the skeptics were not capable of disturbing it, I judged that I could receive it, without scruple, as the first principle of the philosophy I was seeking.[16]

The philosophy he sought was one in which the foundation was not subject to doubt, especially not subject to the foibles and snares of sense experience. To that end, he opposes Aristotle and the scholastics such as Thomas Aquinas by holding that the *res cogitans*, the thinking thing, the human mind, has no need of the physical world, the *res extensa*, for its existence. The *res cogitans* is a complete substance and, as such, is self-guaranteeing of its existence and its knowledge. The thinking self comes equipped with innate ideas of such power that they are able to reconstruct the existence of God and of the material world with indubitability. In order to achieve this power, however, Descartes began a tradition known as psycho-physical dualism, which shattered the experiential unity of the human self and caused serious disarray in the behavioral sciences until the middle of the nineteenth century and the birth of experimental psychology.

Nonetheless, Descartes bequeathed also an intriguing possibility, namely, that the human mind has innate powers which are independent of sense experience and which are independent of the physical place that the mind occupies at any given time. Further, as with Plato, he holds that we can know infinitely more than we do, even to knowing the ultimate principles of reality equivalent to the knowledge of perfect being. This is a heady claim, but we should not forget that Descartes was the father of modern mathematics. As we of the twentieth century know, modern mathematics creates physics, and physics makes worlds of which nature knows not nor even dreamt. Looked at from a traditional view, Pascal was right, infinite space does terrify us. In the philosophy of Descartes, however, even infinite space is but a local box, potentially transcended by the power of the human mind.

V. IMMANUEL KANT: THE SELF AS CONSTRUCTING THE WORLD

Not all philosophers accepted the claims of Descartes or of the two major thinkers who continued his work, Spinoza and Leibniz. I refer especially to the British tradition in philosophy, which had always stressed the irreducible importance of sense experience in the activity of human knowing. Beginning with Francis Bacon, and on through Hobbes and Locke, the empirical method of observation was regarded as necessary if reason were to function in a trustworthy way. It was the eighteenth-century philosopher David Hume, however, who issued the most trenchant critique of the European continental philosophers. Focusing on the principle of causality, Hume made it clear that judgments proceeding from the intuitive power of reason were faulty. Hume's opponents were the Newtonians, who, following the philosophical speculation rather than the empirical physics of Newton, had promulgated increasingly unlikely hypotheses. The chastising and skeptical voice of Hume was heard across the English Channel by the German philosopher Immanuel Kant (1724–1804). Awoken from his "dogmatic slumber" by the attack of Hume, Kant set out to address his criticism and save Newtonian physics.

However much they disagreed on fundamental issues, Descartes, Spinoza, and Leibniz did agree that the human mind had access to the principle of causality. For David Hume, the principle of causality was a mock-up due to habit and custom rather than to any intuitive grasp of the mind. Hume admitted that we can say that A caused B, again and again, but he denied that we experienced the principle of A causing B. What we experience is a series of repetitive acts, no one of which provides reason with the right to claim that such a causal nexus will always be so. If Hume were right, scientific propositions would be limited to single elements. Correspondingly, Newtonian physics would be shipwrecked. Despite the extensive and intense outcry against Hume, Kant, for one, was wise enough to admit that he was fundamentally correct. A way had to be found to accept Hume's criticism and yet save science. Kant's move in this direction is not only a mark of genius but also of speculative ingenuity. He rightly refers to his work in this regard as a second Copernican revolution.

There is considerable complexity in Kant's response to Hume, but I shall trim the sails and set it out in bald terms. Hume insisted that propositions which were analytic, a priori, had no merit. By this he meant that any proposition which claimed more than a single event or sense datum could reveal was an illegitimate claim. To the contrary, the only propositions of merit were synthetic, a posteriori, by which Hume meant a description of our sense of experience, that could be accounted for only by single sense impressions. Kant accepted Hume's dictum that legitimate propositions had to be based on experience. But Kant sought also to have these propositions function as a priori, that is, as universal laws, which did not have to be evaluated on each appearing occasion. The latter was necessary if Newtonian science were to prevail. Kant's strategy was to develop an entirely new type of proposition, one which was synthetic but also a priori. This proposition would be based on experience and yet would function as a universal law. How in the name of all that was sacred in the two-thousand-year history of epistemology would such a hybrid be possible? In fact, nothing less than a philosophical Copernican revolution would suffice if Kant were to succeed.

As early as his "Inaugural Dissertation" in 1770, Kant anticipates this revolution in consciousness. In a series of extraordinary claims, Kant turns the history of philosophy and science upside down:

The idea of time does not originate in the senses, but is presupposed by them.

Time is not something objective and real.

The concept of space is not abstracted from outer sensations.

Space is not something objective and real.[17]

In technical terms, Kant holds that space and time are presensuous intuitions had by us prior to our experience of the physical world. In a more simple format, Kant tells us that space and time are homemade blankets which condition all of our experience. We time the world and we space the world. If we, as human life, did not exist, then neither would time nor space. His answer to Hume is now clear. All of our a priori judgments on the physical world, as found in physics and mathematics, are based on experience, for they always assume the existence of space and time, which we experience as presensuous intuitions, had by each human being.

The world is experienced as it appears, that is, as phenomenal. It comes to us already contexted by our formulation of space and time. In this way, synthetic a priori propositions are possible in physics and mathematics, for they are laws which are nonetheless based on common experience. Science is saved. The concession made by Kant is both beguiling and serious. The world which does not appear in space and time cannot be known with apodictic or scientific certainty. So we have only indirect knowledge of the existence of God, the immortality of the soul, and the eternality of the world. In fact, because these concerns are not limited to space and time, they are antinomic and can be both supported and opposed equally, by reason. Metaphysics, then, is not a science.

Kant has taken the first step in the second Copernican revolution. The world we experience is a construct of the human imagination. Its laws are home-grown and have no ultimate or even astral significance. He does not take the second step, although it will be taken in subsequent centuries. The universe will become a construct of human imagination and so too, in the twentieth century, will God become one of our imaginative formulations, and nothing will have any meaning unless we endow it with meaning.

VI. KARL MARX: HUMAN LIFE AS SELF-DECEIVED AND ALIENATED

In spite of the inordinate brilliance of philosophy from the early Greeks to the nineteenth century, one naive strand awaited challenge. Philosophy, and other disciplines as well, assumed that events took place one after the other, in serial fashion, playing out the transcendent rubric of Judaism, Christianity, or Islam. Until the eighteenth-century thought of Vico and Herder, the inner, complex fabric of historical forces was largely unsung. This naivete about the complexity of history was given a rude awakening by the publication of the philosophy of Hegel, who introduced us to the dialectic of historical events and who put into perspective the power of historical forces which transcend the intentions and interpretations of human chronicle. For Hegel, history is a matrix in and through which all persons and all events are given their meaning. Hegel was the first to see history, correctly, as a "slaughter-bench," in which the private affairs of human life are carried on in the context of forces over which they have no control. He writes:

> But in contemplating history as the slaughter-bench at which the happiness of peoples, the wisdom of states, and the virtue of individuals have been sacrificed, a question necessarily arises: To what principle, to what final purpose, have these monstrous sacrifices been offered?[18]

To this question, there are any number of responses, and they range from the Pollyanna attitude of the religious zealot to the laissez-faire cynicism of the determinist. A more realistic and creative response emerges from the thought of Karl Marx (1818–83), who studied Hegel's writings with care. The central philosophical position of Marx was brilliantly paradoxical. On the one hand, he accepted the Hegelian view that human life is in the inextricable throes of history. On the other hand, he, like the Jews and the Christians, believed in *kairos*, a moment in historical time which can be seized such that the flow of history is irreversibly changed. Marx was the first genuine and intentional revolutionary of consciousness in the history of philosophy.

Schopenhauer once said that anyone who studied philosophy and was unaware of Kant was in a state of innocence. I agree, but I add that in the twentieth century, anyone who studies anything and is unaware of Marx is in a state of innocence, or as the Roman Catholicism of my childhood would say, in a state of vincible ignorance, that is, guilty of not knowing what one should know in order to make an intelligent moral decision.

I concentrate here on only two of Marx's salient contentions: first, that institutions condition consciousness rather than the reverse; second, that our fundamental situation is to be in a state of alienation. For the first, I cite the famous passage from Marx's 1859 work, "A Contribution to the Critique of Political Economy."

> The mode of production of material life conditions the social, political and intellectual life process in general. It is not the consciousness of men that determines their being, but, on the contrary, their social being that determines their consciousness.[19]

Marx is telling us that we come to consciousness in a maelstrom of competing institutional conditions. For him, it was church and state, bourgeois and proletariat, capitalist and worker, that formulated our consciousness. For us in twentieth-century America, additionally it is male and female, urban and rural, black, brown, and white, East and West, North and South, having access to money and education and being denied such access, which conditions our coming to consciousness. Marx's point is clear. Who we are is a function of our anticipations, expectations, and the burdens promulgated by those around us, who accept or reject our efforts at becoming either like them or different from them. The self-generating, self-motivating individual is largely a myth, as we find ourselves slotted into one groove or another, for the good of the family, the economy, the nation, or some religious or political ideology, none of which function on behalf of individuals.

It is no wonder that originality, imagination, and boldness on behalf of social and political change are hard to come by, for, as Marx points out, the social structure so conditions us that we regard such changes as anathema. Given this lamentable state of affairs, we find that Marx, perhaps surprisingly, is in the tradition of Plato, Augustine, and Spinoza, for he, like they, holds that only a moral conversion will free us from the fetters of social conditioning and illegitimate expectation. Remarkably, Marx calls upon us to seize the process of history, enter into its bowels, and redirect society toward human liberation. To this end, in continuity with the entire tradition of moral epistemology, it is necessary for us to become aware of how we have been had. And this leads to a second important insight of Marx, the deleterious character of our alienation from our own humanness.

Although the experience of human alienation has been made notorious by the existentialists Sartre and Camus, its original explication traces to Marx's early "Economic and Philosophic Manuscripts of 1844." The manuscripts are a brilliant analysis of a broken promise. Contexted by the

Industrial Revolution, they detail how "workers" become estranged from their work and in time from nature, from other workers, and finally from themselves.[20] Marx's complex and detailed argument centers around the failure of society to structure social and economic life such that we fulfill our *Gattungswesen*. Awkwardly translated as species-consciousness or species-being, *Gattungswesen* is best explored through its referent: "worker." Because of the rise of laissez-faire capitalism, the free-market economy, and the economic exploitation of surplus value, the interpretation of workers as equivalent to overhead became accepted policy. In time, workers became estranged or alienated from their work, for the products were not distinctively theirs and they became estranged from each other by virtue of piecework competition. Due to land enclosure and the development of the urban factory system, the workers became alienated from nature. Finally, stung with the burden of what the classical economist David Ricardo approvingly calls the capitalist necessity of sustaining a subsistent lumpenproletariat, the worker became alienated from himself/herself. Although considerable controversy has been generated relative to Marx's appraisal of industrial capitalism, we should not allow this to distract us from the universality of Marx's notion of alienation. The greatest offense is for those in power to promise that which they have neither the power nor the intention to redeem. This is as true of socialism as it is of capitalism, as true of religion as it is of egalitarian democracy. Marx is right. The major offense is to structure a society in which promises are made but knowingly aborted. Political, social, and religious power exists as dependent on the rampant, imposed self-deception of the common person. This is an egregious offense against humanity which can be changed only by an extensive revolution in human consciousness. Marx had the courage to call for that change. His commentary on his philosophical predecessor, Ludwig Feuerbach, is apropos: "The philosophers have only *interpreted* the world, in various ways; the point, however, is to *change* it."[21] Ironically, Marx was too modest about philosophy, for philosophy has always changed the world, and he as a philosopher has changed the world more than any other single person.

VII. NIETZSCHE: LIVE DANGEROUSLY

As surprising as it might be to casual students of modern intellectual history, Marx was not the radical thinker of the nineteenth century. That designation is more appropriately applied to either Sören Kierkegaard (1813–55) or Friedrich Nietzsche (1844–1900). Marx believed that the lumpenproletariat would be redeemed if we were to have a systemic extirpation of social mores. Kierkegaard and Nietzsche, to the contrary, had no such confidence in the possibilities of the common person. Although all three thinkers showed a contempt for organized religion, bureaucracy, and the faceless ideologies of their time, a contempt shared by their peer, the great Russian novelist Fyodor Dostoevsky, nonetheless, Kierkegaard and Nietzsche saw hope only for those few among us who were able to break through the systematic hypocrisy of modern religion, society, and politics. I focus here on Nietzsche.

From the time of Jean Jacques Rousseau, in the middle of the eighteenth century, until the middle of our own century, we have witnessed an extraordinary rash of creative thinkers and artists whose personal lives, predilections, and attitudes, to say the least, have been neurotic. In this tradition, which I refer to as that of the tangled genius, Nietzsche is clearly the dominant figure.

As a young man in his twenties, Nietzsche was hailed as the greatest philologist in the history of the European languages. Yet from the time of the publication of his first work, *The Birth of Tragedy*, in 1872, Nietzsche was progressing toward the insanity which was to claim him in 1888, some twelve years before his death. There are scholarly arguments over the cause of his insanity, with the three favored explanations being a syphilitic infection contracted in his youth, a brain lesion resulting from an early fall, and genetically induced paranoid schizophrenia. Whatever may be the correct cause, it is unsettling to read that Freud speaks of Nietzsche as knowing more about himself than anyone in the history of literature. Still more unsettling is that to read Nietzsche is to read someone who knows more about me than I know about myself, indeed, knows more about us than we know about ourselves.

In one of his last writings, Nietzsche tells us that "since Copernicus, man has been rolling from the center toward X."[22] In effect, we have lost our hold on the life force necessary to a fully human and liberated culture. For Nietzsche, civilization makes a tragic mistake when it advances the cause of Apollo, the God of order and form, over that of Dionysus, the God of eros and energy. Nietzsche cites the paradox that when Apollo is supreme, we have neither creative energy nor form, but when Dionysus is supreme, the Apollonian call to order is present and enhancing. Nietzsche is the most strident figure in the history of philosophy, because of his doubt about the significance of clear reason. He contends that Socrates, by virtue of his introduction of the rational method of philosophical questioning to Greek culture, single-handedly brought about the demise of Greek tragedy, namely, the move from the supreme madness and magic of Aeschylus and Sophocles to the *deus ex machina* of Euripides.[23]

It is not germane to the present discussion that we adjudicate the scholarly controversies over Nietzsche's inflammatory interpretation of the evolution of Greek tragedy. To the point, however, is that Nietzsche, in siding with the Sophoclean chorus, which foretells the doom of Oedipus, also encourages acceptance of the underground energies available to us as a gift from Dionysus, if we had but the will to shuck off the tired truisms of our politics, our religion, and our ethics. Nietzsche's call, to each of us, is for a *Versuch einer Umwertung aller Werte*, an attempt at a transvaluation of all values. In order to bring off the instituting of new values, we must overcome our primary opponent, bourgeois Christian ethics, especially as found in the glorification of humility and self-abnegation. Nietzsche charges Christianity with the historical guile of convincing its followers to be humble, whereas its leaders were the acme of pride and arrogance.

For Nietzsche, the traditional hierarchy of values is to be inverted. The supreme values are the aesthetic, especially the dance, whereby the entire body resonates through our consciousness. He anticipates the momentous film of Ingmar Bergman, "The Seventh Seal," in which the flagellants do the dance of death as their response to the plague. In Nietzsche, as in Bergman, better to dance to the death than to humbly accept the will of God. No surprise here, for it is Nietzsche who is the first modern thinker to announce the death of God. In a brilliant parody of the Gospel of St. John, Nietzsche writes in *The Gay Science*:

> Have you not heard of that madman who lit a lantern in the bright morning hours, ran to the market place, and cried incessantly, "I seek God! I seek God!" As many of those who do not believe in God were standing around just then, he provoked much laughter. Why, did he get lost? said one. Did he lose his way like a child? said another. Or is he hiding? Is he afraid of us? Has he gone on a voyage? or emigrated? Thus they yelled and laughed. The madman jumped into their midst and pierced them with his glances.
>
> "Whither is God" he cried. "I shall tell you. We *have killed him*—you and I. All of us are his murderers. But how have we done this? How were we able to drink up the sea? Who gave us the sponge to wipe away the horizon? What did we do when we unchained this earth from its sun? Whither is it moving now? Whither are we moving now? Away from all suns? Are we not plunging con-

tinually? Backward, sideward, forward, in all directions? Is there any up or down left? Are we not straying as through an infinite nothing? Do we not feel the breath of empty space? Has it not become colder? Is not night and more night coming on all the while? Must not lanterns be lit in the morning? Do we not hear anything yet of the noise of the gravediggers who are burying God? Do we not smell anything yet of God's decomposition? Gods too decompose. God is dead. God remains dead. And we have killed him. How shall we, the murderers of all murderers, comfort ourselves? What was holiest and most powerful of all that the world has yet owned has bled to death under our knives. Who will wipe this blood off us? What water is there for us to clean ourselves? What festivals of atonement, what sacred games shall we have to invent? Is not the greatness of this deed too great for us? Must not we ourselves become gods simply to seem worthy of it? There has never been a greater deed; and whoever will be born after us—for the sake of this deed he will be part of a higher history than all history hitherto."

Here the madman fell silent and looked again at his listeners; and they too were silent and stared at him in astonishment. At last he threw his lantern on the ground, and it broke and went out. "I come too early," he said then; "my time has not come yet. This tremendous event is still on its way, still wandering—it has not yet reached the ears of man. Lightning and thunder require time, the light of the stars requires time, deeds require time even after they are done, before they can be seen and heard. This deed is still more distant from them than the most distant stars—*and yet they have done it themselves*."

It has been related further that on that same day the madman entered divers churches and there sang his *requiem aeternam deo*. Led out and called to account, he is said to have replied each time, "What are these churches now if they are not the tombs and sepulchers of God?"[24]

What an extraordinary text. Tombs and sepulchers indeed! What are we to do? Nietzsche tells us, straight out, that we are to become *Übermenschen*, that is, we are to transcend the banalities of our lives and drink deeply of the saving energies of Dionysus, the god of eros. Above all, we are to avoid being seduced by the fraud, the hokum, the hypocrisy, and the false promises which surround us. We are called, as the Gospel of Jesus teaches us, to come unto ourselves, to be ourselves and to transcend the petty bureaucracies which dominate our lives, be they Christian, democratic, or socialist. Above all, we should avoid living second-hand lives handed down to us by parents, teachers, ministers, and assorted functionaries. Nietzsche reminds us of the parable of the snake and the need to shed our skin, regularly. "The snake that cannot shed its skin perishes. So do the spirits who are prevented from changing their opinions; they cease to be spirit."[25] More, we must risk our lives and our values, if we are to prevail as human. "For believe me, the secret of the greatest fulfillment and the greatest enjoyment of existence is: to *live dangerously*! Build your cities under Vesuvius! Send your ship into uncharted seas."[26] And, if I read Nietzsche right, do not turn back.

VIII. WILLIAM JAMES: TO BE HUMAN IS TO RISK

Despite the vast disparities of style and deep disagreements on fundamental issues, a common thread binds the thinkers just considered. And that thread would wend through most other philosophers of the period in question. Each of them in his own distinctive way, was convinced of the certitude of his respective positions. With William James (1842–1910), we come upon an entirely new phenomenon in philosophy, one for whom pluralism was not a fall from grace but rather a permanent and positive condition of human inquiry. In 1876, James published an essay in *The Nation* entitled "The Teaching of Philosophy in Our Colleges." Midway through that piece, he wrote:

> If the best use of our colleges is to give young men a wider openness of mind and a more flexible way of thinking than special technical training can generate, then we hold that philosophy . . . is the most important of all college studies. However sceptical one may be of the attainment of universal truths . . . one can never deny that philosophic study means the habit of always seeing an alternative, of not taking the usual for granted, of making conventialities fluid again, of imagining foreign states of mind. In a word, it means the possession of mental perspective. Touchstone's question, "Hast any philosophy in thee, shepherd?" will never cease to be one of the tests of a well-born nature. It says, Is there space and air in your mind, or must your companions gasp for breath whenever they talk with you? And if our colleges are to make men, and not machines, they should look, above all things, to this aspect of their influence.[27]

The search for alternatives characterized both the life and thought of William James. As a young man, under the baleful influence of his father, who insisted that he choose a career, James underwent a series of profound personal disturbances, which forced him to consider suicide as an alternative to the bland Protestant ethic that suffused his early conscious life. After undergoing an intense vastation experience, dramatized by the appearance to his consciousness of a loathsome creature, James realized "*that shape am I,* I felt, potentially."[28] Convinced of the utter fragility of his personal self, he subsequently writes in his diary that he is trapped between living out the bequest of a stale, inherited ethic on the one hand and suicide on the other. Faced with Scylla and Charybdis, James makes a bold personal move to extricate himself. In his diary entry of April 30, 1870, he rejects suicide and writes:

> Now, I will go a step further with my will, not only act with it, but believe as well; believe in my individual reality and creative power. My belief, to be sure, *can't* be optimistic—but I will posit life (the real, the good) in the self-governing *resistance* of the ego to the world. Life shall be built in doing and suffering and creating.[29]

James remained loyal to this provocative announcement in his diary. His subsequent life and thought was based on two active assumptions. First, he was convinced that human beings have extraordinary reservoirs of untapped energy which can be brought into play by an act of the will. In this regard, he had confidence also in the wisdom of common people, and he shared the belief of his philosophical colleague, Josiah Royce, that "the popular mind is deep, and means a thousand times more than it explicitly knows."[30] James was especially fond of drawing from the insights and experiences of underground, bizarre, or highly idiosyncratic people. In his "Introduction" to his father's *Literary Remains*, James wrote that "the sanest and best of us are of one clay with lunatics and prison-inmates."[31] In this vein, James's popular essays, among them "The Will to Believe," "Is Life Worth Living?," "The Sentiment of Rationality," and "The Energies of Men," constitute an effort on behalf of a nineteenth-century American philosophical evangelism. Unfortunately, they have been often misunderstood because they have been read apart from James's second and more important assumption, namely, that the nature of reality and the human process of knowing has been dramatically misconstrued by the history of philosophy.

Proceeding from his brilliant study of the psychology of human behavior, which culminated in his classic work *The Principles of Psychology*, James contended that reality was not made of things, substances, or blocks of any kind. Rather, the key to understanding the nature of reality was relations. Before we absorbed the philosophical import of modern art, quantum mechanics, depth psychology, and modern mathematics, James had told us of the narrowness and misplaced emphases of classical metaphysics and epistemology. The cardinal insight of James occurs in 1884, in an essay entitled "Some Omissions of Introspective Psychology." Therein he affirms that our prehension of reality does not occur through the denotation of separate objects but rather is best described by a stream of consciousness, by which our experience of the relational transitions between objects is as affectively real as our experience of the objects themselves. James's phenomenological description of how we actually experience the world as a processive, relational field is not given full justice until James Joyce's magnificent version of the stream of consciousness appears in *Ulysses*.

James cuts between the ideational pretensions of the classical idealist philosophy, in which our common, ordinary experience is distrusted, and the narrow, unimaginative claims of the British empiricists, for whom the world comes as a simple, contiguous string of single sense perceptions. To the contrary, for James, the world is thicker and is teeming with inferences, anticipations, and leads, each of which awaits our active, constituting presence. James writes:

> In our cognitive as well as in our active life we are creative. We *add*, both to the subject and to the predicate part of reality. The world stands really malleable, waiting to receive its final touches at our hands. Like the kingdom of heaven, it suffers human violence willingly. Man *engenders* truths upon it.[32]

James's commitment to the active and constituting presence of the human mind in any version of reality leads to several radical conclusions. First, the world as we know it is inseparable from how we know it. Second, shifts in the human version of the world result in nothing less than shifts in the world itself. Third, and most extraordinary, a diagnosis of the history of philosophy, speculative science, and the arts is equivalent to a diagnosis of the evolution of reality. In short, the history of human life is a history of reality, for without human life, the source of intelligence so far as we now know, the blunt existential reality of the physical world, would have no meaning whatsoever.

James's philosophy is unashamedly anthropocentric. He calls it radical empiricism, for it is based on experience undergone and it takes at full cognizance the equivalent experiential character of relations to that of things and objects. James is unabashedly post-Copernican. He regards the world as ultimately unintelligible, fraught with chance and novelty, and subject to the constitutive role of human life. In 1903, James made the following entry in a notebook.

> All neat schematisms with permanent and absolute distinctions, classifications with absolute pretensions, systems with pigeon-holes, etc., have this character. All "classic," clean, cut and dried, "noble," fixed, "eternal," *Weltsanschauungen* seem to me to violate the character with which life concretely comes and the expression which it bears of being, or at least of involving a muddle and a struggle, with an "ever not quite" to all our formulas, and novelty and possibility forever leaking in.[33]

The fundamental contribution of William James to any morphological analysis of the human condition is that he thickens the discussion. Radical empiricism involves an acceptance of a far wider range of continuous and experienced relationships than that usually associated with the normal confines of the human self. It gives to novelty and chance a much greater role in our understanding of the fabric of the world. The philosophy of James calls for a never-ending series of descriptions and diagnoses, each from a specific vantage point but no one of them burdened with having to account for everything. For James, the world is much like "the pattern of our daily experience,"[34] loosely connected, processive, and pluralistic. The crucial factor in our understanding of the world in which we live is the affective experiencing of relations. So multiply involved are we that the attainment of deep insight to our "inner life" leads us to participate in no less than the very rhythm of the world at large. If we live at the edge, what we most find in this rhythm are surprises, relational novelty everywhere. Nothing is clear until the last of us has our say and the last relation is hooked. Rare among philosophers, William James believed this.

> In principle, then, as I said, intellectualism's edge is broken; it can only approximate to reality, and its logic is inapplicable to our inner life, which spurns its vetoes and mocks at its impossibilities. Every bit of us at every moment is part and parcel of a wider self, it quivers along various radii like the wind-rose on a compass, and the actual in it is continuously one with possibles not yet in our present sight.[35]

IX. CONCLUSION

The message of William James is that there are possibilities "not yet in our present sight." That is also the message of philosophy. We could have chosen seven other thinkers to represent the dramatic importance of philosophy. Philosophy abounds with troublemakers; thinkers who are restless about the status quo and who bring the human mind to bear upon our situation with an attitude of skepticism, belligerence, and openness to new ideas, resolutions, and possibilities unheard and even undreamt.

Finally, a personal note. How can anyone who speaks a Western tongue, especially those among us who purport to be educated, afford not to study philosophy? I ask you! I implore you! Quo vadis? Whither goest thou without any understanding of whence we have come and who we are? And this is to say nothing of where we hope to go. In the works of Voltaire, we find a reference to a letter from Henry IV, the King of France, to an ill-knighted person by the name of Crillon, who, most unfortunately, arrived after a great battle had been fought. To the tardy Crillon, Henry IV wrote: "Hang yourself, brave Crillon! We fought at Arques, and you were not there."[36]

We stand today on the edge of another great battle, that between humanistic learning in our nation and in our universities on the one hand, and the shallow, opportunistic, and personally aggrandizing appeal to the bottom-line principle of sheerly economic accountability on the other hand. Unlike Crillon, I plan to be at this battle and I trust that you will do likewise, for to do less is to abandon all that is distinctively human. I tell this to our children and to my students. I ask them to pass the message to their children and to their students. Philistines and purveyors of the shallow are everywhere. They pervade the university as well as the marketplace. It is our task to sustain and celebrate the wisdom of the past on behalf of our obligation to make possible the wisdom of the present. More than seventy years ago, William James said that philosophy bakes no bread. True enough, nor does it build bridges or clone cells. Yet a society that only bakes bread, builds bridges, and clones cells is a society that has failed to realize its deepest mission. The ancients knew well that time will seize us, in time. Our task is to think deeply about the most quixotic of all cosmic events, namely, the utterly transient yet powerful existence of a human life. Three millennia of philosophical speculation have addressed that paradox. And it is to that same ambivalence between power and fragility that we address ourselves once again. Ultimate conclusions are beyond our reach, but the quality of our endeavor is a gauge of the worthiness of our cause. Those of us who have bartered the present for a paradisiacal future, much less a career, have missed the drama of the obvious. Philosophy teaches us that every day, everyone has access to the depth of being human. We should not await salvation while the parade passes by. The nectar of a guaranteed human future is illusory and the height of self-deception. Our death is imminent. Philosophy sanctifies our reflective effort to ask why and, above all, philosophy makes an effort to tell the truth. In our time, what could be a more outlandish and coveted activity?

2 Spires of Influence

THE IMPORTANCE OF EMERSON FOR CLASSICAL AMERICAN PHILOSOPHY

And, striving to be man, the worm
Mounts through all the spires of form.
RALPH WALDO EMERSON, "Nature"

Perhaps the title of this chapter should be "Why Emerson?" as that would better reflect how I came to write this piece. It is not so much that I have had to become convinced of the singular importance of the thought of Emerson, for the writing and teaching of Joseph Blau[1] and Robert C. Pollock[2] long ago made that clear to me. Rather the query about "Why Emerson?" proceeds from my study of the classic American philosophers, especially William James, Josiah Royce, and John Dewey. Despite their differences and disagreements, often extreme in both personal style and doctrine, these powerful and prescient philosophers did have at least one influence in common—the thought of Ralph Waldo Emerson.

Another major figure of the American classical period, George Santayana, seems to be a case apart. Santayana had an abiding interest in Emerson's thought and refers frequently to Emerson in his own writings. His judgments on Emerson vary from admiration and affection to pointed and even harsh criticism. I do not think that Emerson was a significant influence on Santayana. Nonetheless, his published assessments of Emerson at the beginning of the twentieth century are contextually interesting, especially as they contrast with those of James, Royce, and Dewey.

The remaining two major figures of the classical period, C. S. Peirce and G. H. Mead,[3] appear to be much less directly influenced by Emerson.

Parenthetically, however, we do find a text in Peirce about Emerson which is intriguing and perhaps merits further inquiry in another context. In "The Law of Mind," published in 1892, Peirce wrote:

> I may mention, for the benefit of those who are curious in studying mental biographies, that I was born and reared in the neighborhood of Concord—I mean in Cambridge—at the time when Emerson, Hedge, and their friends were disseminating the ideas that they had caught from Schelling, and Schelling from Plotinus, from Boehm, or from God knows what minds stricken with the monstrous mysticism of the East. But the atmosphere of Cambridge held many an antiseptic against Concord transcendentalism; and I am not conscious of having contracted any of that virus. Nevertheless, it is probable that some cultured bacilli, some benignant form of the disease was implanted in my soul, unawares, and that now, after long incubation, it comes to the surface, modified by mathematical conceptions and by training in physical investigation.[4]

The wary and tough-minded response of Peirce is not atypical of a philosophical assessment of Emerson. Indeed, even those philosophers who acknowledge their debt to Emerson lace their remarks with dubiety about his fundamental assumptions and unease about much of the rhetoric of his formulation. Nonetheless, James, Royce, Dewey, and Santayana, each in his own way, find it necessary to evaluate the importance of Emerson in the light of their own developing positions. Before turning to these judgments, it should be helpful if I sketch the Emersonian project in cultural and philosophical terms.

The central theme of Emerson's life and work is that of *possibility*. In an anticipation of the attitude of Martin Buber, Emerson believes that 'we are really able', that is, we and the world are continuous in an affective and nutritional way. It is human insight which is able to "animate the last fibre of organization, the outskirts of nature."[5] Emerson's persistent stress on human possibility is fed from two sources: his extraordinary confidence in the latent powers of the individual soul when related to the symbolic riches of nature and his belief that the comparatively unarticulated history of American experience could act as a vast resource for the energizing of novel and creative spiritual energy. The often oracular style of Emerson should not cloak the seriousness of his intention when he speaks of these possibilities. In this regard, the key text is found in his Introduction to the essay "Nature."

> Our age is retrospective. It builds the sepulchres of the fathers. It writes biographies, histories, and criticism. The foregoing generations beheld God and nature face to face; we, through their eyes. Why should not we also enjoy an original relation to the universe? Why should not we have a poetry and philosophy of insight and not of tradition, and a religion by revelation to us, and not the history of theirs? Embosomed for a season in nature, whose floods of life stream around and through us, and invite us, by the powers they supply, to action proportioned to nature, why should we grope among the dry bones of the past, or put the living generation into masquerade out of its faded wardrobe? The sun shines to-day also. There is more wool and flax in the fields. There are new lands, new men, new thoughts. Let us demand our own works and laws and worship.[6]

We of the twentieth century may not grasp the radical character of Emerson's invocation, standing as we do on the rubble of broken promises brought to us by the great faiths of the past, be they scientific, social, or religious. But Emerson made no such promise and cannot be accused, retroactively, of bad faith. His message was clear. We are to transform the obviousness of our situation by a resolute penetration to the liberating symbolism present in our own experience. We are not to be dependent on faith hatched elsewhere out of others' experiences, nor, above all, are we to rest on an inherited ethic whose significance is due more to longevity and authority than to the press of our own experience. Surely, Emerson's nineteenth century, which was barely able to absorb the recondite theology responsible for the transition from Presbyterianism to Unitarianism, had to blanch at his bypassing the issue entirely, while calling for a homegrown "revelation." The radical character of Emerson's position at that time was given historical credence by the reception given to his Divinity School Address, delivered two years after "Nature" and one year after "The American Scholar." Using a tone more modest than either of those, Emerson in effect told the graduating class of Harvard Divinity School that the tradition they had inherited was hollow and the Church to which they belonged "seems to totter to its fall, all life extinct."[7] As in "Nature," he again called for a "new hope and new revelation."[8] The upshot of this address was that for nearly thirty years Emerson was unwelcome as a public figure in Cambridge.

Now, more to the point of the present discussion is Emerson's doctrine of experience and his emphasis on relations, both central concerns of the subsequent philosophical thought of James and Dewey. In his essay "The American Scholar," Emerson points to three major influences on the development of the reflective person: nature, history, and action or experience. In his discussion of the third influence, Emerson provides a microcosmic view of his fundamental philosophy. He makes it apparent that he does not accept the traditional superiority of the contemplative over the active life. Emerson tells us further that "Action is with the scholar subordinate, but it is essential. Without it he is not yet man. Without it thought can never ripen into truth."[9] It is noteworthy that accompanying Emerson's superb intellectual mastery of the great literature of the past and his commitment to the reflective life is his affirmation that "Character is higher than intellect."[10] Living is a total act, the functionary, whereas thinking is a partial act, the function. More than twenty years after the publication of "The American Scholar," Emerson reiterated his commitment to the "practical" and to the "experiential" as the touchstone of the thinking person. In his essay "Fate" he considers those thinkers for whom the central question is the "theory of the Age." In response, Emerson writes: "To me, however, the question of the times resolved itself into a practical question of the conduct of life. How shall I live? We are incompetent to solve the times."[11] The human task for Emerson is not so much to solve the times as to live them, in an ameliorative and perceptive way.

Emerson's generalized approach to inquiry is clearly a foreshadowing of that found subsequently in James, Dewey, and Royce. Too often, Emerson's anticipation of these thinkers is left at precisely that general bequest, whereby the undergoing of experience is its own mean and carries its own peculiar form of cognition.[12] What is less well known is that Emerson also anticipated the doctrine of "radical empiricism," which is central to the philosophy of James and Dewey. I do not contend that Emerson's version of relations had the same psychological or epistemological genesis[13] as that of either James or Dewey. Yet, *mutatis mutandis*, Emerson did affirm the primary importance of relations over things and he did hold to an aggressive doctrine of implication. Further, his metaphors were more allied to the language of continuity than to that of totality or finality. Finally, Emerson shared that modern assumption which began with Kant and is found repeated in James and Dewey—namely, that the known is, in some way, a function of the knower.

Emerson's attitude toward implicitness, relations, and the partially constitutive character of human inquiry helps us to understand him in other ways as well. Why, one might ask, would Emerson, a New England

Brahmin, have a proletarian epistemology? That is, how could Emerson write as he did in "The American Scholar," a paean of praise to the obvious, to the ordinary? The text, as read to the audience at the Phi Beta Kappa celebration of 1837, was startling.

> I embrace the common, I explore and sit at the feet of the familiar, the low. Give me insight into to-day, and you may have the antique and future worlds. What would we really know the meaning of? The meal in the firkin; the milk in the pan; the ballad in the street; the news of the boat; the glance of the eye; the form and gait of the body; . . .[14]

Emerson immediately provides the response to the rhetorical question posed above. For the "ultimate reason" why the affairs of the ordinary yield insight traces to Emerson's belief that "the sublime presence of the highest spiritual cause lurks, as always it does lurk, in these suburbs and extremities of nature."[15] His version of the world is not characterized by hierarchies, nor by fixed essences, each to be known as an object in itself. Rather he stresses the flow of our experience and the multiple implications of every event and every thing for every other experience had or about to be had. Nature brings with it this rich symbolic resource, enabling all experiences, sanctioned and occasional, to retract potentially novel implications of our other experiences. The novelty is due both to the unpredictability of nature[16] and to the creative role of human imagination. Of the first Emerson writes:

> Nature hates calculators; her methods are saltatory and impulsive. Man lives by pulses; our organic movements are such; and the chemical and ethereal agents are undulatory and alternate; and the mind goes antagonizing on, and never prospers but by fits. We thrive by casualties. Our chief experiences have been casual. The most attractive class of people are those who are powerful obliquely and not by the direct stroke; men of genius, but not yet accredited; one gets the cheer of their light without paying too great a tax. Theirs is the beauty of the bird or the morning light, and not of art. In the thought of genius there is always a surprise; and the moral sentiment is well called "the newness," for it is never other; as new to the oldest intelligence as to the young child; . . .[17]

The malleability and novelty-prone capacity of nature feeds the formulating and constructive powers native to the human imagination. Emerson, like James and Dewey, sees this transaction between the open nature of nature and the "active soul" as the necessary context for meaning. In his *Journals*, Emerson writes:

> This power of imagination, the making of some familiar object, as fire or rain, or a bucket, or shovel do new duty as an exponent of some truth or general law, bewitches and delights men. It is a taking of dead sticks, and clothing about with immortality; it is music out of creaking and scouring. All opaque things are transparent, and the light of heaven struggles through.[18]

We should not mistake Emerson's position for a flight of fancy or for the poetic stroke in the pejorative sense of that word. Emerson is a hard-headed empiricist, reminiscent of the Augustinian-Franciscan tradition for whom the world was a temporal epiphany of the eternal implications and ramifications of the eternal ideas. For Emerson, "A fact is the end or last issue of spirit."[19] Such facticity, paradoxically, comes to us only on behalf of our grasping and formulating the inherent symbolic features of our life.

> We learn nothing rightly until we learn the symbolical character of life. Day creeps after day, each full of facts, dull, strange, despised things, that we cannot enough despise—call heavy, prosaic and desert. The time we seek to kill: the attention it is elegant to divert from things around us. And presently the aroused intellect finds gold and gems in one of these scorned facts—then finds that the day of facts is a rock of diamonds; that a fact is an Epiphany of God.[20]

The epiphanic, for Emerson, is not a result of human quietism. It is we who constitute these "facts" by our forging of relations. "Every new relation is a new word."[21] The making of words for Emerson, as for James, is the making of the world of meaning. Words are not simply grammatical connectors. As the embodiment of relations they do more than define. They make and remake the very fabric of our world as experienced. "The world is emblematic. Parts of speech are metaphors, because the whole of nature is a metaphor of the human mind."[22] This text mirrors the binary strands found in subsequent American philosophy: the idealist-pragmatic epistemology of James, Royce, Dewey, and Peirce, each with an original emphasis of one strand over another.

If we read the Emersonian project as one which focuses on the dialectic between the raw givenness of nature and the symbolic formulations of the human imagination, then we have a direct line of common interpretation from Emerson to the classic American philosophers. I grant that each of the American philosophers in question contexts this dialectic differently, yet even a cameo version reveals the similarity. The thought of Peirce, for example, exhibits a life-long tension between his acceptance of the irreducibly "tychistic" (i.e., chance-ridden) character of the world and of the inevitably fallibilistic character of human knowledge, and his extreme confidence in the method of science. And it is the tough-minded Peirce who writes that "without beating longer round the bush let us come to close quarters. Experience is our only teacher." And "how does this action of experience take place? It takes place by a series of surprises."[23]

The philosophy of John Dewey reflects a similar tension between a confidence in empirical method and the acknowledgment of novelty and unpredictability as indigenous to the history of nature. Dewey states that "Man finds himself living in an aleatory world; his existence involves, to put it baldly, a gamble. The world is a scene of risk; it is uncertain, unstable, uncannily unstable. Its dangers are irregular, inconstant, not to be counted upon as to their times and seasons. Although persistent, they are sporadic, episodic."[24]

Still, when faced with this extremely open and even perilous version of nature, Dewey calls upon philosophy to act as an intelligent mapping, so as to reconstruct, ameliorate, and enhance the human condition. Dewey's project is Emersonian, for the affairs of time and the activities of nature are the ground of inquiry, rather than the hidden and transcendent meaning of Being. Just as Emerson broke with the theological language of his immediate predecessors and many of his peers, so too did Dewey break with the ecstatic religious language of Emerson. This break in language should not hide from us that Dewey's understanding of the relationship which exists between nature and human life, echoes that of Emerson: always possibility, often celebration, frequently mishap and never absolute certitude.

As for an Emersonian analogue in Royce, readers of that indefatigable polymath know that cameo versions of any of his positions do not come easy. Nonetheless, Royce's long speculative trek away from the absolute and toward a theory of interpretation, ever reconstructed by the community, echoes Emerson's emphasis on the conduct of life. Royce was forced to abandon the doctrine of the absolute mind because he finally accepted the judgment of his critics that he could not account for the experience of the individual on either epistemological or metaphysical grounds. In his last great work, *The Problem of Christianity*, Royce has come full circle and awarded to the individual the task of formulating the "real world" by virtue of the relationship between "self-interpretation" and the "community of interpretation." Emerson wrote that "we know more from nature than we can at will communicate."[25] Similarly, Royce writes that "the popular mind is deep, and means a thousand times more than it explicitly knows."[26] In my judgment, Royce's mature thought, under the influence of Peirce, structures philosophically the earlier informal approach of Emerson. Although the content is Emersonian, the following passage from Royce brings a heightened philosophical sophistication.

> Metaphysically considered, the world of interpretation is the world in which, if indeed we are able to interpret at all, we learn to acknowledge the being and the inner life of our fellow-men; and to understand the constitution of temporal experience with its endlessly accumulating sequence of significant deeds. In this world of interpretation, of whose most general structure we have now obtained a glimpse, selves and communities may exist, past and future can be defined, and the realms of the spirit may find a place which neither barren conception nor the chaotic flow of interpenetrating perceptions could ever render significant.[27]

It is with William James, however, that the Emersonian dialectic between the creative and constructive character of the human mind and the apparently intransigent character of the physical world most explicitly comes to the fore. James, like Emerson, holds to a relationship of congeniality between nature and human power. They both avoid the alternate interpretations, which, in turn, would stress either the complete objectivity of the meaning of nature or a completely subjective version in which nature has an existence only at the behest of the human, or failing that, the absolute mind. In some ways, James outdoes Emerson in his stress on the "powers" and "energies" of the individual, although we should remember that he also emphasizes "seeing and feeling the total push and pressure of the cosmos."[28]

William James is profoundly aware of these alternate versions of our situation and often evokes them in an extreme way. Two texts from *Pragmatism* stand out in this regard, and if we put them back to back, the poles of the Emersonian dialectic are thrown into bold relief.

> Woe to him whose beliefs play fast and loose with the order which realities follow in his experience: They will lead him nowhere or else make false connexions.[29]

> In our cognitive as well as in our active life we are creative. We *add*, both to the subject and to the predicate part of reality. The world stands really malleable, waiting to receive its final touches at our hands. Like the kingdom of heaven, it suffers human violence willingly. Man *engenders* truths upon it.[30]

Obviously, both of these texts cannot stand at one and the same time. James was very much aware of this conflict and continued to pose it, even though he was simultaneously working his way out of the dilemma. In an earlier entry in an unpublished notebook, he gives a reason for maintaining this conflict. "Surely nature itself and subjective construction are radically opposed, one's higher indignations are nourished by the opposition."[31] Emerson, of course, would approve of both the "indignation" and the "nourishment." It should be noted, however, that James goes beyond Emerson at this point and develops his formal doctrine of radical empiricism to mediate this "opposition." The genesis and content of James's radical empiricism is a long and complicated story, but in his conclusion to his essay on "A World of Pure Experience," James sets out the dramatic presence of the knowing self in a world both obdurate and malleable.

> There is in general no separateness needing to be overcome by an external cement; and whatever separateness is actually experienced is not overcome, it stays and counts as separateness to the end. But the metaphor serves to symbolize the fact that experience itself, taken at large, can grow by its edges. That one moment of it proliferates into the next by transitions which, whether conjunctive or disjunctive, continue the experiential tissue, cannot, I contend, be denied. Life is in the transitions as much as in the terms connected; often, indeed, it seems to be there more emphatically, as if our spurts and sallies forward were the real firing-line of the battle, were like the thin line of flame advancing across the dry autumnal field which the farmer proceeds to burn. In this line we live prospectively as well as retrospectively. It is "of" the past, inasmuch as it comes expressly as the past's continuation; it is "of" the future in so far as the future, when it comes, will have continued *it*.[32]

So much for the refractions of the Emersonian dialectic in some of the classical American philosophers. At this point, the reader may well ask why I have not cited these philosophers on this central theme in Emerson? The response, alas, is quite simple. Our philosophers did not write very much on Emerson and when they did, the focus was often on other, if related, themes. I turn now to James, Santayana, Royce, and Dewey on Emerson, directly.

I I

At the age of three months, William James was visited by Ralph Waldo Emerson at the James family's home on Washington Square in New York City. This prepossessing and perhaps burdensome presence of Emerson lasted throughout most of the life of William James. In the decade following 1870, James read virtually everything Emerson wrote and at one point in 1873 made the following entry in his diary: "I am sure that an age will come when our present devotion to history, and scrupulous care for what men have done before us merely as fact, will seem incomprehensible; when acquaintance with books will be no duty, but a pleasure for odd individuals; when Emerson's philosophy will be in our bones, not our dramatic imagination."[33] Apparently, Emerson's thought had already reached the "bones" of James, for the above sentiment about the past is shared by Emerson. In "The American Scholar" he wrote that "I had better never see a book than to be warped by its attraction clean out of my own orbit and made a satellite instead of a system. The one thing in the world, of value, is the active soul."[34]

Some thirty years after his diary entry, in 1903, James was called upon to deliver the address at the centenary celebration for Emerson in Concord.[35] This occasion caused James to reread virtually all of Emerson's writings. Frankly, with regard to the question of the influence of Emerson on James, the address is disappointing. As one would expect, James is laudatory of Emerson's person and work.[36] And, as he often did in such pieces of encomium, the text is largely made up of long passages from Emerson. Despite these limitations, an important theme runs beneath the baroque prose of James and that of Emerson as selected by James. As we might expect, it is the theme of "possibility," of the hallowing of the everyday. James is struck by the radical temporality of Emerson's vision. He offers a brief collage of that attitude: " 'The Deep to-day which all men scorn' receives thus from Emerson superb revindication. 'Other world! There is no other world.' All God's life opens into the individual particular, and here and now, or nowhere, is reality. 'The present hour is the decisive hour, and every day is doomsday.' "[37]

James cautions us that Emerson was no sentimentalist. The transformation of stubborn fact to an enhanced symbolic statement of richer possibility was an activity that James found very compatible with his own stress on novelty and surprise. Emerson had written, "So is there no fact, no event, in our private history, which shall not sooner or later, lose its adhesive, inert form and astonish us by soaring from our body into the empyrean."[38] On behalf of this and similar passages, James comments that Emerson "could perceive the full squalor of the individual fact, but he could also see the transfiguration."[39]

Aside from this important focus on Emerson's concern for "individuals and particulars," James's address is taken up with praise of Emerson's style as a literary artist. I note the irony here, for such praise of style is precisely what has taken up much of the commentaries on the thought of James, often to the detriment of an analysis of his serious philosophical intent. It is unfortunate that James never undertook a systematic study of Emerson, especially as directed to his notions of experience, relations, and symbol. James would have found Emerson far more "congenial"[40] and helpful than many of the other thinkers he chose to examine. A detailed study of Emerson as an incipient radical empiricist is a noteworthy task for the future.

The response of Santayana to Emerson's thought was more censorious than that of James and Dewey. On several occasions, James compared the thought of Emerson and Santayana, to the detriment of the latter. In a letter to Dickinson S. Miller, James comments on Santayana's book, *The Life of Reason:*

> He is a paragon of Emersonianism—declare your intuitions, though no other man share them; . . . The book is Emerson's first rival and successor, but how different the reader's feeling! The same things in Emerson's mouth would sound entirely different. E. receptive, expansive, as if handling life through a wide funnel with a great indraught; S. as if through a pin-point orifice that emits his cooling spray outward over the universe like a nose-disinfectant from an "atomizer."[41]

We learn from a letter written by Santayana that James apparently had expressed similar sentiments to him as he had in the letter to Miller. Santayana was not pleased and in his response issues a devastating criticism of Emerson.

> And you say I am less hospitable than Emerson. Of course. Emerson might pipe his wood-notes and chirp at the universe most blandly; his genius might be tender and profound and Hamlet-like, and that is all beyond my range and contrary to my purpose. . . . What did Emerson know or care about the passionate insanities and political disasters which religion, for instance, has so often been another name for? He could give that name to his last personal intuition, and ignore what it stands for and what it expresses in the world. It is the latter that absorbs me; and I care too much about mortal happiness to be interested in the charming vegetation of cancer-microbes in the system—except with the idea of suppressing it.[42]

Although not quite so caustic as his rebuke to James, Santayana's writings on Emerson always had a critical edge to them. In an early essay, written in 1886, Santayana comments judiciously on Emerson's optimism, which he traces more to his person than to his doctrine. Yet, Santayana's sympathetic treatment of Emerson concludes with a damaging last line: "But of those who are not yet free from the troublesome feelings of pity and shame, Emerson brings no comfort, he is a prophet of a fair-weather religion."[43]

In 1900, as a chapter in his *Interpretations of Poetry and Religion*, Santayana published his best-known essay on Emerson. This piece has been frequently cited on behalf of those who are condescending to Emerson or severely critical of him. I believe this use of Santayana's essay to be a misreading. Certainly, Santayana was more indulgent of Emerson in 1900 than he was in 1911, when he published his famous essay on "The Genteel Tradition in American Philosophy." In 1911, Santayana lumps Emerson with Poe and Hawthorne as having "a certain starved and abstract quality." Further, their collective "genius" was a "digestion of vacancy."

> It was a refined labour, but it was in danger of being morbid, or tinkling, or self-indulgent. It was a play of intramental rhymes. Their mind was like an old music-box, full of tender echoes and quaint fancies. These fancies expressed their personal genius sincerely, as dreams may; but they were arbitrary fancies in comparison with what a real observer would have said in the premises. Their manner, in a word, was subjective. In their own persons they escape the mediocrity of the genteel tradition, but they supplied nothing to supplant it in other minds.[44]

In 1900, however, when Santayana addresses Emerson's thought directly, his evaluations are more favorable. Admitting of Emerson, that "at bottom he had no doctrine at all," Santayana writes that "his finer instinct kept him from doing that violence to his inspiration."[45] Santayana repeats his earlier contention that Emerson's power was not in his "doctrine" but rather in his "temperament." And that Emersonian temperament was, above all, antitradition and antiauthoritarian. Even though he was a classic instance of the "Genteel Tradition" and held many positions which were anathema to Santayana, Emerson nevertheless pleased Santayana by his refusal to professionalize and systematize his thought. Further, Santayana, with poetic sensibilities of his own, was taken with Emerson's style. He writes of Emerson: "If not a star of the first magnitude, he is certainly a fixed star in the firmament of philosophy. Alone as yet among Americans, he may be said to have won a place there, if not by the originality of this thought, at least by the originality and beauty of the expression he gave to thoughts that are old and imperishable."[46]

Still more to the point, and less known, is that Santayana shared Emerson's celebration and embracing of the "common." In 1927, as part of a chastising letter sent to Van Wyck Brooks, Santayana writes: "I therefore think that art, etc. has better soil in the ferocious 100% America than in the intelligentsia of New York. It is veneer, rouge, aestheticism, art museums, new theatres, etc. that make America impotent. The good things are football, kindness, and jazz bands."[47] It turns out that Santayana, like Whitman, learned something from Emerson.

Before examining John Dewey's essay on Emerson, I offer a brief interlude with a comment on Josiah Royce's assessment of Emerson. Although Royce was a voluminous writer[48] and ventured interpretations of an extremely wide range of problems and thinkers, he rarely spoke of Emerson. And yet, Royce thought far more of Emerson than we could have divined from his publications. In 1911, Royce delivered a Phi Beta Kappa oration in honor of William James, who had died the previous year. The theme of Royce's essay was that James was the third "representative American Philosopher." It was in Royce's opening discussion of the first two candidates that his version of Emerson emerged:

> Fifty years since, if competent judges were asked to name the American thinkers from whom there had come novel and notable and typical contributions to general philosophy, they could in reply mention only two men—Jonathan Edwards and Ralph Waldo Emerson. For the conditions that determine a fair answer to the question, "Who are your representative American philosophers?" are obvious. The philosopher who can fitly represent the contribution of his nation to the world's treasury of philosophical ideas must first be one who thinks for himself, fruitfully, with true independence, and with successful inventiveness, about problems of philosophy. And, secondly, he must be a man who gives utterance to philosophical ideas which are characteristic of some stage and of some aspect of the spiritual life of his own people. In Edwards and in Emerson, and only in these men, had these two conditions found their fulfillment, so far as our American civilization had yet expressed itself in the years that had preceded our civil war. . . .
>
> Another stage of our civilization—a later phase of our national ideals—found its representative in Emerson. He too was in close touch with many of the world's deepest thoughts concerning ultimate problems. Some of the ideas that most influenced him have their far-off historical origins in oriental as well as in Greek thought, and also their nearer foreign sources in modern European philosophy, but he transformed what ever he assimilated. He invented upon the

basis of his personal experience, and so he was himself no disciple of the orient, or of Greece, still less of England and Germany. He thought, felt, and spoke as an American.[49]

Again, we are left with a judgment as to Emerson's importance, notably in this case as a philosopher, but without subsequent or sufficient analysis. A search through the papers and publications of Royce does not cast much more direct light on this influence of Emerson. Royce's remarks do convince me, however, that Emerson wrought more in the lives of the classical American philosophers than written evidence can sustain.

Among the centenary addresses of 1903, we find another by an American philosopher, John Dewey. This essay sets out to rescue Emerson from the condescension implied when he is described as not a philosopher. Dewey complains that "literary critics admit his philosophy and deny his literature. And if philosophers extol his keen, calm art and speak with some depreciation of his metaphysic, it is also perhaps because Emerson knew something deeper than our conventional definitions."[50] The first of Dewey's complaints is now out of date, for Emerson is taken very seriously as a literary artist. The second complaint still holds, although with important exceptions as noted above in the work of Blau and Pollock.

In Dewey's judgment, Emerson has been misread and misunderstood. He takes as Emerson's project the submitting of ideas "to the test of trial by service rendered the present and immediate experience."[51] Further, Dewey contends that Emerson's method is consistent with this experimental endeavor. "To Emerson, perception was more potent than reasoning; the deliverances of intercourse more to be desired than the chains of discourse; the surprise of reception more demonstrative than the conclusions of intentional proof."[52]

It is intriguing that Dewey, whose own style is anything but oracular, would praise this approach of Emerson. One might rather expect this indulgence from those reared in the language of the existentialists or of twentieth-century religious thinkers, such as Buber, Berdyaev, and Marcel. A closer look at Dewey's text, however, provides some source of explanation. Similar to James's emphasis, Dewey states that the locus of Emerson's inquiry is the "possibility" inherent in the experience of the "common man." Against the opinions of other commentators, Dewey holds that Emerson's "ideas are not fixed upon any Reality that is beyond or behind or in any way apart, and hence they do not have to be bent. They are versions of the Here and the Now, and flow freely."[53]

Dewey is especially sympathetic with Emerson's attempt to avoid the "apart."[54] And he is convinced that Emerson knew, as few others, of the enervating and diluting effect often had by theory on the richness of common and concrete experience. Dewey's text on this issue is crystal-clear and can be read as well as a critique for much of what passes for philosophical discourse in our own time.

> Against creed and system, convention and institution, Emerson stands for restoring to the common man that which in the name of religion, of philosophy, of art and of morality, has been embezzled from the common store and appropriated to sectarian and class use. Beyond any one we know of, Emerson has comprehended and declared how such malversation makes truth decline from its simplicity, and in becoming partial and owned, become a puzzle of and trick for theologian, metaphysician and litterateur—a puzzle of an imposed law, of an unwished for and refused goodness, of a romantic ideal gleaming only from afar, and a trick of manipular skill, of specialized performance.[55]

Dewey took Emerson's task as his own. Although his prose lacked the rhetorical flights so natural to Emerson, he too wrote out of compassion for the common man and confidence in the "possibility" inherent in every situation. By the time of Dewey's maturity, the world of New England high culture had passed. Dewey, despite being born in New England, was a child of industrial democracy. He alone of the classic American philosophers was able to convert the genius and language of Emerson to the new setting. John Dewey, proletarian by birth and style, grasped that Emerson's message was ever relevant. In the conclusion to his essay on Emerson, Dewey captures that message and carries it forward to his own time. I offer that we should do likewise.

> To them who refuse to be called "master, master," all magistracies in the end defer, for theirs is the common cause for which dominion, power and principality is put under foot. Before such successes, even the worshippers of that which to-day goes by the name of success, those who bend to millions and incline to imperialisms, may lower their standard and give at least a passing assent to the final word of Emerson's philosophy, the identity of Being, unqualified and immutable, with Character.[56]

3   The Promethean Self and Community in the Philosophy of William James

Surely the individual, the person in the singular number, is the more fundamental
phenomenon, and the social institution of whatever grade, is but secondary and ministerial.
WILLIAM JAMES, *Memories and Studies*

From the outset, we should make it clear that readers of the writings of
William James are hard put to find a doctrine of community therein. In
fact, the basic cast of his thought runs not only against social conglom-
erates but against simple aggregates as well. In a letter of June 7, 1899,
he writes:

> As for me, my bed is made: I am against bigness and greatness in all their forms,
> and with the invisible molecular moral forces that work from individual to indi-
> vidual, stealing in through the crannies of the world like so many soft rootlets, or
> like the capillary oozing of water, and yet rending the hardest monuments of
> man's pride, if you give them time. The bigger the unit you deal with, the hol-
> lower, the more brutal, the more mendacious is the life displayed. So I am
> against all big organizations as such, national ones first and foremost; against all
> big successes and big results; and in favor of the eternal forces of truth which
> always work in the individual and immediately unsuccessful way, under-dogs
> always, till history comes, after they are long dead, and puts them on the top.[1]

James was an unabashed and indefatigable champion of sheer individuality. Many have interpreted him as the paragon of a philosophical version

of the mythic American claim to rugged individualism, despite his own proclivities being due more to the genteel Brahmin experience than to that of the more fabled frontier sort. Nonetheless, James's version of the individual has much to teach us about a doctrine of community, especially as it is worked out in the fabric of American life.

It is unquestionable that a central theme in all of James's life and thought has to do with the nature of self-consciousness and the meaning of human activity. The remarkable upshot of this long-standing theme is that James collapses the first concern, self-consciousness, into the second, human activity, so that John Dewey can write of "the vanishing subject in the psychology of James."

> There is a double strain in the "principles of psychology" by William James. One strain is official acceptance of epistemological dualism. According to this view, the science of psychology centers about a subject which is "mental" just as physics centers about an object which is material. But James's analysis of special topics tends, on the contrary, to reduction of the subject to a vanishing point, save as "subject" is identified with the organism, the latter, moreover, having no existence save in interaction with environing conditions. According to the latter strain, subject and object do not stand for separate orders or kinds of existence but at most certain distinctions made for a definite purpose within experience.[2]

Dewey is fundamentally correct in the interpretation of the *Principles*. He, like other subsequent commentators, was able to spot James's early dubiety about the existence of a substantial self, because of the later position taken in *Essays in Radical Empiricism*.[3] It is made clear in those essays that James, while writing the *Principles*, had adopted a methodological dualism between self and world only because he would not resolve the question of consciousness at that time. It is not until some fifteen years later that James presents his mature position on these matters, especially in "Does Consciousness Exist?" (1904) and "The Experience of Activity" (1905). This line of intellectual development from the *Principles* to *Essays in Radical Empiricism* is now a commentator's truism and I do not oppose it. Yet there is another strand in this development, and, when noticed at all, it is not sufficiently integrated into James's radically empirical doctrine of human activity. I refer here to the evocative language of his personal crisis and his ensuing attempt to pose the human will as cognitive. In short, I see James's self as one that is self-creating in its transactions with the environment. Although it is true that James's focus was distinctively and aggressively individual, it will not take much transformation to show that his phenomenology of the *Lebenswelt* can be understood in a social matrix. John Dewey, for one, had no difficulty in overlooking just that transformation of James's position, without, however, so acknowledging.

Proceeding now, *seriatim,* I wish to consider the developmental stages in James's doctrine of the self: a) his crisis texts, b) material from *The Principles of Psychology,* and c) his radical empiricism. I shall then attempt to illustrate the social and communal significance of James's position, as if he had chosen to do so himself.

At this point in the James literature, his crisis texts are comparatively well known, although aspects of them have not been adequately studied. We have three texts extant, of which two are diary entries of February 1, 1870, and April 30, 1870. The third is more difficult to place chronologically, although the experience on which it was based most likely occurred sometime between the two diary entries mentioned above.[4] The actual publication of this third text occurred in *The Varieties of Religious Experience* under the guise of a communication from an anonymous French correspondent. We now know this to be an autobiographical version of an experience undergone by James some thirty years earlier.

It is difficult to know exactly the cause of James's period of depression from 1868 until 1870, although this has not stilled the frequent speculation as to a correct diagnosis of his malady, especially as he and his family have left so very many private papers and letters.[5] One of the most intriguing and plausible interpretations is that of William Clebsch, who attributes to James an advanced case of acedia. Considering James's situation from 1868 until 1870, Clebsch writes:

> In an earlier era this plight would have been recognized as acedia, or torpor. Catholic moralists wrongly combined this eighth deadly sin of the early monks with sloth, mistaking the inability to act for laziness. Acedia was rather an overscrupulous wondering about what one ought to do. It prevented one from doing anything. It tempted one to suicide as the only escape from the ennui and the guilt of inactivity. Victims of acedia could love nothing, could hate only themselves and could hate themselves only for their inability to love anything, including themselves.
>
> In the history of Western spirituality acedia had been treated by placing its victims under the absolute spiritual authority of another. Martin Luther's confessor dealt with such scrupulosity in the young monk by ordering him to teach biblical theology in Wittenberg. But James had no Doctor John Staupitz. The

sole authority he could find was his own ability to believe that he might command his own will. Having envisioned the only escapes from acedia as committing suicide or having a shriveled soul, James became his own spiritual director. Reciting verses of comfort in the crisis of fear had held James back from insanity and suicide, but God had not delivered him. He began saving himself from acedia, a feat traditionally held impossible. He became, as it were, at once the sick-souled patient and his own absolving confessor. Nor does it detract from the feat to point out that his indulgent father could afford to let this thirty-one-year-old son teach or rest, work or travel, as best pleased him. The fiscal ease that allowed for this cure must also have deepened the malady.[6]

In his diary entry of February 1, 1870, James states his plight:

Today I about touched bottom, and perceive plainly that I must face the choice with open eyes: shall I frankly throw the moral business overboard, as one unsuited to my innate aptitude, or shall I follow it, and it alone, making everything else merely stuff for it? I will give the latter alternative a fair trial. Who knows but the moral interest may become developed. . . . Hitherto I have tried to fire myself with the moral interest, as an aid in the accomplishing of certain utilitarian ends.[7]

In my judgment, James here laments his second-handedness. Burdened by his father's overwhelming presence and his pressure on James to adopt a career, he entertains the possibility of abandoning his inherited ethic for a hedonistic life. James's complaint about the "moral business" is that it functioned only in a utilitarian way and was not deeply rooted as a personal commitment. His inability to cut between these options of hedonism and second-handedness made him ripe for an intense personal experience undergone sometime in the early spring of 1870. As James tells it:

Whilst in this state of philosophic pessimism and general depression of spirits about my prospects, I went one evening into a dressing-room in the twilight to procure some article that was there; when suddenly there fell upon me without any warning, just as if it came out of the darkness, a horrible fear of my own existence. Simultaneously there arose in my mind the image of an epileptic patient whom I had seen in the asylum, a black-haired youth with greenish skin, entirely idiotic, who used to sit all day on one of the benches, or rather shelves against the wall, with his knees drawn up against his chin, and the coarse gray undershirt, which was his only garment, drawn over them inclosing his entire figure. He sat there like a sort of sculptured Egyptian cat or Peruvian mummy, moving nothing but his black eyes and looking absolutely non-human. This image and my fear entered into a species of combination with each other. *That shape am I,* I felt; potentially. Nothing that I possess can defend me against that fate, if the hour for it should strike for me as it struck for him.[8]

The key line in this text is James's warning, *"that shape am I,* I felt, potentially."* James is hereby denying the existence of a fixed, inherited self as a given. The choice of the word "shape" is crucial here, for it attributes an almost chameleonlike character to self-identity. The self that we accept ourselves to be is but one tenuous shaping, which is vulnerable to forces that can upend it and cause us to present ourselves to the world in a multiple number of profoundly different ways. The task is obvious. We must seize the world on behalf of our own version and it is this version that is to become our self. This is not to be an act of intellect but rather an act of will. On April 30, 1870, James records this decisive step.

I think that yesterday was a crisis in my life. I finished the first part of Renouvier's second "Essais" and see no reason why his definition of Free Will—"the sustaining of a thought *because I choose to* when I might have other thoughts"—need be the definition of an illusion. At any rate, I will assume for the present—until next year—that it is no illusion. My first act of free will shall be to believe in free will. . . .

Not in maxims, not in *Anschauungen,* but in accumulated *acts* of thought lies salvation. *Passer outre.* Hitherto, when I have felt like taking a free initiative, like daring to act originally, without carefully waiting for contemplation of the external world to determine all for me, suicide seemed the most manly form to put my daring into; now, I will go a step further with my will, not only act with it, but believe as well; believe in my individual reality and creative power. My belief, to be sure, *can't* be optimistic—but I will posit life (the real, the good) in the self-governing *resistance* of the ego to the world. Life shall [be built in] doing and suffering and creating.[9]

The die is cast for James's future in both life and thought. Not seduced by any form of Pollyanna optimism,[10] James affirms the creative character of the human organism in positing the meaning of the world as inseparable from how we "have" the world, that is, how we experience the world. We are not to the world as a spectator is to a picture but rather as a sculptor to matter.[11]

If the crisis texts yield an impressionistic view of the fragility of the self, James's scientific dubiety of the fixed self is found in *The Principles of Psychology.* In the chapters in "The Stream of Thought" and "The Consciousness of Self," he rejects the classical doctrine of the substantial soul, and the idealist transcendental ego. And although he expresses some admiration for Hume's treatment of personal identity,[12] he condemns the ensuing associationist philosophy as being unable to account for how the self "comes to be aware of itself."[13] Two years after publishing the *Principles,* James was forced to condense his thoughts on the self for presentation in his *Psychology—Briefer Course.*

> The consciousness of Self involves a stream of thought, each part of which as 'I' can remember those which went before, know the things they knew, and care paramountly for certain ones among them as 'Me,' and *appropriate to these* the rest. This Me is an empirical aggregate of things objectively known. The *I* which knows them cannot itself be an aggregate; neither for psychological purposes need it be an unchanging metaphysical entity like the Soul, or a principle like the transcendental Ego, viewed as 'out of time.' It is a *thought,* at each moment different from that of the last moment, but *appropriative* of the latter, together with all that the latter called its own. All the experiential facts find their place in this description, unencumbered with any hypothesis save that of the existence of passing thoughts or states of mind.[14]

The self that is appropriative in the stream of thought is the physiological correlate to the Promethean self of the crisis texts. Further, this self is anticipatory of the self that risks belief in hypotheses so as to elicit data unavailable were an agnostic position adopted. Consequently, James's much maligned essay on "The Will to Believe" is simply an epistemological version of what he earlier affirmed in deeply personal terms and then accounted for in the context of physiological psychology.[15]

The next step in James's development of his notion of the self comes with his doctrine of radical empiricism. Its most clear formulation is found in his preface to *The Meaning of Truth,* published in 1909.

> Radical empiricism consists first of a postulate, next of a statement of fact, and finally of a generalized conclusion.
>
> The postulate is that the only things that shall be debatable among philosophers shall be things definable in terms drawn from experience. [Things of an unexperienceable nature may exist ad libitum, but they form no part of the material for philosophic debate.]
>
> The statement of fact is that the relations between things, conjunctive as well as disjunctive, are just as much matters of direct particular experience, neither more so nor less so, than the things themselves.
>
> The generalized conclusion is that therefore the parts of experience hold together from next to next by relations that are themselves parts of experience. The directly apprehended universe needs, in short, no extraneous trans-empiri-

cal connective support, but possesses in its own right a concatenated or continuous structure.[16]

Both the "statement of fact" and the "generalized conclusion" are significant for our present concerns. The "fact" is that relations become experienced equivalent to the objects experienced. This yields a tissue of continuous transition, in which the human organism is never wholly other from the relations that intend or lead from the world of objects. This continuity is affectively experienced, always, in such a way that it is never necessary or warranted to posit as "a generalized conclusion" that there be an external principle of accountability, be it God, the Absolute Mind, or some eternal law of Nature. The significance of James's position is that the human self, as it were, is on its own for its own creation within the flow of experience. That is, the human self is on its own for the formulation of its peculiar "shape" as wrested from the "push and pressure of the cosmos."[17] Actually, forging the self is a scramble, characterized by the interplay of environ and presence, with novelty and mishap lurking everywhere. So strongly does James believe this version, that in a footnote to his essay on "The Experience of Activity," he portrays the vaunted "I" as but a pronoun of position, struggling to maintain its presence in an ever shifting relational flow.

The individualized self, which I believe to be the only thing properly called self, is a part of the content of the world experienced. The world experienced (otherwise called the 'field of consciousness') comes at all times with our body as its centre, centre of vision, centre of action, centre of interest. Where the body is is 'here'; when the body acts is 'now'; what the body touches is 'this'; all other things are 'there' and 'then' and 'that'. These words of emphasized position imply a systematization of things with reference to a focus of action and interest which lies in the body; and the systematization is now so instinctive (was it ever not so?) that no developed or active experience exists for us at all except in that ordered form. So far as 'thoughts' and 'feelings' can be active, their activity terminates in the activity of that body, and only through first arousing its activities can they begin to change those of the rest of the world. The body is the storm centre, the origin of coordinates, the constant place of stress in all that experience-train. Everything circles round it, and is felt from its point of view. The word 'I', then, is primarily a noun of position, just like 'that' and 'here'. Activities attached to 'this' position have prerogative emphasis, and, if activities have feelings, must be felt in a peculiar way. The word 'my' designates the kind of emphasis. I see no inconsistency whatever in defending, on the one hand, 'my' activities as unique and opposed to those of outer nature, and on the other hand in affirming, after introspection, that they consist in movements in the head. The 'my' of them is the emphasis, the feeling of perspective-interest in which they are dyed.[18]

A careful reading of this text shows that James's Promethean self is still tinged with the fragility that emanates from the "crisis" texts. If the "my" of myself is dependent on how I "feel" the messages of my environment, then we are perilously close to a derivative self. Yet James insists that in our conscious life we are active; welcoming, selecting, and choosing all the while. After all, "each of us dichotomizes the Kosmos in a different place."[19]

For casual readers of James, the term "Kosmos" may seem rather prepossessing. Indeed, it is nothing less than the cosmos that is the immediate environ. Nonetheless, such an environ must be experienced in distinctively personal terms. For James, "so long as we deal with the cosmic and the general, we deal only with the symbols of reality, but *as soon as we deal with the private and personal phenomena as such, we deal with realities in the completest sense of the term.*"[20]

We must admit that James seems to miss a crucial context at this point. On the one hand, consciousness has access to nothing less than the wider range of consciousness "from which saving experiences flow in."[21] On the other hand, our "inner state is our very experience itself; its reality and that of our experience are one."[22] Yet, as we of the twentieth century know all too well, it is the filtering of these cosmic and personal experiences through the social matrix that is how we have our being. To the contrary, James is quite intractable on this matter, for even when he describes the social context of our experience, he asserts the irreducibility of the distinctively personal. He writes:

A conscious field *plus* its object as felt or thought of *plus* an attitude towards the object *plus* the sense of a self to whom the attitude belongs—such a concrete bit of personal experience may be a small bit, but it is a solid bit as long as it lasts; not hollow, not a mere abstract element of experience, such as the 'object' is when taken all alone.[23]

All is not lost, however. What would happen if we were to describe James's radically empirical self in distinctively social terms? Let us contend that the relational environ is so irreducibly social that James's descriptive tension between the Promethean self and a wider range of consciousness is mediated by social transactions. In direct terms, James is not much help on this matter. In the almost 1,400 pages of text in his *Principles of Psychology,* he devotes litle more than two pages to the "social self." His version of the social self sounds quaint to our contemporary awareness. He writes that "*a man's Social Self* is the recognition which he gets from his mates. . . . Properly speaking, *a man has as many social selves as there are individuals who recognize him and carry an image of him in their mind.*"[24] Although this statement is the line of prose and thought that provided the impetus for G. H. Mead to develop his own important doctrine of the self as social, it is not the direction I wish to take.

My contention is that if we take James's radical empiricism as our point of departure, we can develop a notion of the social self that can be of fundamental assistance to contemporary social thought.[25] The self in James's thought is both aggressive and fragile. Its home-made character poses a challenge to forge a series of mooring points in an ever-changing flow of experience. These moorings are vantage points rather than pylons. The self casts about for the optimum relational choices, seeking to advance the interest-oriented concerns of the organism. To fail to make relations yields three pejorative results. The self is either cut adrift as flotsam in the flow, or is mired while the flow rushes by, impervious to our needs, or still again, more dangerously, is cast out of the flow and remains discarded as jetsam. When the self is self-creative, it moves hand over hand through the relational fabric, pointing, intending, leading, and constructing all the while. For the self to be without novel relations is for it to be subject to enervation and severe shrinkage, somewhat like the proverbial "raisin in the sun." Relation amputation and relation starvation threaten the capacity of the self to energize and reshape in response to the novel press of experience. In reverse, relation saturation and relation seduction are characterized by an accosting of the self with more than it can handle, either quantitatively or qualitatively.[26] The making of relations is not done out of whole cloth, for each relation has its own set of demands and prices. In effect, the self proceeds from its own transient locale, physically and psychologically, and, as such, confronts relational possibilities and implications intended to be consonant with its own interests. These relations, however, often have other fish to fry. They teem with hidden novelty and obligations to still other relations not directly in the purview of the self.

James is quite aware of these novelties, for he writes: "Our fields of experience have no more definite boundaries than have our fields of view.

Both are fringed forever by a *more* that continuously develops and continuously supersedes them as life proceeds."[27] The "more" of which James
speaks is not a mere accretion. Rather it begets still further novelty. In
a kaleidoscopic fashion, each turn of the wheel, each new relation begets
not only "more" relationships but retroactively changes the relationships
previously undergone. For James, "there can *be* no difference anywhere
that doesn't make a difference elsewhere."[28] Whereas the common assumption is that we stand relatively fixed, somewhat as an observer, while
things and situations change "around" us, James's perception of our situation is radically different. The self, as present to the world, is more of
a permeable membrane than a spectating redoubt. Relational changes do
not happen "around" us as mere external ports of call. Rather, they penetrate the very fabric of our being and, optimally at least, demand that we
reshape, reassess, reconnoiter, rework, and revisit each of our previous
relations undergone. For the most part, we do not act this way, lapsing
rather into an Archimedean point of view as a spectator of a picture. In this
latter way, relations are only external to us, shorn of their febrility and
capacity to transform. We move through the world as ghouls, looking but
not seeing. We are dead, not only to the press of experience, but to ourselves as well.

Now to the point at issue, the Jamesian self and its relationship to the
experience of community. Just as the self is a bundle of relations, so more
so is the community. Communal relations differ from the ongoing fabric of
relations, *überhaupt,* in that they are self-conscious and often intentionally
reflective. James failed to focus on the fact that my own self-consciousness
comes into being inseparable from how I am consciously "had" by others.
He was unaware of Marx's notion of the *Gattungswesen,* or species-
consciousness, which is the single most potent influence on how I come to
understand who I am. James was correct in stressing the creative, interested, and assertive character of the human organism. He neglected, however, the formative power of the social situation, which, despite our
Promethean protestations, conditions all of our versions of what we are
doing, including and especially those we contend to be distinctively independent of such influence. In a word, James was not aware of the blanket-
ing presence of self-deception, a notion so central to twentieth-century
thought as a bequest from Marx, Dostoevsky, Nietzsche, and Sartre.

Still, James is not without significant contributions on this matter.
Twentieth-century social thought, when sophisticated, is largely an attack

on the naive tradition of a substantial self, operating independently of its social environment. James never held such a position. Somewhat ironically, then, it turns out that although James does not take into sufficient consideration the significance of the social context, his empirical description of the human self is strikingly akin to that of twentieth-century thought. Specifically, James's self is functionally rather than ontologically derived. Although his point of departure is physiology, James duplicates the position of existential thought, namely, that the human self has no fixed place from which to proceed. In fact, it is precisely this lack of an inherited place that distinguishes James's notion of the self from classical philosophical and psychological positions, and which therefore makes James's thought so relevant to contemporary social thought. Indeed, the only notion of the self that is viable in our century is one that is functional rather than ontological in its principle of accountability. And that is precisely the position of James. Let us look at the potential significance of James's thought on this issue, as directed to the important contemporary problem of "having a place."

In my judgment, the crucial difference between Aristotelianism and Copernicanism traces to the doctrine of place. In the Aristotelian perspective, everything had a natural place, and the human organism was not an exception. Copernicanism dealt a devastating blow to this living-room version of the cosmos, by casting deep doubt on the fixed character of the planets. The intervening centuries between Copernicanism and the twentieth century witnessed an effort at temporary repair by Newtonian physics. But the die was cast and the full implications of Copernicanism finally arrived in our century, sustained by quantum mechanics, a new cosmology, and the socially derived collapse of religious, political, and ideological eschatologies. In a word, the deepest contemporary ontological problem is that of homelessness. Pascal anticipated our situation when he wrote: "The eternal silence of these infinite spaces frightens me."[29]

James, to the contrary, was not put off by the collapse of the Aristotelian world view. He never assumed that we had a place, for, as such, there is no place as proper place. If James is correct, as I think he is, then we have no place, for, in fact, there is no place. A place, like time in the famous adage, must be seized. To seize a place is not only to affirm that this is my place. It is also to deny a host of relations, such as, for example, this is your place, some other place, or no place at all. It is true that to be is to be in place, that is, in some place rather than another place. What is less obvious, however, is that every place seized is a place denied. Every relation accepted is a relation denied, or held up, or held off, and, therefore, the place we have is by no means the one we must have, although we come to think of it that way. Epistemologically, our strongest tendency by far is to assume that the way things are is the way they should be, or even must be. In James's philosophy, this is not so, for the way things are is most often a path of least resistance, a result of having said a precipitous "no" to countless alternatives. Saying "yes" to a relational posibility often has the unfortunate consequence of having to deny that we have said "no" to a series of competing relational possibilities. Having denied that we have said "no," it is too infrequent that we reopen the conversation, tending rather to accept our situation as inevitable and fixed. We receive little help here from our peers, since they for the most part function similarly. Further, all of us seem to treat each other as though our own fixations, *mutatis mutandis,* belong to them as well.

The social science of community, or even of general human gatherings, has not been of much help here. Categories abound: mother, father; black, white; parent, child; male, female; rural, urban; blue and white collar; each cleaves to its own peculiar separation, oblivious that such distinctions crisscross and render dubious any subsequent generalization. In a word, we have come to accept sameness rather than relational novelty as the order of the day.

On behalf of this contention, let us ask the following questions: What is it to say that someone lives *there* or *here* or *somewhere?* What is it to say that someone went *there* or *someplace?* Again, what do we mean when we say that someone is from *there* or *here* or *someplace?* In general, there is a tendency to think that we know what we mean by such identifications, such placeholders. To the contrary, in empirical terms, I think that we assert what we do not, in fact, know, but only assume as a fallout of the generic meaning of the placeholder. In effect, we affirm a name, a location, an identity as a way of salvaging and negating most of the relationships that any event, place, or person necessarily entails. Thereby, we trade off sterile, nominating concepts as a substitute for the richness of actual situations. In Jamesian terms, these nominations are but placeholders, barely representative of the relational fullness with which life concretely comes. For James, as we have mentioned, even the *I,* the *me,* is but a stand-in for the rush of competing selves that both occupy and relent in our stream of consciousness. Things, and all the more so, selves, are not singles. Rather, they are knots of competing relations, fluid and not definable as separate from how they are experienced in the consciousness of others. Yet with rare, albeit important exceptions,[30] the social sciences still assume that things exist as such, that objects exist as such, and that names are descriptive of events, places, and artifacts, rather than as substitutes for processes. And, of course, the converse is also held, namely, that unless named, our experiences do not exist.[31] The relationship between such an attitude and the ascendancy of quantitative method in the social sciences should not be overlooked.

James's approach is decidedly different. In his thought, there are no singles outside the network, the web, or the concatenated context, which is never known as an *All-einheit*. Rather, to know the world is to know it as *durcheinander,* through and through, in which everything, every place, every event is freighted with a "more," a coming and a going, a saving and a losing. And we speak here on the level of the obvious, saying nothing at this time of the subterranean recesses of our conscious life, or our dreams, tics, and functionally repressed secrets.

Returning to our concern with the doctrine of place, let us deepen our analysis somewhat. Where are you? You answer, I am here. Yet here to you is there to me. What is it for you to be there, that is, to be in place, in that place? Your response, however prosaically jejune it may be, nonetheless has got to be relation-saturated. Supposing our site is a town, a village, a neighborhood, a farm, a block, that is, some version of a *Lebenswelt*. I now ask myself, did I start here? Or did I come here? Do I want to be here or am I backing and filling? Am I here on behalf of my leaving? Or, would my leaving betray my wanting to stay? And what of memories? Are they selective? If so, are they on behalf of my leaving or my staying? Perhaps I am that kind of person for whom memories are called upon not to justify what I want to do but rather to justify what I do.

Now it turns out that I leave from here in order to live there. From the side of leaving, why did I go? Was it a response to a need and if so, of what kind? Was it a response to a fantasy or to a Walter Mitty fulfillment? Again, could it not have been an escape? Perhaps it was only a drifting as in going from one place to another, in a form of personal flotsam. So too, from the side of arriving there from here, similar ambiguities crop up. Am I here because I wanted to come or because I have been forced to come, called by the lure and pull of others? Am I here on the way to somewhere else or as an exile, soon to return whence I came? Perhaps I am very unusual for an American, and I am here to stay. At least, so I think—now.

I can be still more specific. Let us take the case of a young child who is moved from one neighborhood, home, room, to another. This move is a "step up," as they say. The neighborhood is better, the home is nicer, and the room is bigger. Yet a deep loneliness sets in and our child cries itself to sleep each evening. Some would say that the obvious reason is a loss of friends, but I believe that to be too one-dimensional for a sufficient cause. Rather, the relations severed are more subtle. The Jamesian "penumbra," the "halo of relations," has been abandoned. Lost is the familiar creak of a stair, a shadow cast by the bough of a tree, and the play of light in the child's room, dusk to dawn. Each of them, among countless other sounds and shapes, has acted as a mooring for the ever floating consciousness. Psychically, we are originally weightless and it is necessary for us to hook ourselves to a series of things, artifacts, and images, which in turn tell us where we are and even who we are.

The social psychologists and the social anthropologists are correct. We are creatures formed in the cauldron of the other, selves, things, shadows of all shapes, rings of tones, scent of smells, and above all the double-barrelled touch of touch. James failed to stress sufficiently this context of other. Nonetheless, they fail to stress what James knew all too well, that the active self is hydra-headed and brimming with sensorial capacities, each of them capable of rendering distinctively personal even the most obvious of commonness.

Marx, Durkheim, Mead, Dewey, have it right. The self is a social construct. But James has it right as well. It is the personally idiosyncratic seeker of relations who puts a distinctive cast on the world. Marx tells us that institutions condition consciousness, but who more than Marx himself intruded his personal version of the world on these very same institutions. The social and the communal are intrusive, but so too is the personal. Nothing is final. To this, James attests over and over.

> Everything you can think of, however vast or inclusive, has on the pluralistic view a genuinely 'external' environment of some sort or amount. Things are 'with' one another in many ways, but nothing includes everything, or dominates over everything. The word 'and' trails along after every sentence. Something always escapes. 'Ever not quite' has to be said of the best attempts made anywhere in the universe at attaining all-inclusiveness.[32]

Above all, the escape is perpetrated by the individual, especially the Promethean self. In the last analysis, the critical question is *how* do we feel and *how* we do feel *about*? In the contemporary stress on social conditioning let us not forget James's warning:

> Individuality is founded in feeling; and the recesses of feeling, the darker, blinder strata of character, are the only places in the world in which we catch real fact in the making, and directly perceive how events happen, and how work is actually done.[33]

Two

THE AMERICAN ODYSSEY AND ITS BEQUEST
AS CHAMPIONS OF SURPRISE

The human journey is a paradox, for unless one believes that we are to be rescued by a *deus ex machina* subsequent to our death, then it is a trip with an ending that culminates in oblivion. Nonetheless, the journey motif is central to world culture and especially to world literature. One can read the marvelous sixteenth-century version of the journey of the Chinese monk Hsüan-tsang, who from 596 to 664 sought the wisdom of Buddhist scriptures in India. Known in English as *The Journey to the West*, this literary and cultural classic reveals in endless detail the saga of seeking, trekking, and reaching out to an unknown future, so as to articulate the meaning of our present and to knit only apparently alien places and traditions into a common quest. In Western civilization, the journey motif is the font of our most powerful literature: the *Odyssey* of Homer, the *Aeneid* of Virgil, the *Divine Comedy* of Dante, and the interior wanderings of the *Faust* of Goethe. Countless other versions exist in the travel and exploration literature of the modern European age, when the "journey to the West" took as its task to cross the great ocean and "found" a New World.

The United States of America, known to the world however inaccurately as simply America, is a result of these journeys. America was born as a child of the journey west, an event which bequeathed bewilderment, terror, and finally destruction of the American Indian people for whom the land in question was their home. The arrival of the European settlers in America began still another odyssey to the West, one inspired by the Hebrew Bible as reinterpreted by Calvinist puritanism. The trek through the American wilderness, carrying as it did bold political and social values, has been responsible for building the most awesome and influential civilization in the modern world.

The newest of the great civilizations in the history of the world, America has the advantage of being dedicated to novelty and experiment, while not being burdened by many centuries of encrusted tradition. Yet this very freedom to improvise has caused America to often lack a necessary reflective attitude, which in turn has generated an arrogance and an insensitivity to aged cultures whose strength is in continuity rather than in adaptation.

America, as a culture, is a complex affair. Multiethnic, multireligious, and made up of virtually every persuasion and outlook, America represents, in anticipation, the look of global culture in the next century. The succeeding essays attempt to probe the potential bequest of America to the next century. In my judgment, the contribution of America to the future of world culture is no longer dependent on whether America itself can institutionalize its own best wisdom. The human message of the American odyssey over the last three centuries is of such importance that it transcends America's ability to realize its own insight in the fabric of daily activities. America sees clearly the need for a positive provincialism, a melioristic politics, a vibrant pluralism, and a commitment to growth while yet attending to the less fortunate.

Taken in the round, America is a culture of transiency. It was born as a result of an exploring journey and its history is one of continental trekking. Diverse in both origin and experience, the American people, for the most part, are committed to a pluralistic version of the important questions and consequently, are chary of any single, intractable, assured version of the human condition. In these essays, I attempt to probe the underlying assumptions of American culture and then assess their significance for a global future. Despite the existence of some self-preening and ideological religious rhetoric, I hold that America is made up of people for whom life is basically a journey, transient and worthy of meaning for its own sake and not for a posthumously requited future. Also, I believe that the American style of resolving disputes, despite occasional setback, is characterized by compromise, melioration, and a deep sense of multiple possible interpretations. This style, rendered in hard political decisions, strikes me as propitious for the future of humankind.

4 *Transiency and Amelioration*

AN AMERICAN BEQUEST FOR
THE NEW MILLENNIUM

The stark and startling residual wisdom of our collective past tells us that for the most part, by far, all great movements of the past have been on behalf of a definite goal—in short, an eschatology. Further, conversely rare has it been for the multitude to devote themselves to a cause whose message was the celebrating of the finite, the generational, and especially, sheer transiency.

I take as my head text lines from the poet Adrienne Rich, in her *Dream of a Common Language:* "I have to cast my lot with those who age after age, perversely, with no extraordinary power reconstitute the world."

Given the contemporary American scene, the call to reconstitute the world rings with the cadence of a faded antiquity. Seemingly bereft of both imagination and energy, the American political center gropes about, alternating between nostalgia for the previous decade and cynicism about the future. A diagnostic map of the last twenty years leads us from possibility to enervation; from Camelot to Watergate; from Selma to Sun Myung Moon and the political innocence that surrounds being "born again"; from involvement and social concern to anomie and hands-off; from innovation to the bottom line and the bludgeon of accountability; from the febrile and the intense to the flaccid; from Marx with an *x* to

Marks with a *ks;* from imagination and personal energy to fixed roles and second-handedness, from hope to cynicism.

Some among us[1] hold that our present situation is representative of the inevitable phase in the inexorable workings of a historical and cultural cycle. According to this belief, the benighted achievements of our past will be repeated, however different may be the rubric or the historical setting. I do not so believe, and I offer two reasons for my skepticism on this matter. First, the doctrine of history as cyclical focuses only on identities or similarities, thereby downplaying or missing the radical novelties that constitute the distinctively human character of historical development.[2] Second, and more germane to the present discussion, something different is at work in contemporary American culture. America is undergoing a change in its most important and profound commitment. America is experiencing a pervasive erosion in its belief in the myth of progress. This subtle jeopardy is no longer the mark of a Luddite fringe, but rather now makes itself felt across religious, racial, ethnic, social, and economic lines. For what it is worth, although I am as committed to the American myth of progress as anyone has ever been, I too experience an ontological twilight, a brownout of my consciousness, in the America of the recent seventies. Put directly, the religious and metaphysical originality of America is strapped to its belief in the sacredness of time, its celebration of journey and transiency, and its aversion to ideology, eschatology, and final solutions. The inversion of this order of priorities will sink us as a culture. We shall move either in the direction of emptiness, self-satisfaction, and narcissism[3] or toward self-righteousness and ideological certitude. Both of these tendencies have lurked at the extremes in our culture, but they have been held at bay by a vibrant, pluralistic center that, however unwittingly, invoked the maxims of C. S. Peirce, always fallibilism, always chance, and those of Emerson and Dewey, always possibility, always a new day.

Now before deepening the analysis of this contemporary cultural situation, allow me to allay some potential misapprehensions about my view of America and the myth of progress. I am not a cultural chauvinist nor a jingoist. The history of America is pockmarked with first-rate offenses. Need we repeat the litany: the devastation of the American Indian; the slavery of black Americans; the repression of religious, racial, and ethnic minorities; the vulgarity of American corporate capitalism, with its inequities generation after generation. I do not speak of America as a superior culture. I do speak of America as an originating culture, indeed, as one of the handful of genuinely novel cultures in the history of the world, for better and for worse. As for the meaning of the word *progress*, it is, like so many important American words, bumptious, homely, and subject to cliché versions.[4] Nonetheless, it masks a profound cultural attitude. From a classical point of view, the American use of the word *progress* seemingly harbors a contradiction, for it affirms growth while denying the existence of an ultimate goal, or the redemption of human death. In fact, we have no contradiction here, for despite Jessica Mitford and the practitioners of the academic death and dying industry, America does understand death, and thus rarely speaks of it. Death is the context for human life and like Dylan Thomas, as a people, we most often exhort:

> Do not go gentle into that good night
> Rage, rage against the dying of the light.

Or idiomatically, ignore death—grow. The upshot of this is that contrary to most commentators, the American myth of progress is not a yahoo, Pollyanna doctrine. Rather, it is an ameliorative response to the irreducible sadness of being human. Witness, for example, the version of Josiah Royce on our fundamental situation:

> Contemplate a battle field the first night after the struggle, contemplate here a vast company the equal of the population of a great town, writhing in agony, their groans sounding at a great distance like the roar of the ocean, their pain uneased for many hours, even death, so lavish of his favors all day, now refusing to comfort; contemplate this and then remember that as this pain to the agony of the world, so is an electric spark drawn from the back of a kitten to the devastating lightning of many great storms; and now estimate if you can the worth of all but a few exceptional human lives, such as that of Caius.
>
> Briefly and imperfectly I state the case for pessimism, not even touching the economical and social argument, drawn from a more special consideration of the conditions of human life. Such then, is our individual human life. What shall we call it and whereunto shall it be likened? A vapor vanishing in the sun? No, that is not insignificant enough. A wave, broken on the beach? No, that is not unhappy enough. A soap bubble bursting into thin air? No, even that has rainbow hues. What then? Nothing but itself. Call it human life. You could not find a comparison more thoroughly condemning it.[5]

II

I return now to the discussion of our present cultural situation. Historically, when in trouble, the American tradition was to issue a jeremiad, a lamentation over the fall from grace. As early as the third generation of the

New England Puritans, Increase Mather issued such a warning on behalf of the Boston Synod of 1679. Perry Miller writes of Mather's pronouncement, "The Necessity of Reformation," as the first in a long history "of investigations into the civic health of Americans." "The land was afflicted, it said, because corruption had preceded grace; assuredly if the people did not quickly reform, the last blow would fall and nothing but desolation be left."[6] Mather's version of the jeremiad articulates one of the two types of warning, namely, that doom befalls those who abandon previously held beliefs and values. American cultural history harbors a second version of the jeremiad, that is, the prophecy of doom resulting from inability or reluctance to convert the novelties of our experience into a transformation of our beliefs, assumptions, and expectations.[7] The classic statement of the second form of lamentation is found in the writings of Emerson, who in 1836 asked of Americans, "Why should not we also enjoy an original relation to the universe?"[8] Chastising Americans for their dependence on the whited sepulchers of the past, Emerson writes in "The American Scholar" that "perhaps the time is already come when it ought to be, and will be, something else; when the sluggard intellect of this continent will look from under its iron lids and fulfill the postponed expectation of the world with something better than the exertions of mechanical skill."[9] Closer to our own time, Alfred Kazin notes that our modern writers "have had to discover and rediscover and chart the country in every generation, rewriting Emerson's 'The American Scholar' in every generation" and yet "still cry America! America! as if we had never known America. As perhaps we have not."[10]

After Emerson, the first to rewrite "The American Scholar" was Whitman. And he was also the most explicit in combining the two strands of the jeremiad. In his *Democratic Vistas* of 1871, he echoes the sentiments of Increase Mather and the Boston Synod.

> For my part, I would alarm and caution even the political and business reader, and to the utmost extent, against the prevailing delusion that the establishment of free political institutions, and plentiful intellectual smartness, with general good order, physical plenty, industry, etc. (desirable and precious advantages as they all are), do, of themselves, determine and yield to our experiment of democracy the fruitage of success. With such advantages at present fully, or almost fully, possessed—the Union just issued, victorious, from the struggle with the only foes it need ever fear (namely, those within itself, the interior ones), and with unprecedented materialistic advancement—society, in these States, is

cankered, crude, superstitious and rotten. Political, or law-made society is, and private, or voluntary society, is also. In any vigor, the element of the moral conscience, the most important, the verteber to State or man, seems to me either entirely lacking, or seriously enfeebled or ungrown.

I say we had best look our times and lands searchingly in the face, like a physician diagnosing some deep disease. Never was there, perhaps, more hollowness at heart than at present, and here in the United States. Genuine belief seems to have left us.[11]

Yet it is also in *Democratic Vistas* that Whitman assumes that America embodies a "New World metaphysics."[12] And it is the same Whitman who earlier had written to Emerson, "Each age needs architects. America is not finished, perhaps never will be; now America is a true divine sketch."[13] And again, "Always, America will be agitated and turbulent. This day it is taking shape, not to be less so, but to be more so, stormily, capriciously, on native principles, with such vast proportions of parts."[14]

Now just as Emerson differed from Mather and Whitman from Emerson, so too must our jeremiad, *mutatis mutandis,* differ in turn from all three. Our present situation is distinctively different, for we are now far enough along to have a "usable past" of our own. The paradox of this "usable past," however, is that it is not made up of fixed values. Rather, it is characterized by an assumption about the experimental nature of the human quest. In Dewey's phrasing, we have learned to accrue wisdom, warrant assertions, and fund experiences, always within the context of the exigencies of history and the transformation of expectations. The irony here is that this native wisdom is exactly parallel to the speculative breakthroughs of the century at large. As a culture, we have anticipated much of what we have since been taught by modern art, modern physics, contemporary theology, social psychology, and process philosophy. The deeper irony, by far, is that no sooner has the creative thought of this century moved in the direction of the American angle of vision, than we have chosen to abandon our native assumptions. The thrust of our own jeremiad is clear. America is guilty of a failure of nerve and has lost sight of the specific meaning for itself, of the Shakespearean maxim, "to thy own self be true." To say it another way, now that America is faced with the need for spiritual rehabilitation without the luxury of physical relocation, it has begun to ape the manners of Old World civilizations without having access to the advantages of their long historical lineage. America has begun to back and fill. In desultory fashion, we seem to await a paradisiacal *deus ex machina,* as if there were available forces other than our own. In turn, we lose confidence in the myth of the journey as its own meaning, thereby leaving ourselves open to the acceptance of the dehumanizing implications of an eschatology. This approach is not only counter to the deepest commitments of our traditions, but if I read this century right, it is also out of step with the best of contemporary thought. At this point, a comparison of the philosophical underpinnings of the American tradition with some of the contentions of the last century should assist us in our cultural diagnosis.

III

Although distinctively a child of America, I am also a stepchild of Auschwitz and Hiroshima. And my generation came to consciousness under the spell of Marx, Nietzsche, Freud, Camus, and Sartre. We inherit as well the claims and versions of Albert Einstein, Werner Heisenberg, Franz Kafka, Marcel Duchamp, and Louise Nevelson, to mention only a few who symbolize the revolution in the parameters and possibilities of our consciousness.

(Like so many of my peers, I knew virtually nothing as a young man of American culture, let alone American philosophy. Yet significantly, I believe, I found the import of the intellectual revolution of the European thinkers to be obvious if dramatic. Further, their attack on the classical assumptions of Western culture interested me historically but did not threaten my own experience, which, albeit unreflective, was American. Of particular importance here was that I felt no loss in accepting the biting continental critique of social and religious hierarchy and of epistemological certitude.)

It is beyond the scope of this paper to detail the major implications of European speculative thought of the last 100 years, nor could I guarantee the agreement of others on those implications. Nonetheless, in my judgment at least, certain themes emerge not only as important but as directly relevant to an understanding of the reflective American tradition.

The first is that of place, as in having no natural place. More directly, the deepest contemporary ontological problem is that of homelessness. Copernicanism, born in the sixteenth century, finally arrives in the twentieth century. The macro-coziness of Newtonian physics can be sustained only as an earth construct. The human abode becomes a jerry-built neighborhood in the vast reaches of cosmic unintelligibility. Our sky is a diaphanous roof to nowhere. "Seize the time" is now joined by "seize the place," for neither is given to us. Human life is home-made. The literature and art of the century provide their own versions of this revolution in physics. Can one ever forget a first reading of Kafka? To be human is to be put on trial for no cause. The castle of salvation is out of reach, or perhaps even an illusion. The labyrinth of streets in Prague, back and forth across the Ulna, from the courthouse to the castle, symbolizes the human journey, without an exodus. For Gabriel Marcel, we are *homo viator*, people of the journey. He writes:

> Perhaps a stable order can only be established if man is acutely aware of his condition as a traveller, that is to say, if he perpetually reminds himself that he is required to cut himself a dangerous path across the unsteady blocks of a universe which has collapsed and seems to be crumbling in every direction.[15]

The most trenchant statement of the experience of deracination and the ensuing confrontation with temporality as the human way is to be found in the work of Karl Jaspers, "The Spiritual Crisis of our Times."

> As compared with man in those eras, man to-day has been uprooted, having become aware that he exists in what is but a historically determined and changing situation. It is as if the foundations of being had been shattered. How self-evident to the man of old seemed the unity of life and knowledge has become plain to us now that we realize that the life of our fellows in the past was spent under conditions in which reality was, as it were, veiled. We, on the other hand, have become able to see things as they really are, and that is why the foundations of life quake beneath our feet; for, now that the identity of thought and being (hitherto unchallenged) has ceased to exist for us, we see only, on the one hand, life, and, on the other, our own and our companions' awareness of that life. We do not, as did our forefathers, think merely of the world. We ponder how it is to be comprehended, doubting the validity of every interpretation; and behind every apparent unity of life and the consciousness of life there looms the distinction between the real world and the world as we know it. That is why we live in a movement, a flux, a process, in virtue of which changing knowledge enforces a change in life; and, in turn, changing life enforces a change in the consciousness of the knower. This movement, this flux, this process, sweeps us into the whirlpool of unceasing conquest and creation, of loss and gain, in which we painfully circle, subject in the main to the power of the current, but able now

and then to exert ourselves within a restricted sphere of influence. For we do not only live in a situation proper to mankind at large, but we experience this situation as it presents itself in specific historical circumstances, issuing out of a previous situation and progressing towards a subsequent one. [16]

Texts similar to the one above abound in the writings of twentieth-century thinkers. In my view, the fallout reads something like this: If the world as known is in some way a function of the knower, then introspection, sociology, and cosmology are of a piece. Further, if self-deception is an irreducible presence in human judgment, the test for meaning is communal and processive. Reality is not ultimately intelligible, for it cannot be understood from a single point of view, in that every point of view is a viewpoint. Existential philosophy, modern physics, and modern art join in common rejection of a world found or inherited. Making, relating, formulating, constituting, journeying become the strategies for survival and the source of intelligibility.

Returning to the parallel mentioned above, this revolution in European thought is anticipated experientially by the American tradition. Philosophically, it is also anticipated by the metaphysics of James and Dewey, although we did not understand that until after the advent of recent continental thought. A further parallel can be drawn, although its width necessarily houses exceptions. I do not think that European life has absorbed the significance of its own thought during the twentieth century. Conversely, I do not think that thought in America, especially in philosophy, has absorbed the insights of American life. I grant that this schizophrenia on both sides of the modern *mare nostrum* is not new. What is new, however, is that American culture now seems ready to abandon its own "form of life." That would be tragic for two reasons. First, the American "form of life" strikes me as the paradigm for the twenty-first century. Second, the American "form of life" has not been sufficiently articulated in a philosophical way, so that should America falter, its bequest could be re-enacted. Let us look further into the American angle of vision.

IV

To speak straight out, America never did believe in a doctrine of natural place. Nor did it abide inherited hierarchies. As early as the seventeenth century, we expressed a loathing for royalty, Anglican bishops, popery, and the Dutch feudal settlements of that century. And when pressed by authority or inherited doctrine, more often than not, we moved. Known in our literature as trekking or wending, it is described by de Tocqueville in the following way:

> Thus the European leaves his cottage for the transatlantic shores, and the American, who is born on that very coast, plunges in his turn into the wilds of central America. This double emigration is incessant! It begins in the middle of Europe, it crosses the Atlantic Ocean, and it advances over the solitudes of the New World. Millions of men are marching at once towards the same horizon; their language, their religion, their manners differ; their object is the same. Fortune has been promised to them somewhere in the West, and to the West they go to find it.[17]

Or again, witness this ambiguous text of Santayana. He deplores American transience and yet affirms that such a "form of life" generates remarkable and creative human possibilities.

> Consider now the great emptiness of America: not merely the primitive physical emptiness, surviving in some regions, and the continental spacing of the chief natural features, but also the moral emptiness of a settlement where men and even houses are easily moved about, and no one, almost, lives where he was born or believes what he has been taught. Not that the American has jettisoned these impedimenta in anger; they have simply slipped from him as he moves. Great empty spaces bring a sort of freedom to both soul and body. You may pitch your tent where you will; or if ever you decide to build anything, it can be in a style of your own devising. You have room, fresh materials, few models, and no critics. You trust your own experience, not only because you must, but because you find you may do so safely and prosperously; the forces that determine fortune are not yet too complicated for one man to explore. Your detachable condition makes you lavish with money and cheerfully experimental; you lose little if you lose all, since you remain completely yourself. At the same time your absolute initiative gives you practice in coping with novel situations, and in being original; it teaches you shrewd management. Your life and mind will become dry and direct, with few decorative flourishes. In your works everything will be stark and pragmatic; you will not understand why anybody should make those little sacrifices to instinct or custom which we call grace.[18]

The shift from the vertical social, political, and religious organization of the European West to the horizontal wanderings of Americans is of great significance. We must not forget that America was founded and given a theme early by the dissenting, convenanting Calvinists. For them the invisible, paradisiacal church of the Catholic tradition was anathema. They were of the visible church, in time and on the land. In American life, the covenant was sacred and pluralistic. Calvinist theology was, after all, known as Federalist theology. Secularization of the covenant changed the rhetoric but not the fundamental assumption. As early as the banishment of Anne Hutchinson, the die was cast in favor of a covenant of works, that is, what and how we do, here, is who we are. The line is straight from Winthrop to Edwards, Adams, Jefferson, Emerson, Royce, and Dewey. For them, the religious question is a temporal question, one of geopolitics and of the human transaction with the environment.[19] In American history, philosophers and theologians of the eternal are second-rate thinkers. Rather, covenanting takes place in the bowels of time, replete with the exigencies, possibilities, and ever lurking disasters that lace our journey. It is noteworthy as a generalization that our social and political thinkers and our classical philosophers have stressed the needs and possibilities of experience, whereas our writers and poets have focused on the disasters. In that vein, a contrast of the philosophy of William James with Melville's trenchant critique of the American philosophy of experience, in *The Confidence Man,* proves illuminating.

Contrary to common received wisdom, American thought is not Pollyannaish. If your philosophy of history is that history has no ultimate meaning and that time is meaningful by its own means, then, *sub specie aeternitatis,* the human situation is necessarily tragic. Yet, it is precisely and only for that reason that time becomes sacred. Our activities take on meaning not because they are endowed by the eternal but because they are not endowed by the eternal.[20] It is for this reason that the motif of the journey, so central to American life, turns up our most important metaphor, frontier, along with a host of allied and culturally significant terms: *experiment, chance, edge,* and *novelty.*

v

The trek "west" has been at the center of modern culture at least since the explorations of the late Renaissance. Inadvertently, America turned out to be the great discovery of that journey west. In our time, however, it has turned out to be the end. The Thoreau who wrote that when he walks, he walks west so as to be free, for to walk east is to be trapped, is now out of date. Whitman's song of the open road must now be put against the poem

of Louis Simpson, "At the End of the Open Road."[21] California is the end
of the trek and the end of the American physical journey. California is
America turned back on itself, introverted and bewildered, for open space,
horizontal and accessible, no longer stretches before us. Visually, California announces China and reflectively, it forces us back onto our own
intellectual traditions, beginning with John Winthrop, and in turn, back
further to the wisdom of antiquity. In a word, California announces a new
world, a global world, a world in which the trek has doubled back on itself.
And that shattering event of our own time makes of America an old world.

From the perspective of a philosophy of culture, the burning question
has to do with our bequest to the new world of global culture. What are we
to offer a new world? Are we to repeat, inversely, our earlier burden and
pose now as a parent? Is not there little difference in the term *colony* from
the more recent one, *undeveloped nation*? Does not the phrase *third world*
connote an increased maturity in global consciousness, dispensing as it
does with the simplistic distinction between old and new as well as with the
invidious comparisons attendant on that distinction? Some of us worry
that despite changes in language, we have appropriated for our own use
a masked version of the older form of arrogant mercantilism, be it economic or ideological. Do we, in fact, have anything to offer a new world?

One way to respond to these difficult questions is to monitor the role of
America in matters of economic and political responsibility, asserting the
need over and over for integrity, understanding, and compassion, and for
a genuine sense of global rather than simply national consciousness. Without gainsaying these irreducibly necessary political and diplomatic approaches to world culture, we point to still another response, this a philosophical bequest from the American angle of vision.

The question confronting us is not so much the prospect of philosophy
in the new world, nor is it the prospect of America in the new world.
Rather we should focus on those philosophical dimensions of American
culture that deserve to become operative factors in the formulation of
a new world culture. Worthy of detailed analysis, these warranted assumptions of our cultural history are presented here on behalf of further
scrutiny so as to assess their future viability. Taking them *seriatim*, I would
single out the following commitments:

   1. *Pluralism* as a positive and nonlamentable characteristic of the human
   condition. Pluralism is not a fall from grace or a style biding time for a future

unity. Ethnic, religious, racial, social, and aesthetic pluralism is a fundamental and fecund characteristic of the human condition. Patterns of unity, however intellectually desirable, are inevitably imposed, usually in a procrustean manner. Pluralism lacks neatness, but unity lacks compassion, and, being stingy, often misses the potentialities of loose ends.

2. *Provincialism* has a positive side. Surely we know in our time that to think only in terms of ourselves, our race, our nation, is to be cut off from insight and nutrition. Yet if we do not feel and think deeply about our intimate experiences, what chance do we have of global experience? As twentieth-century America has learned, to its chagrin, bigger is not better. Put simply, neighborhoods are sacred and so too are all the provincial experiences of all the people in global culture.

3. *Interrelatedness* is unavoidable. For every step forward, there is one sideways, if not backward. Life is lived not in lineal jumps, but rather in a complex of relations. Modern America, devoted as it is to science and technology, is slowly learning that even majestic breakthroughs often hide time bombs, set to go off generations hence. The miracle drug of one decade is the uterine cancer of a subsequent decade. One generation's pesticidal success is another's silent spring. As the Greeks knew long ago, mythologically, and Americans now discover scientifically, time extracts a price. The wisdom yielded is that we should think not so much in terms of objects and goals as in terms of implications and relations.

4. *Transience* as the "form of life" can be celebrated. As an anticipation of contemporary cosmology, the local journey mirrors the entire human odyssey, which is intense but transient. As a bequest, America offers a dramatically egalitarian evaluation of culture, one in which the quality of experience is not hierarchized by *a priori* judgments or the prepossessions of the past. For us, novelty is crucial and even failure and mishap are to be integrated into the pedagogy of history. At our best, we set our sights on amelioration rather than salvation.

5. *Anti-eschatology* can be constructive. The most important operative contention of American cultural history has to do with the ultimate meaning of history, or rather, with the absence of such finality. American culture is chary of ideology, particularly that of an eschatological cast. Calvinist in origin and, therefore, indebted more to the Hebrew than to the Christian scriptures, America has more interest in saving experiences than in salvation outside of time. We are a people deeply skeptical of final solutions and philosophies of history that provide principles of total accountability. Although we tarry and dally with salvation cults of every kind, none seems able ever to get the upper hand. Indeed, in keeping with our pluralism, we have set one nostrum against another, in effect, trimming the claim of each by the indulgence of many. We believe in healing and amelioration, while persistently doubting the presence of any ultimate resolution. It may very well be that we have stumbled on the only viable philosophy of history for a pluralistic world culture.

To come full circle, the land is one but the people are many. What is the New World to make of itself? A self-conscious planet in an infinite abyss, we alternate between self-preening centrality and cosmic triviality. Perhaps our best strategy, prospect, if you will, is to trim our sails and think in earth terms, albeit with cosmic horizons. The American Thoreau prophesied our collective future.

> All things invite this earth's inhabitants
> To rear their lives to an unheard of height
> And meet the expectation of the land.[22]   DISINGENUOUS

In so meeting the expectation of the land, however, we should not forget the American experience and expect too much. Even the world-renowned poet T. S. Eliot, while searching for English origins, reflects rather his childhood in a border state, Missouri—smack in the middle of America. The New World should listen carefully to these American lines of Eliot.

> There is only the fight to recover
>   what has been lost
> And found and lost again and again;
>   and now, under conditions
> That seem unpropitious. But perhaps
>   neither gain nor loss.
> For us there is only the trying. The rest is not our business.[23]

5 *America*

THE LONELINESS OF THE QUEST

Wee shall finde that the God of Israell is among us, when tenn of us shall be able to resist a thousand of our enemies, when hee shall make us a prayse and glory, that men shall say of succeeding plantacions: the lord make it like that of New England: for wee must Consider that wee shall be as a Citty upon a Hill, the eies of all people are uppon us; soe that if wee shall deale falsely with our god in this worke wee have undertaken and soe cause him to withdrawe his present help from us, wee shall be made a story and a by-word through the world, wee shall open the mouthes of enemies to speake evill of the wayes of god and all professours for Gods sake; wee shall shame the faces of many of gods worthy servants, and cause theire prayers to be turned into Cursses uppon us till wee be consumed out of the good land whether wee are goeing.

JOHN WINTHROP, "A Model of Christian Charity"

America. Surely no culture in the history of civilization has attained such global notoriety and yet been so adrift as to its own identity. We are a people who take as our historical refrain the amazed utterance of J. Hector St. John de Crèvecoeur in the eighteenth century: What then is the American, this new man?[1] What, who, indeed! What is the source of our identification as Americans? Religious identification fails. Ethnic identification fails. Racial identification fails. Regional and linguistic identifications fail. Political and social identifications fail. No, the identity in question is far more complex, far more subtle, and, potentially, far more enriching.

The identity of which we speak is not that of Aristotle but rather that of Hegel. The world of Aristotle submits to categories and to the doctrine of natural place, in which everything is what it is and not other, and everything was either in place or out of place, for everything had a place, a proper place. The world of Hegel is profoundly different. Post-Copernican, anticipating Darwin and cosmic DNA, Hegel proposes a cultural matrix in and through which history generates consciousness. For Hegel, things are not only what they are, but, at the same time, they can be other. Hegel dramatically alters the fabric of consciousness and the clarity of reason. Process replaces substance as the major metaphor. Activity, historical activity, replaces stasis as the *summum bonum*. Identity is no longer a noun, but a development, an achieving en route. This Hegelian bequest to the future of human consciousness has its most telling formulation in the saga of America, or rather "Americaning."

As long ago as the obscure philosopher of the obscure, Heraclitus, we were told that you cannot step into the same river twice and that we are most human when we are in a state of tension between claiming opposites. In my view, America is at its best when it is in this state of tension as to both mission and constituency. America is at its worst when it decides to define both mission and the qualifications for constituency. With regard to the deep human questions, the goal of clarity is a sham. The Renaissance philosopher Nicholas of Cusa knew this better than most, for to him the richest vein in human inquiry is the field of the *coincidentia oppositorum*, which is always present in the fabric of time. Put simply although irretrievably irresolute, even if the world is eternal and space is infinite, we do experience time. Neither the logic of theology nor that of physics allows for this, yet we do experience time. No clarity here, just human experience.

Now, with regard to the problem of modern individualism and the quest for community, I offer the following caveats and some ensuing diagnosis. Our first warning is to avoid geometric thinking, by which I mean the pervasive tendency to render rich and thick terms in simplistic spatial imagery. The individual is not a single entity, apart, alone in geometric isolation. To the contrary, the individual is a social construct, a creation of thousands of years of human history. Single persons, far back into antiquity, storied by fame, fortune, and the idiosyncratic turn of the historical wheel, have bewitched us into thinking that the individual was ever thus. Not so, for they are unrepresentative of the teeming masses whose faces and peculiarities are lost to the selective scythe of historical recollection. The individual as face, the individual as body, is not given proper due until the Renaissance. The emotionally charged faces of Leonardo da Vinci, the surging bodies of Michelangelo and the haunting portraits of Albrecht Dürer, amidst countless others, all attest to the emergence of individuals as the *dramatis personae* of the human quest. In his *Oration on the Dignity of*

Man,[2] the Renaissance philosopher Pico della Mirandola praises God for having made us in his image such that, like chameleons, we can become as gods ourselves.

A powerful parallel to this anthropocentric view of the world occurred in the sixteenth century during the Lutheran Reformation, when the person was given extraordinary powers of self-presence and self-determination. No longer was salvation dependent on the priest, the *mediator dei,* who managed the hierarchical chain of being from God to laity. For Luther, salvation took place in time and could be seized by the individual, independent of the structures of the Church.

Americans, however, are descendants neither of the flamboyant humanists of the Renaissance nor of Luther. Our roots are in a more subtle bequest, that of English Calvinism, historically known as puritanism. The intense and complex dialectic between the individual and the community is an essential ingredient in classical puritanism, especially in its American form. Despite the original Calvinist contention that one could do *nothing* to deserve salvation, this stricture slowly changed in America so that the reverse became true. The signs of conversion soon became anticipatory rather than codifying. The stark warnings of the Hebrew scriptures soon became replaced by the aggrandizing text of the Christian scriptures, "By their fruits ye shall know them." Further, a successful personal conversion experience allowed one to enter the covenanted community, the saints in light. This community, a "congregation" of believers, had a remarkable ability to preserve the integrity of individuals in the context of social and political organization. In fact, American puritanism developed the tradition of federal theology, in which the individual was paramount, the congregation the source of institutional gathering, and the presbytery the larger and intercommunity arbiter of disputes. Although my judgment is controversial, I believe that the federal theology of the covenanted congregationalists is more the historical model for the American constitution than the works of Locke, the Scottish school, or the French philosophes. Nevertheless, American Calvinists we were and in a deep, albeit hidden, way we still are. The upshot of which is that we believe in the inalienable rights of individuals, especially if deeply held, and in the necessity of such individuals to be sanctioned and evaluated by any one of a vast plurality of community structures, each inevitably narrow, and inevitably parochial, but together constituting a marvelous amalgam of human strategies for survival. Individual in constituency but plaid in fabric, as Americans we have tried the impossible. We have tried to make it possible for all to count, each in his or her idiosyncratic way, all the while knowing that the personal counting is inseparable from building a homogeneous community.

Much more could be said about the positive character of our Puritan heritage, for despite the long-standing denigration of their achievements and their style, they built into our lives a profound sense of the delicate balance between the fulfillment of the individual and the need to structure a community whose task was, ironically, to protect the individual against the excesses of the environment, be it social, political, or natural. The struggle of the seventeenth-century Puritans on this behalf was played out, over and again, in constantly shifting settings, although the theme was constant. The Great Awakening of the eighteenth century, with the life and thought of Jonathan Edwards as its centerpiece, was the first major revisiting of the Puritan dialectic. The years surrounding the American Revolution constituted a second version, this time with dramatic political effects. Still another scenario was played out in the epoch of the American Renaissance, with Emerson and Thoreau as leading protagonists for an imaginative reconstruction of the distinctively American relationship between the individual and the community.

Emerson's doctrine of self-reliance was especially influential on the American mind of the mid-nineteenth century. The most intellectually cosmopolitan of the American thinkers, Emerson forged a triple relationship between the self, nature, and society. He invoked Americans to have "an original relation to the universe" and stressed the hidden power of the interior life. Some of Emerson's aphoristic remarks are now considered quaint, but in the time of the frontier movement west by way of Conestoga and buckboard, his urging us to "hitch our wagon to a star" had the ring of authenticity. And it was too little known that the telling phrase of the mid-twentieth century counterculture movement, "do your own thing," was original with Emerson.[3]

At a deeper level Emerson was ever alert to the rich possibilities available to us in the living of the everyday. Due to the power of the individual imagination, each of us has access to the multiple symbols which potentially characterize the world in which we find ourselves. He tells us that "we learn nothing rightly until we learn the symbolical character of life."[4] The transcendent implications of the everyday are celebrated by Emerson in one of his *Journal* entries, where he calls upon each of us to use "this power of imagination" to clothe the "dead sticks" with immortality and to find the music in "creaking and scouring."[5]

It is with Walt Whitman, however, that the real power of the poet of the ordinary comes to the fore. Whitman had Emerson's sympathies and pre-dilections, but he had a boldness unknown to Emerson. Further, Whitman understood America as few before or since. For Whitman, "America is not finished, perhaps never will be; now America is a divine true sketch."[6] He had an uncanny sense of the need for America to articulate its own native genius.

> The old men, I remember as a boy, were always talking of American inde-pendence. What is independence? Freedom from all laws or bonds except those of one's own being, controlled by the universal ones. To lands, to man, to woman, what is there at last to each, but the inherent soul, nativity, idiocracy, free, highest poised, soaring its own flight, following out itself?
>
> At present, these States, in their theology and social standards (of greater importance than their political institutions) are entirely held possession of by foreign lands. We see the sons and daughters of the New World, ignorant of its genius, not yet inaugurating the native, the universal, and the near, still import-ing the distant, the partial, and the dead. We see London, Paris, Italy—not original, superb, as where they belong—but second-hand here, where they do not belong. We see the shreds of Hebrews, Romans, Greeks; but where, on her own soil, do we see, in any faithful, highest, proud expression, America herself? I sometimes question whether she has a corner in her own house.[7]

The major stumbling block to this articulation of American genius was born of its most auspicious undertaking: the regnancy of the individual within the framework of the body politic. This too, Whitman understood.

> We shall, it is true, quickly and continually find the origin-idea of the singleness of man, individualism, asserting itself, and cropping forth, even from the op-posite ideas. But the mass, or lump character, for imperative reasons, is to be ever carefully weighed, borne in mind, and provided for. Only from it, and from its proper regulation and potency, comes the other, comes the chance of indi-vidualism. The two are contradictory, but our task is to reconcile them.[8]

Reconciliations, however, are hard to come by, especially in the hands of great thinkers, who often deal in extremes. Despite the picaresque char-acters of the American frontier movement, the aftermath of the Civil War and the rise of the industrial revolution were to render the individual some-thing of a cipher on the American scene. Into this setting entered the most extraordinarily evocative and rhetorically brilliant of the American philos-ophers, William James. His position on the individual was dramatically one-sided and his innocence of the social matrix by which we became single selves was most unusual for a late nineteenth-century thinker. Nonetheless, James pressed forward with a philosophical, psychological, ethical, and religious individualism seldom, if ever, equalled in Western thought. As late as 1905, James wrote this paean to the individual: "Surely the individual, the person in the singular number, is the more fundamental phenomenon, and the social institution of whatever grade, is but secondary and ministerial."[9] Written in the century after the work of Hegel, Marx, Durkheim, and the founding of American sociology, this text of James has a stubborn naivete about it. Still, it represented a heartfelt attitude deep within the American psyche. In a letter written in 1899, James declares himself "against bigness and greatness in all their forms . . . against all big organizations as such, national ones first and foremost." Giving vent to what he calls his "ebullient spleen," James states his case forthrightly "in favor of the eternal forces of truth which always work in the individual. . . ."[10]

We would be severely mistaken if we were to dismiss James's position as unabashedly sentimental. Rhetoric aside, James's doctrine of the individual proceeds from an extensive altering of centuries of assumptions about human behavior. He is, after all, the architect of the controversial doctrine of the will to believe, a doctrine which awards to persons the Promethean capacity to forge meaning in situations traditionally regarded as beyond our ken. And James insists on the irreducible presence of chance in the cosmic, natural, and social setting in and through which we build our lives. Continuous with Emerson and with a pervasive refrain in American life, James affirms the constant presence of possibility and of novelty.[11]

Undoubtedly, the potential prowess of the individual as advanced by William James is extremely attractive. Unless we are to abandon all hope in the quagmire of a social determinism, no social philosophy can afford to be without a doctrine of the human self as engaging, creative, and constitutive, no matter what the acknowledged restraints. From among the many powerful efforts to develop such a philosophy in classical American thought, I choose, however briefly and peremptorily, to focus on two versions, that of Josiah Royce and that of John Dewey.

Although a philosopher of the first rank, Royce is comparatively unsung in the annals of American thought. A polymath and autodidact, Royce was a man of an indefatigable intellectual energy which he directed to virtually every discipline extant. Of more importance for the present discussion, and less well known, is the fact that Royce had a lifelong fascination with the varieties, strengths, and weaknesses of American communal life. Because of his many writings on German philosophy and literature, Royce was regarded as a Europhile. It is true that his philosophical writing and scholarship was rooted in European thought, but it is equally true that his social writings and his deepest personal concerns were rooted in America. In one of his last public utterances, Royce tells us that "my deepest motives and problems have centered about the Idea of the Community."[12]

As on most important issues, Royce's early thought was in diametric opposition to that of William James. In his history of California, he sets out a position which holds the social order to be supreme:

> After all, however, our lesson is an old and simple one. It is the State, the Social Order, that is divine. We are all but dust, save as this social order gives life. When we think it our instrument, our plaything, and make our private fortunes the one object, then this social order rapidly becomes vile to us; we call it sordid, degraded, corrupt, unspiritual, and ask how we may escape from it forever. But if we turn again and serve the social order, and not merely ourselves, we soon find that what we are serving is simply our own highest spiritual destiny in bodily form. It is never truly sordid or corrupt or unspiritual; it is only we that are so when we neglect our duty.[13]

These are stern words, more reflective of the ethics of Kant than of the freewheeling individuality of the mining camps in which Royce was born, high in the Sierra Nevada mountains of California. Royce's thought on these matters, however, was to evolve. Under the press of philosophical criticism, especially by James and C. S. Peirce, and due, as well, to an increasing dissatisfaction with the inequities of the American social system, Royce structured a more mature and accommodating philosophy of the community. In his last major work, *The Problem of Christianity,* Royce put Peirce's triadic logic to work in an effort to forge a viable rapprochement between the individual and the community. He introduces the mediative notion of interpretation, whereby the community of persons evolves by virtue of the resolution of obstacles through the common acceptance of an interpreter of each to the other. In this way, a diarchy of hard and fast positions yields to a higher ground, with the intention of pragmatic resolution rather than the specter of obdurate confrontation. In language more conciliatory than that found earlier in his work on California, Royce points to the obligation of the individual to the social will.

A man's own case is usually not *merely* his own. It also concerns some social order to which he belongs. The litigant stands in presence, not merely of his own rights and wrongs, but of the whole social will. The decision of his case will affect many besides himself, and sometimes might save or wreck a nation. The patient's illness is not merely a medical phenomenon, and not merely an individual misfortune, but also is an event of social moment. His family, and perhaps his country, may be affected by what is done with this single case. . . .

When a man's affairs deeply concern other people besides himself, the only way to deal justly with the case is to interpret this man's own individual views and interests to some fitting representative of the social will, in order that the matter may be arbitrated, or in order that the wills of all concerned may be, as far as possible, both harmonized and expressed. A Community of Interpretation must exist or must be formed.[14]

Ironically, Royce's brilliant detailing of the future of the human community occurred at the outset of a cataclysmic event, the First World War, an event regarded by many to prophesy the doom of a viable human future. Royce died in the middle of the war, broken, bewildered, and on the bottom rung of his "hope" for the coming of the beloved community. Further treatment of Royce's philosophy of community occurs in the following chapter.

Let us attend to one last thinker in the classical American tradition as an aid to an understanding of our contemporary situation. Certainly, the most sustained and remarkably accurate diagnosis of American society in the first half of this century is to be found in the writings of John Dewey—a series of trenchant books and a flood of articles, each addressed to one or more of the educational, political, and social problems afflicting America. One of his most recurrent themes was the relationship between the individual and the community. This was especially true of his 1927 work, *The Public and Its Problems,* and that of the 1930 book *Individualism Old and New.*

Similar to Royce, Dewey also came under the sway of Hegel when young. After the publication of James's monumental *Principles of Psychology,* Dewey broke with Hegel's doctrine of the absolute mind, yet he remained committed to a Hegelian emphasis on the social and historical matrix as a condition for understanding not only events but philosophical ideas. Consequently, Dewey assumed that the ideal person should have a flair for life, and for novelty and moral courage as brilliantly extolled by James. Further, Dewey held that this Promethean self should build in concert with others a social community, with the responsibility to assure that all members of the society would have at least the opportunity and access to so live. The spiritual profundity and egalitarian character of this human community is quite startling, yet Dewey saw nothing utopian about it, and, indeed, held it to be realizable.

It is a truism that Dewey provided a social setting for James's Promethean self. Dewey's contribution, however, is far deeper and more painfully honest, for he knew the pervasive obstacles to building a human community. There is little sentimentality or naivete in the thought of John Dewey. Listen to Dewey on the significance of the twentieth century for the individual in America.

> The shift that makes the older individualism a dying echo is more marked as well as more rapid in this country. Where is the wilderness which now beckons creative energy and affords untold opportunity to initiative and vigor? Where is the pioneer who goes forth rejoicing, even in the midst of privation, to its conquest? The wilderness exists in the movie and the novel; and the children of the pioneers, who live in the midst of surroundings artificially made over by the machine, enjoy the pioneer life idly in the vicarious film. I see little social unrest which is the straining of energy for outlet in action; I find rather the protest against a weakening of vigor and a sapping of energy that emanate from the absence of constructive opportunity; and I see a confusion that is an expression of the inability to find a secure and morally rewarding place in a troubled and tangled economic scene.[15]

This is a fifty-year-old text with the ring of immediacy. Dewey points to the ostensibly invisible erosion of the old American individualism by isolating those baleful signs of its disappearance, particularly vicarious living. Dewey was a master diagnostician of those social currents which take from us our moorings and offer as replacements mere media pap.

> It would be difficult to find in history an epoch as lacking in solid and assured objects of belief and approved ends of action as is the present. . . .
> Individuals vibrate between a past that is intellectually too empty to give stability and a present that is too diversely crowded and chaotic to afford balance or direction to ideas and emotion.[16]

The message here is clear, for as we said at the outset of this discussion, the term "individual" is not fixed. It has to be reconstructed generation by generation, lest it become a vapid creature of vicious nostalgia. Just as the nature and desiderata of the social community evolve, so too must the needs, expectations, and possibilities of the individual change. In Dewey's

view, the social method by which this can occur is face-to-face communication, a characteristic of small, albeit heterogeneous, gatherings.
This is a decidedly different method from the leveling and external equity
which represents the approach of mass media to the process of democrati-
zation. As early as 1927, long before television, Dewey saw the importance
of this difference.

> Equality does not signify that kind of mathematical or physical equivalence in
> virtue of which any one element may be substituted for another. It denotes effec-
> tive regard for whatever is distinctive and unique in each, irrespective of physical
> and psychological inequalities. It is not a natural possession but is a fruit of the
> community when its action is directed by its character as a community.[17]

It is precisely this activity of the community in its local, face-to-face
gatherings which enables a society both to evolve and to protect the inalienable rights of its citizens. The stakes are high in Dewey's version, for
"the clear consciousness of a communal life, in all its implications, constitutes the idea of democracy."[18] The key word, of course, is democracy.
Whether it be social democracy, socialist democracy, capitalist democracy, or libertarian democracy, if the rights of the individual are repressed
or even attenuated, personal growth will be at best idiosyncratic, heroic or
accidental. And at worst, which historically is more likely, personal
growth will be illusory.

In the tumultuous although comparatively short history of America,
from Massachusetts Bay until the present, many thinkers have cast light on
our unique effort to create an original body politic, with alternating and
paradoxically equal stress on the individual and the community. Of these
thinkers, Dewey was the most sophisticated, honest, and imaginative. As
with his predecessors Winthrop, Edwards, Jefferson, Lincoln, Emerson,
Whitman, Royce, and James, Dewey's wisdom is a precious resource in
our historical conscience and consciousness. We, however, as Americans,
are children of Auschwitz, Hiroshima, Vietnam, and Watergate. Dewey
would have appreciated the difference, and it is that difference to which we
now turn.

II

We live in the penultimate decade of the twentieth century. More imposing, we live in the penultimate decade of the fifth millennium of recorded

history and the second millennium of the Christian era. Who are we? What seek we? What have we done and what can we do?[19] Who is this, this present American?

America has always sent mixed signals to its citizens. On the one hand, all is possible; on the other, the possibilities seem to be for someone else, somewhere else, somehow else. I was a child of the Great Depression, a period that raised serious questions about the merit of our journey and a period that considerably cut into our long-standing self-righteousness. The heady days of our triumphant presence in the First World War were but khaki memories. The personally explosive years of the twenties had receded into the memoried vault of tattered silk stockings and abandoned touring cars. Writing of the year of my birth, my beginning as homo Americanus, William Manchester proceeds as follows:

> In the desperate summer of 1932, Washington, D.C., resembled the be-sieged capital of an obscure European state. Since May some twenty-five thousand penniless World War veterans had been encamped with their wives and children in District parks, dumps, abandoned warehouses, and empty stores. The men drilled, sang war songs, and once, led by a Medal of Honor win-ner and watched by a hundred thousand silent Washingtonians, they marched up Pennsylvania Avenue bearing American flags of faded cotton. Most of the time, however, they waited and brooded. The vets had come to ask their govern-ment for relief from the Great Depression, then approaching the end of its third year; specifically they wanted immediate payment of the soldiers' "bonus" authorized by the Adjusted Compensation Act of 1924 but not due until 1945. If they could get cash now, the men would receive about $500 each.[20]

I trust that you know the fate of this Bonus Expeditionary Force. Doomed by orders of President Herbert Hoover as carried out by Amer-ican military heroes such as Douglas MacArthur, Dwight Eisenhower, and George Patton, they were gassed, burned out, beaten, and dispersed. Their ragged journey to Washington became their ragged presence among the Potomac cherry trees and the leftovers of the high bourgeoisie of the previ-ous decade. They soon beat a ragged retreat to a ragged existence in the America of the thirties. Such was my first year as an American.

From 1938, I have a vivid memory of the relationship of the individual to the body politic. Please notice that I do not speak of the individual and the community, merely of the body politic. I was not to discover the differ-ence between the woodenness and artificiality of the body politic and the loyalty and warmth of the community until much later in my life. I was eight years of age and a student in a public school in New York City. It was an imposing building for anyone, let alone a little boy, little in both stature and experience. The stairwells were iron, and metal grates reached high into the air at every turn. As has been made literarily famous by Bel Kaufman, there was an up and down staircase and woe to those who violated the narrowness of that geometric order. In any event, it was a spring day. As was proper for that time of year, the giant windows were raised so as to allow a breeze into the already stuffy rooms. Suddenly the clop of a horse and a voice, shrill and inviting, came into the room. Even though trapped in my seat, bolted to the floor, I resonated to its plea. Ay, junk*a*! Ay, junk*a*! Give me your junk*a*! This was carefully interspersed with the sound of a cowbell and the periodic clip-clop of an old and valiant horse. How I longed to be that man. To me, truthfully although innocently, he was free: free of rote; free of the Euclidean world into which I was being dragged; above all, free of competition, for this was his street, his neighborhood, his place. As the oldest of then six children, I had already been introduced into head-to-head competition. School reaffirmed the existence of that all-too-pervasive human activity and despite my youth, I had learned what I was to later find confirmed by Darwin, namely, only the fittest survive. The remainder are antiquities in their own time.

I trust that you have garnered the inordinate and double-barrelled sadness in this story. My innocence about the quality of life available to the junk man is outdone only by the fact that I made no such move to freedom and in fact became an established member of the very hierarchy which I intuitively loathed in my childhood. Now, aside from an autobiographical wistfulness, the point of the story is that Americans have traditionally been subject to the following dialectic. We are among the most herded, organized, prepackaged, and goal-oriented of all peoples. Over against this imposing array of forces which urge us on, we have a strident though often hidden urge to be the Marlboro man, free of entanglements of any kind and self-individuating. Few if any of us achieve this in any permanent way. We, therefore, are a very grouchy and frustrated people. America, then, becomes an archetype of disappointment for its natives, whereas it is a Valhalla of opportunity for its newly arrived immigrants. Sufficient to the day is the analysis of the surface. Let us turn now to the problems afflicting our contemporary scene.

For a number of reasons, America may be finished. If we contrast the claims made by America with the reality of the contemporary situation, we find that the above judgment, despite its excessive posture, may be true.

First, America throve on its appellation as a *mundus novus*. Europe, reluctantly and—given Renaissance cartography—miraculously, gave birth to a child, neither expected nor wanted. The movement of peoples and cultures from east to west was a thousand-year hegira. We believed that its apex was America. Did we not know that human history has no regard for self-acclaimed geographical finality? Pearl Harbor symbolized the reemergence of the Orient. Our inability to quell the ancient restiveness of the Vietnamese and the strident reappearance of China have convinced us that the planet earth yields to no privileged place for more than the time of passing occupancy. No, America is not Mount Hebron and it cannot guarantee its future by sacerdotal geography. Paradoxically, the place of America in the future of the human community will trace to its activity and not to its place. The meaning of the quest for Zion in the Wilderness, a classical American theme, is no longer the quest for a physical or geographical place. This event renders us bereft of one of our most cherished and trusted assumptions, that of the uniqueness of our land. No longer can we assume that who we are is where we are, although where we are is a glorious and multisplendored evocation of the earth. The Puritans' bequest was the claim that the land, America, was waiting for us and for us alone, to do as we would. The contemporary task is to show that we deserve the opportunity and shall realize its potential not only for ourselves but for the world community as well.

A second reason to sound the potential death knell for America has to do with our drive to impress, to preen, if not to control. For those transitory ends, we married ourselves to our skill, technology. Did we not know that technology, lacking spiritual originality, can be emulated, learned, repeated, and sent back to us with another national label? And did we not know that our technological genius would raise aspirations for our citizens, aspirations too often blunted by the vagaries and mysteries of the market economy? The Japanese and others have taught us that a first-rate technological society must have as a central ingredient the sanctioned worthiness of the worker, the family, and some guarantee of a fertile future.

Third, our salvific role in the Second World War led Americans to believe that we were a breed apart. The Holocaust signified the corruption of the "Old World" and we took upon ourselves the mantle of Western morality. The flush of victory and the self-righteousness of our cause prevented us from realizing the ominous implications of Hiroshima. It was not until Vietnam, and especially the massacre at My Lai, that Americans began to identify with the endemic and global sickness that plagued efforts to build a human community. Added to this sense of participation in an international capacity for self-deception as to the rightness and justice of one's cause was the shocking revelation that our domestic politics, at the highest level, revealed chicanery, hypocrisy, deceit, and the manipulation of power in a way totally unrepresentative of the American ideal.

The fallout from these events has been considerable and important. The bequest of the Nixon administration is the presence of a dubiety, even a cynicism, about the political process and—more devastating—an erosion of trust in representative government. Even more threatening to our self-image is the fact that we now recognize ourselves as the founders and major proponent of the nuclear age. We are the people of the bomb. Our vaunted apocalyptic tradition has now moved from Zion to Armageddon. In short, the long hallowed appellation, *America,* has changed. It has changed for us and for all who inhabit the planet earth. The aspirations of the individual and the nature of the community in America have changed as well.

III

What is it to be an American in this penultimate decade of the twentieth century? Surely, the strutting and the chauvinistic arrogance of the postwar period has been trimmed. There is an unfortunate pathos in this remark, but we seem to have been reduced to proper size. No longer the nation which strides atop the world scene, we now find ourselves hoisted on our own petard. Champions of equality, no matter the size, America has suddenly acquired a complex of companions on the world scene, externally inferior, although by our own doctrine clearly our equals. Despite protestation from the political right, this development is salutary and in the long run necessary for the spiritual and mental health of America.

The question before us is whether Americans of the present time, no matter what their age, can come of age. We ask then whether Americans, stripped of their traditional *raison d'être,* can maintain their uniqueness or whether they will be reduced to just other faces in the world scene. Paradoxically, the loss of previous ideological support presents us with our most propitious opportunity. Given our macho history, it may come as a surprise to the reader, yet our future as Americans is to become the spiritual leaders of the world community. This task, this quest, has a superb unreality and an empirical loneliness attached to it. Allow me to repeat; the quest of Americans for America is lonely. The quest of Americans for world domination is over. The quest of Americans for world presence as persons, as free, as helpful, as harbingers of a new order, is before us. To abandon the self-aggrandizing struts of a previous epoch is hard. To abandon the doctrine that all will go well, if we but show up, is hard. To abandon the long-standing assumption that Americans were at one and the same time rugged individuals and complaisant devotees of an unending series of loyal communities, is hard. To face the fact that it is we, the Americans, who are the founders, the architects, and major proponents of nuclear obliteration, is hard. The chant starts in our bowels, rises to our lungs, and bursts out from our bewildered lips: where to go, what to do.

Let us say it straight out. Disarm and pledge ourselves to the future of the world community in which the individual person is inviolable. Dewey, in 1922, had it right.

> Within the flickering inconsequential acts of separate selves dwells a sense of the whole which claims and dignifies them. In its presence we put off mortality and live in the universal. The life of the community in which we live and have our being is the fit symbol of this relationship. The acts in which we express our perception of the ties which bind us to others are its only rites and ceremonies.[21]

Can we live with this commitment to the affairs of time? Can we live with this secular liturgy, stunningly apart from a meaning transcendent of our everyday affairs? As Americans, can we start over?

Why not? Why not start over? Why not build an America which speaks the voice of the forgotten, the voice of the repressed, the voice of the new beginning. We, after all, are the supreme new beginners of the modern world. Why not tell the truth? Human life is fraught with conflict and oppression. Why not say that we will share our struggles as well as our accomplishments. We are the home of the *proletarian individual*. Any nation can be the home of the bourgeois individual, the few. We, historically, have celebrated the many—individuals *en masse*—and it would be in keeping with our best wisdom if we were to export that globally. We are the people who believe in the educability of all, no matter what the origin or situation or previous failure. We are the champions of surprise.

A community, be it local, natural, or global, is worth its salt only insofar as it can provide for an integral voice of its members, no matter what their persuasion. The individual is paramount. Yet without a communal sanction the individual festers, often in self-deception about his or her worth. America has the potential capacity to structure a communal forum for individual life, second to none. Of necessity, given the world scene, this will involve community organizations which go against the grain and whose primary feature is the barb and the put-down. Although this may be painful at times, especially for the more traditional of us, this self-criticism is our strength and our noblest contribution.

We cannot deny that the American dream has lost much of its glitter. Nor can we deny that our role in the global scene is infinitely more complex and controversial than we had expected. Yet no nation in the history of the earth has ever undertaken a more arduous and worthwhile task. We seek nothing less than to enable a wide variety of peoples, rooted in virtually every racial, ethnic, religious, and political tradition, to form a community in which each person lives out the uniqueness of his or her heritage and persuasion in a spirit of harmony and justice. This American nation cannot expect such communities to occur at the end of a gun or a rocket, nor can this nation use economic manipulation to carry such a profound message. To the contrary, only complete equity of opportunity for the individual will assure that America is building a bona fide community, one that will cast spiritual light on a deeply troubled world. We should seek to be emulated not for our power, but for our compassion. We should not seek to create a Leviathan which features the war of all against all and mindless violence. Let us pursue the path of Royce's beloved community and let us reinvigorate the advice of John Dewey, building slowly, from the ground up, face-to-face, and with empathy for one another. Without the other person, there is no community. The quest for America, resembling the human quest, is often lonely and ultimately sad, for being finite the quest ends in death. The nectar, therefore, is in the journey, and only the community can sustain that nectar by the presence of sharing, thereby assuaging our loneliness.

6 Classical American Philosophy

A REFLECTIVE BEQUEST TO THE
TWENTY-FIRST CENTURY

Seeking to conquer a larger liberty, man but extends the empire of necessity.
HERMAN MELVILLE, "The Bell Tower"

A new century, nay, a new millennium is upon us. We are beholden to offer
a bequest to this new epoch so that the human odyssey will continue in ever
more fruitful and creative ways. Some bequests are obvious, such as a
more sophisticated technology and enhanced capacity for the less fortunate nations and people of the world. Surely America has much to offer in
this regard, and I trust and hope that international politics will not prevent
us from sharing our considerable ability in economic, agricultural, and
applied scientific knowledge. In this arena, however, we are not alone;
several European nations and especially the Japanese have both imagination and technical ability worthy of global emulation. In short, the technological prowess of America, although notable and far-reaching, is not our
distinctive bequest.

What then, is sufficiently distinctive about American culture to be a
worthy bequest to the next century? One could point to our form of consti-
tutional government; but recent events in Vietnam, Lebanon, and Central
America indicate that not every nation finds our approach compatible
with long-standing cultural mores and political assumptions. One could
point as well to our national and praiseworthy commitment to equality;
but here too dubiety arises, for our history is stained with the destruction

of American Indian culture and our present is conflicted with our inability to integrate all black Americans into the social and economic mainstream of our culture.

I suggest that we take a different course of action. It would be wise if we were to probe our past and render as a bequest our wisest, albeit most critical, tradition, that of classical American philosophy, particularly but not exclusively as found in the thought of William James, Josiah Royce, and John Dewey. I do not see this tradition as salvific, but I do believe that its wisdom is directly related to the problems facing global culture in the twenty-first century.

II

The twenty-first century will not begin totally anew. Symbolically, it is a calendar milestone. Yet it will inherit the massive problems now facing us at the end of the twentieth century. In the area of human equity, the availability and distribution of food will loom large, as will the preservation of our ecosystem and the judicious use of our natural resources. The seriousness of these human problems will increase geometrically in direct proportion to the growth of world population, a growth that is foreboding and dangerous to human survival. The fact that efforts to curtail population growth are often met with opposition, either cultural or religious, does not foretell a sanguine outcome of this potential crisis. In the past, famine, infectious disease, and war acted as population growth deterrents, historically depressing as that may be. Of these, infectious disease is now under the scrutiny of the powerful scientific knowledge of modern medicine. Further, were the affluent nations of the world to address the issue of famine with a resolve independent of political considerations, famine could also be significantly alleviated. As for war, it now has escalated into the arena of possible nuclear obliteration, which is unthinkable, although ironically we are now duty bound to think of virtually nothing else until its specter is obviated.

The burden of our immediate future has a sharp clarity to it. People of the twenty-first century will live longer, need more food, use more resources, and confront a staggering increase in population as well as an increased strain on our already beleaguered ecosystem. Modern technology and modern medicine have the capacity to remedy both famine and disease, thereby still further increasing the number of people who will live and live longer. Obviously, nuclear war is intolerable as a resolution of the problem of overpopulation. Thus we are faced with more of us needing more. Consequently, more of us must share more and do more if all, and in the long run if any, of us are to survive in a genuinely human way.

The above scenario is neither startling nor new. The literature of prognostication, complete with charts of extrapolation, is vast and easily available. Nations now struggling for economic survival—such as India, Mexico, Kenya, and Bangladesh—will double, triple, and even quintuple their population by the year 2030, when, by conservative estimates, the population of the world will reach 7 billion human beings.[1]

A further extrapolation has to do with potential nuclear war. The sophisticated and noncommercial film, *The Last Epidemic,* sponsored by Physicians for Social Responsibility, details the grim, no-win results of even a one-megaton nuclear bomb exploding over the city of San Francisco. This film is instructive because it features commentary by high-ranking military and intelligence personnel, all of whom cite the extraordinary excess of the number and power of the weapons now extant in the world. Robert Jay Lifton and Kai Erickson detail the results of even moderate escalation, namely, to one twenty-megaton nuclear bomb.

> A twenty-megaton bomb, for instance, if detonated over New York City, Chicago, or Leningrad, would vaporize, crush, incinerate, or burn to death almost every person within a radius of five or six miles from the center of the blast—two million people, perhaps. Within a radius of twenty miles, a million more or so would either die instantly or would suffer wounds from which they could not recover. If the bomb exploded on the ground, countless others who live miles away, far beyond the reach of the initial blast and searing heat wave, would be sentenced to a lingering death as radioactive fallout drifted quietly down onto people, buildings, water and food supplies, and the earth itself.[2]

Now, despite an occasional optimistic futurologist or the pronouncements of the politically motivated Pollyanna predictions of the Hudson Institute as represented by the work of the late Herman Kahn, it does not take an intelligent person very long to ascertain that serious trouble clouds our collective future. In addition to the usual run of human vices, which will always be with us, we seem to have run afoul of a virulent case of *hubris,* or stubborn pride. The Greeks, as early as Homer, diagnosed this fault as the most serious of human failings, for it prevents healing even when compromise is available. Both Judaism and Christianity focus on the severity of the sin of pride, and Western literature from Augustine to Goethe details it baleful consequences. The twentieth century, succumbing to the jargon of the social sciences, has a tendency to mask human failing, human vice, human sin, with a set of vague, neologistic euphemisms. In my lexicon, *hubris* is but a name for stubborn pride, for Achilles sulking in his tent, for adolescent, self-destructive protest, for self-preening, and for citations from one scripture or another to justify miscreant behavior. Above all, *hubris* is a name for our refusal to face our own finitude, the imminence of your death and my death. I grant that my approach is classical, traditional, and more hard-hitting than the pusillanimous vagaries of social science terminology. Yes, I believe in sin. Yes, I believe that human beings are potentially dangerous—to themselves, to their self-interest, and to others. Yes, I believe that human beings are seduced by nation, by turf, by religion, by the alleged sanction of cultural longevity, by the primacy of their own language, and by whatever else they can elicit as a cause to inflict damage on other human beings who have the same loyalties but to different gods and traditions. In this regard, self-righteousness, be it religious, social, political, ethnic, racial, linguistic, regional, or cultural, is profoundly dehumanizing, for it separates the human community into hostile and even warring camps. The paradox, however, is that the opponents in these conflicts never face up to the irresolute character of these disputes, holding rather to the need for closure, for some final solution, in which only one party to the dispute can be totally victorious and justified.

Self-righteousness would be a mere mask for conflict if it were not for the underlying drive for closure and total solutions. Despite the obvious plurality of positions taken and deeply believed by countless human gatherings, we still have a tendency to view all others as out of step if they do not emulate our values and our beliefs. Unfortunately, there are good historical reasons for this depressing state of affairs. After all, it has been rare for the multitude to devote themselves to a cause whose message was the healing and celebration of the finite, the generational, the transient. This historical contrast also reveals that the pursuit of absolutes generates moral self-righteousness, fanaticism, violence, and, today, global terrorism.

Day by day, the beginning of the twenty-first century and a new millennium comes into focus. I do not believe that the strategies and attitudes of the past are sufficient or even salutary for a response to the collective problems of the next century. Our problems are now global in implication, for we are knit together as never before, both in solidarity and in opposition. A crisis anywhere in the world has the capacity to force an escalation and involve the world at large. Given this global mosaic, single-minded solutions, from whatever source, however noble in intent, are bound to come up short for some people, somewhere. This is true even of scientific and technological resolutions of global problems, an approach which continues to elicit considerable confidence in spite of our growing awareness of the negative byproducts of pesticides and pharmacological nostrums. In a prescient text, as long ago as 1907, William James warned us against overconfidence in a sheerly scientific advancement.

> The scope of the practical control of nature newly put into our hand by scientific ways of thinking vastly exceeds the scope of the old control grounded on common sense. Its rate of increase accelerates so that no one can trace the limit; one may even fear that the *being* of man may be crushed by his own powers, that his fixed nature as an organism may not prove adequate to stand the strain of the ever increasingly tremendous functions, almost divine creative functions, which his intellect will more and more enable him to wield.[3]

It would seem that attempts to effect significant progress in response to the problems facing us in the next century will have to proceed from a more multiple set of sources and feature a basic change in attitude with regard to both possibilities and frustrations. This attitude will have to be more pluralistic, more tolerant, and less committed to ideology, closure, and imposed solutions. In effect, we need less manipulation and a deeper understanding of the pragmatics of step-by-step healing. This will involve a different metaphysics, that is, a move from substance to process as the major metaphor of explication and a heightened sense of the finite in all of our endeavors. In my judgment, the speculative bedding for this change in attitude was begun in nineteenth-century America by William James, continued in the late thought of Josiah Royce, and brought to fruition by John Dewey.[4]

Despite differences in philosophical style and terminology and some disagreement, it is an accurate generalization to say that these thinkers were committed to pluralism, a positive form of provincialism, tolerance, meliorism, a pragmatic epistemology and ethics, the necessity of mediation, and a skepticism about any form of ultimate salvation external to the human effort. Our future, therefore, does not await some natural or divine *deus ex machina*. Consequently, the future rather hangs in the balance, awaiting the outcome of our deliberate, willing, and intelligent efforts to remediate, to heal, and to blunt and shunt those destructive forces which seem inevitably to accompany our journey. Profoundly rooted in the American psyche, these thinkers, nonetheless, had a deep and learned sensibility for cultures other than their own. The tradition of classical American philosophy is one well worth reconsidering as an ally in our entrance to the complexity of the twenty-first century.

III

In speaking of classical American philosophy, George Santayana, himself notoriously ambivalent about America, points to the originating power of that tradition.

> . . . When a way of thinking is deeply rooted in the soil, and embodies the instincts or even the characteristic errors of a people, it has a value quite independent of its truth; it constitutes a phase of human life and can powerfully affect the intellectual drama in which it figures. . . .[5]

It is this double aspect of being rooted in one's culture, while yet providing a philosophical articulation which is transcendent of that culture, that characterizes the influential philosophical movements of the past. One is especially struck by the capacity of the ancient philosophers to turn philosophical speculation about their immediate situation into virtually timeless insights relative to the human condition. Certainly this is the abiding strength of Plato, Epicurus, Lucretius, and Marcus Aurelius, each of whom bequeathed a moral epistemology, a fusing of knowing and doing, a way to live wisely and fruitfully. This is the perspective from which I view classical American philosophy, one in which reflection and action are continuous, of a piece, and in constant need of each other. Following John Dewey, I say, "reflection is native and constant."[6]

The most salient contention of the American philosophical tradition herein under consideration is the steadfast belief in the finite, transitory, and malleable character of the human journey and the accompanying habit of being chary about extra-experiential resolutions of our problems. The tradition takes the finite at dead reckoning,[7] complete with its irresolute character. William James was a life-long opponent of absolutes and of any appeal to solutions which transcended human experience, although his doctrine of experience is the most embrasive ever proposed by a major philosopher. Josiah Royce and John Dewey were early enamored of the absolute mind, coming to consciousness as they did under the eaves of late nineteenth-century Protestant Hegelianism. By the turn of the century, however, primarily due to the influence of William James's *Principles of Psychology,* they turned to a more temporalist context for their metaphysics and especially for their social philosophy. Each thinker, in his own way and at different times in his personal[8] and intellectual life, came up against the stubborn presence of mishap. What is crucial here is that neither James nor Royce nor Dewey was convinced that a posthuman, posthistorical resolution was in the wings. To the contrary, they set out to plot a way by which we can forge a response to the aberrant, to the threatening, and to those forces which prevent us from taking hold of our situation in a way that is placating, healing, and ameliorative. Given the fact that we shall not be rescued from afar, the passing of time, human hopes, foibles, and dreams become the stuff of nothing less than ontology.

In most Western metaphysics, this commitment to the affairs of time obviously occupies a lesser place. The celebration of human experience, especially in its perceptual rather than conceptual activity, strikes a blow at the long-standing assumption as to how one obtains philosophical wisdom. There are predecessors—the Greek and Roman stoics, for example—but in the main, a belief that everyday experience, perceptually undergone, is the touchstone for metaphysics constitutes a minority voice in the cacophonic history of Western philosophy. Yet this was precisely what the classical American philosophical tradition was proposing, namely, that the very transient character of our human lives enhanced, rather than denigrated, the profound inferential character of our values, decisions, and disabilities.

In phenomenological terms, beginning with William James, the task was to diagnose the experience of the individual as we cast about in the flow of experience, bringing a mind set but also getting and begetting as the press of the world filtered into our consciousness. Royce and Dewey took the Promethean self as prescribed by James as an ideal, but they were more sophisticated about the social fabric in which this self came to consciousness. They undertook the task of proposing a community in which the individual would have the flair and personal creativity of the Jamesian self, yet would also be able to manage the complex demands, obstacles, and conflicts inherent in a social setting. This diagnosis of the human self as engaged in the flow of events resulted in a high sensitivity to novelty, to the inordinate lack of clarity on important issues, and in an admission, especially by John Dewey, that our situation is ineluctably problematic. Given this, breakthroughs and occasional consummations are possible; but they too signal the beginning of still another knot confronting us in our journey. The worthiness of our alleged insights, our claim to the truth, is only as significant as their ability to sustain themselves in the consequences which follow. James writes, "There can *be* no difference anywhere that doesn't *make* a difference elsewhere."[9]

The building of a human life, a community, a nation, a world, or (perhaps in the future) a cosmopolis requires that we acknowledge from the outset the permanent relationship between growth and setback. The world is not a "block-universe" composed of inert substances like a set of Legos awaiting definition and management. Rather the world comes to us as a delicately woven fabric, related in a myriad of ways and although susceptible to human change, it carries with it its own set of affairs. Human intrusion into the affairs of nature or into other, alien human affairs generates response and frequently, consequences. The pragmatic method tells us that the worth of our intrusion is tied directly to the worth of the consequences and not to the clarity of the coherent conceptual scheme which originated the involvement. Nor is the worth of our intrusion tied to our self-justifying pronouncements from scriptural sources, whether they be religious or political. For they too must weigh the consequences. Further, as we have now learned at great possible peril to ourselves, consequences do not necessarily show their hand immediately. Often, to the contrary, these developments remain quiescent, buried in the flush of apparent success until in time, their time, they erupt with a vengeance. Compare, for example, the macho sense of power which came upon the heels of the bombs at Hiroshima and Nagasaki with the sense of terror that now afflicts citizens of the globe as they ponder the consequences of the decision to open that Pandora's box. Countless other examples abound in the areas of pharmacology, pesticides, urban renewal projects, pollution, military aid, and technological devices of every stripe.

At bottom, pragmatic epistemology is an attitude; one that does not make truth announcements, let alone pronouncements or manifestos. Rather it is an experimental probing. The pragmatic approach eschews the intuitive and the deductive as licit sources of final knowledge. They are, however, regarded as legitimate points of departure, for no claim is ruled out a priori. Yet even the intuitive and the deductive must stand the test of consequences. Pragmatism has an inductive temper, yet it is far more aware of possible novelty, and it is willing to treat ideas as explorers, ferreting out new ground on which to stand, even at the risk of being severely wrong. It was Dewey who stressed that error and failure, if properly respected, are often profound sources of insight. Pragmatism features a paradoxical combination of epistemic modesty and boldness. It is modest in that no truth claim is final until the last person has his or her say and all of the consequences of the truth claim have shown their hands. Pragmatic truth, then, always has a tentativeness about it, in contrast to the more traditional forms of truth as correspondence or coherence.[10] It is bold in that pragmatism allows truth claims to be floated without sufficient evidence, so as to intensify the search for evidence that would not surface unless the claim were proposed. Empirical evidence to the contrary will, of course, sink the claim.

For purpose of the present context, it is both the tentativeness and the experimental character of pragmatism with regard to truth claims, values, and judgments that has the ring of authenticity as an approach to patterns of future amelioration. The pragmatic approach is precisely the opposite of that characterized by ideology and claims of certitude. When the search for truth is experimental, probing, and open to surprises, novelty, and setback, the tendency is to take a wide view of the evidence and an even wider view of the possible participants who can be of assistance in this search. It is fitting then, that pragmatism is also pluralistic in its epistemology. In his critique of monism or of epistemic absolutes, James sets out the pluralist position.

> Absolute unity brooks no degrees—as well might you claim absolute purity for a glass of water because it contains but a single little cholera-germ. The independence, however infinitesimal, of a part, however small, would be to the Absolute as fatal as a cholera-germ.
>
> Pluralism on the other hand has no need of this dogmatic rigoristic temper. Provided you grant *some* separation among things, some tremor of independence, some free play of parts on one another, some real novelty or chance, however minute, she is amply satisfied, and will allow you any amount, however great, of real union. How much of union there may be is a question that she thinks can only be decided empirically. The amount may be enormous, colossal; but absolute monism is shattered if, along with all the union, there has to be granted the slightest modicum, the most incipient nascency, or the most residual trace, of a separation that is not 'overcome.'[11]

It seems to me perfectly legitimate and instructive to draw a relationship between the pluralism of a pragmatic epistemology and the cultural pluralism of James, Royce, and Dewey. Although as Americans we often violate the commitment to pluralism, it is our most profound tradition and the one which has the most direct and signal significance for the next century. World culture is not a seamless garment knit together from a single bolt of cloth. It is plaid in fabric, with often frayed ends, missed stitches, and clashing colors. World culture is many-hued and in an often riotous arrangement. Just as our cultural maps undergo changes, some subtle, some vast, so too do the lives of the people who find themselves invaded, captured, sold, relocated, or forced to change their external beliefs. Yet, despite these upheavals, most of them against the will of those who are subject to the intrusion, the multiplicity of languages, customs, religions, attitudes, and life-styles persists. Even the bullying of the Red Guards of the Chinese cultural revolution was unable to change the concentric, thousands-year-old history of the open market system of the Chinese. The Jewish people, the Polish people, and many others defy superpower ideology to maintain the quality and integrity of their precious traditions, both personal and communal.

Neither American economic imperialism nor Soviet expansionist communism has a clue to the majesty and the obduracy of the multiple styles of life which constitute global culture. However well intentioned, due to the seduction of self-approving ideology, the superpowers are constantly paraphrasing Henry Higgins by asking, "Why can't they be more like us?" Think of it, if the English had their way, as they very nearly did, all of us would play cricket and drink tea in the afternoon. Whatever the source, and it is usually at the behest of a gun barrel, cultural imperialism is an abomination. The task, of course, is for each culture and subculture to be open to the experience, originality, and value of other cultures. This is only possible if individuals are taught from the outset to be open to experience and to avoid judgments based on conceptual a priori assumptions, inherited truths legitimated only by longevity or by authority. These obstacles to genuine inquiry correspond exactly to Peirce's critique in his paper on "The Fixation of Belief," wherein he chastises the methods of tenacity, authority, and that of the a priori.[12] He then proceeds to develop a doctrine of the community of inquiry which stresses constant experiment and multiple participation. He early anticipated what we now take to be a truism: that the major problems which loom before us rarely will yield to the wisdom of a single observer or even to the activity of a single method or tradition. Peirce's ideal was that someday we would replace competition with cooperation in the arena of scientific inquiry. This is a worthy goal in the arena of social and political inquiry as well.

In our attempt to forge a genuinely pluralistic attitude towards inquiry and to encourage recognition of a plurality of styles and beliefs, it should be made clear that this effort is not a waiting game until all participants agree to agree. Pluralism is not a temporary aberration in the great cosmic scheme, if there be one, nor is it a fall from grace. Following the classical American philosophers, plurality in virtually every arena of activity is a permanent characteristic of the human scene. One way to stress this is to develop a sensitivity to a positive provincialism. The negative side of provincialism is obvious. One example will suffice. Most Americans of this century have been formally educated as though most of the world did not exist. For many Americans, knowledge of other people, other lands, and other languages is notoriously lacking. It is precisely this form of ignorance which leads to xenophobia and which conditions us to succumb to ideology.

On the other hand, human beings come from somewhere, speak a native language, and receive a host of cultural inheritances. Most of us settle somewhere (a nation, a region, even a city or a town or a village), and that place constitutes for us the lineaments of our transaction with time and space. We may travel, but we return home. "Citizen of the world" has a nice ring to it, but it belies the way we think, the provincial source of our beliefs, our values, and our attitudes. In a prophetic essay written in 1902, Josiah Royce distinguishes between a negative and a "wholesome" provincialism.

> My thesis is that in the present state of the world's civilization, and of the life of our own country, the time has come to emphasize, with a new meaning and intensity, the positive value, the absolute necessity for our welfare, of a wholesome provincialism, as a saving power to which the world in the near future will need more and more to appeal.[13]

Royce stresses the need for local communities to develop a sense of pride in their origins and accomplishments. He also encourages communities to build and create a distinctive character. But then—and this is the heart of a genuine pluralism—he urges the members of the community to seek out other communities, especially abroad, and to share the values and the ideals in a common spirit of inquiry. Obviously, this does not always go well, for values and ideals are often conflicted. In order to build a community and a brace of communities and finally a world community, mediation is needed. Royce refers to mediators as interpreters. Where two persons or communities are face to face, it is often necessary for a third to interpret them to each other. In this way, one preserves the integrity of one's own lineage and position while being simultaneously able to reach out and share that of the other. Contrary to Royce's earlier absolute idealism, the path trod here leads not to an absolute nor to a final community as the realization of a fixed eschatology. Royce's goal is more modest and more empirical. He seeks a way to aid us in building a "beloved" community with the virtue of hope, rather than with the more ideological virtue of faith. Remarkably, he writes that *"by the 'real world' we mean simply the 'true interpretation' of this our problematic situation."*[14] Consequently, unless both the interpreter and the community are real, there can be no real world. Further, he denies that

> the real world is anything merely static, or is a mere idea within the mind of a finite self, or is an Absolute that is divorced from its appearances, or is any merely conceptual reality, or is "out of time," or is a "block universe," or is an object of a merely mystical intuition.[15]

If we follow Royce's line of reasoning, the conclusion is inescapable. In building a human community, we are constitutive of nothing less than the world. If our community is in tatters, so too is the world. If our community is self-deceived and illusory, so too is the world. If our community is ongoing, integral, and supportive, so too is the world. Royce has transformed the traditional idealist position, which reads that "the world is as it is thought," to "the world is as it is built to *be*." It is not the goal so much as it is the quality of the interpreted journey which Royce bequeaths to us as the meaning of individual life, inseparable from communal life.

We have no guarantee that any of this will go well, although it is well worth attempting. Put differently, neither optimism nor pessimism seems to be a proper response, for each approach neglects the data generated by the other. Yet, it is characteristic that we are called upon to favor one response or the other, as in the rhetorical question, Are you an optimist or a pessimist? James seeks to avoid such a dichotomy.

Ought not the existence of the various types of thinking which we have re-
viewed, each so splendid for certain purposes, yet all conflicting still, and neither
one of them able to support a claim of absolute veracity, to awaken a presump-
tion favorable to the pragmatistic view that all our theories are *instrumental*,
are mental modes of *adaptation* to reality, rather than revelations or gnostic
answers to some divinely instituted world-enigma?[16]

Following James, neither optimism nor pessimism provides the adap-
tive ability required in our approach to the human situation, for they tend
to be cut off from the reality of setback and possibility, respectively.
Rather, the strategy for effecting concrete and beneficent change should
follow the moral attitude of meliorism, that is, simply, to strive to make
things better. There is no illusion here about the possibility of perfection;
but there is a belief in the growth of sensitivity, of goods, and of enjoyment,
especially the aesthetic, as having to do with living in an environment
which is celebratory, adorned, and able to combine tradition and novelty.
For James, pluralism and meliorism are entwined; the first celebrates
diversity whereas the second aids in the development of originality and adjudication of conflict between a variety of styles. James sees the relationship between meliorism and pluralism as follows:

> The melioristic universe is conceived after a *social* analogy, as a pluralism of
> independent powers. It will succeed just in proportion as more of these work for
> its success. If none work, it will fail. If each does his best, it will not fail. Its
> destiny thus hangs on an *if*, or on a lot of *ifs*—which amounts to saying
> (in the technical language of logic) that, the world being as yet unfinished,
> its total character can be expressed only by *hypothetical* and not by *categorical*
> propositions. . . .
> As individual members of a pluralistic universe, we must recognize that, even
> though we do *our* best, the other factors also will have a voice in the result. If
> they refuse to conspire, our good-will and labor may be thrown away. No in-
> surance company can here cover us or save us from the risks we run in being part
> of such a world.[17]

James is correct about the risk involved in any attempt to effect significant change. The effort must be carried on with a delicacy worthy of the
pluralism and the positive provincialism it espouses. The risk is com-
pounded if the agent of change is naive about the twin, always allied, re-
quirements for successful amelioration. The first requirement we have
stressed in this essay, namely, an abandonment of fixed positions, ideological cant and a priori judgments. This can be brought about only by

what Jewish tradition calls a *teshuvah,* a full turning, a change of heart. This is a moral epistemology, which is rooted in Plato and found recurring in the stoics, Augustine, Spinoza, Bergson, Buber, and especially in classical American philosophy. I foresee no significant social or political breakthrough without this change of heart.

The second requirement for successful human advance has not been discussed here and remains for another setting. I refer to the need for sophistication as to how institutions deflect, co-opt, and dilute change, all the while praising its presence. This warning against massive self-deception is usually attributed to Marx, and correctly, but John Dewey was well aware of its presence. In 1935, Dewey spelled out the need for sophistication about how good works spin their wheels when subjected to the wiles of institutional survival.

> The conditions that generate insecurity for the many no longer spring from nature. They are found in institutions and arrangements that are within deliberate human control. Surely this change marks one of the greatest revolutions that has taken place in all human history. Because of it, insecurity is not now the motive to work and sacrifice but to despair. . . .
>
>   . . . The educational task cannot be accomplished merely by working upon men's minds, without action that effects actual change in institutions. The idea that dispositions and attitudes can be altered by merely "moral" means conceived of as something that goes on wholly inside of persons is itself one of the old patterns that has to be changed. Thought, desire and purpose exist in a constant give and take of interaction with environing conditions. But resolute thought is the first step in that change of action that will itself carry further the needed change in patterns of mind and character.[18]

Global amelioration, then, is possible under the following conditions: 1) awareness of how institutional change takes place, *mutatis mutandis,* in different societies, that is, an avoidance of the innocence or the naivete that thinks that good will is a sufficient agent of change; 2) a profound awareness of the cultural heritage, values, and taboos of other societies as well as an awareness of what they can in conscience yield and what in conscience they must protect; 3) an abandonment of ideology and a concentration on shared values; 4) the willingness of the technologically affluent and politically powerful nations of the world to accept comparable suggestions for amelioration of their own weaknesses and offenses. With these conditions met, perhaps we, the nations of the world, could join in an effort to develop Royce's "beloved community," while keeping an eye directly on famine, population, ecology, and nuclear war. Without an attenuation and developing amelioration of those four problems, the beloved community is a chimera. I believe that we can make a "turning" and begin again. William James says it best:

> If we survey the field of history and ask what feature all great periods of revival, of expansion of the human mind, display in common, we shall find, I think, simply this: that each and all of them have said to the human being, "The inmost nature of the reality is congenial to *powers* which you possess."[19]

In this text of James, the fundamental dialectic of our situation is laid bare in one trenchant sentence. Reality has its givenness, its obduracy, its nature. We, human life, have our powers. Neither triumphs for the good of either. It is congeniality we seek, that is, a community of inquiry characterized by cooperation, insight to the needs of the other, and liberation from arrogance. All philosophy, one way or another, is helpful to us in our plight. Yet classical American philosophy seems to be closest to the mark. We owe it to ourselves to rejuvenate this tradition as an intelligent source for our future global activity. It is very likely that a copy of William James's *Will to Believe* may be more salutary for the future of my grandchildren and their peers than still another missile complete with a nuclear warhead. Philosophy bakes no bread, but it knows white from rye. Or should we wait for attrition and demolition before the plaintive cry reaches to heaven for vengeance or redemption, neither of which, if world history be our guide, will be forthcoming.

As for me, I am on the side of trying!

7 A Relational World

THE SIGNIFICANCE OF THE THOUGHT
OF WILLIAM JAMES AND JOHN DEWEY
FOR GLOBAL CULTURE

Real culture lives by sympathies and admirations, not by dislikes and disdains: under all misleading wrappings it pounces unerringly upon the human core.
WILLIAM JAMES, *Memories and Studies*

One can say with confidence, alas, that systemic intractability, ethnic and religious self-righteousness, and wholesale *hubris* are now endemic to global society. We have only to witness contemporary Lebanon in order to realize how a people can become victimized by the hanging on of ancient rivalries, hates, and jealousies, especially when these are combined with more recent ideological conflicts as sponsored within as well as by scavenging neighbors from without. Like instances abound, east and west, north and south. Lamentably, no end to this strife seems to be in sight, and conflicts like it distract us from the truly awesome problems of population, world hunger, depletion of natural resources and, of course, the specter of nuclear conflagration.

The thought of a single tradition, much less of single thinkers, seems powerless when placed in the context of these sprawling human brush fires, which are both geographically widespread and chronologically repetitive. The extraordinary influence of Buddha, Jesus Christ, Mohammed, and Karl Marx, among others, however, attests to the capacity of one person to offer a message, a viewpoint, a claim, that becomes the staple of common wisdom for subsequent generations. Yet the difficulty with many of the charismatic figures of the past, sometimes through no fault of their own, is that they have generated intense allegiance but precious little tolerance for competing views and persuasions. The contemporary scene requires a very different type of insight, one characterized less by exclusivity and more by relationship and pluralism.

This approach to human conflict, as desirable as it may be, is not easily obtainable. Yet there are thinkers whose work can make a contribution to this dilemma, namely, William James (1842–1910) and John Dewey (1859–1952).

In my judgment, James's thought is the vestibule to the thought and values of the twentieth century. He does not have the philosophical intensity or genius of Heidegger, nor does he have the scope and social/political sophistication of Dewey; but he anticipates much of the contemporary temper—its weaknesses as well as its strengths. In his 1891 essay, "The Moral Philosopher and the Moral Life," James reveals his habit of thinking into the future.

> All the higher, more penetrating ideals are revolutionary. They present themselves far less in the guise of effects of past experience than in that of probable causes of future experience, factors to which the environment and the lessons it has so far taught us must learn to bend.[1]

James's potential contribution to twentieth-century culture is at least fivefold: his doctrines of relations, pluralism, pragmatic contextualism, temporalism, and his suggestion of a moral equivalent to war. Taking them in turn, I shall draw out the ramifications of James's ideas for a viable philosophy of culture.

The metaphysical basis for James's entire philosophical program is to be found in his doctrine of relations, which he called radical empiricism. In 1909, a year before his death, in a preface to his work *The Meaning of Truth*, James clarified his meaning of radical empiricism. The tenets of this position constitute a partial philosophical mapping of the twentieth-century intellectual terrain.

> Radical empiricism consists first of a postulate, next of a statement of fact, and finally of a generalized conclusion.
> The postulate is that the only things that shall be debatable among philoso-

phers shall be things definable in terms drawn from experience. [Things of an unexperienceable nature may exist ad libitum, but they form no part of the material for philosophic debate.]

The statement of fact is that the relations between things, conjunctive as well as disjunctive, are just as much matters of direct particular experience, neither more so nor less so, than the things themselves.

The generalized conclusion is that therefore the parts of experience hold together from next to next by relations that are themselves parts of experience. The directly apprehended universe needs, in short, no extraneous trans-empirical connective support, but possesses in its own right a concatenated or continuous structure.[2]

For James, the direct and affective experiencing of relations obviates the position which holds that the world comes ready-made in a series of objects, essences, or as if we lived in a "block-universe." To the contrary, objects are mock-ups, structured by the mind as a means of managing the perceptual flow. James writes that *"the only meaning of essence is teleological, and that classification and conception are purely teleological weapons of the mind."*[3] The "meaning" of reality is a function of the constitutive activity of the human mind. Existence is finite and unformed, but meaning is constructed and subjected to personal, social, and historical predilection. Above all, we are not trapped in any form of determinism, be it theological, scientific, or historical. The widest and most profound obligation of human pedagogy is to teach ourselves and others how to make relations, that is, how to diagnose both the continuity and discontinuity in our experiences, which he contends are "cognitive of one another." Experience, as such, is potentially pedagogical, if we but pay attention. Everything we perceive teems with relational leads, many of them novel and therefore often blocked from our experience by the narrowness and self-defining, circular character of our inherited conceptual schema. The human task is to let our experiences speak to us in all of their manifold vagueness. Naming, defining, cataloging, quantifying are activities of a last resort and have justification only for purposes of organization—necessary for enabling us to move on to still richer fields of experience—or of survival.

James's doctrine of relations[4] unseats the dominance of the Aristotelian conceptual framework that has suffused common Western consciousness for more than 2,000 years. Further, James's stress on relations rather than on objects and on percepts rather than concepts is congenial to cultures other than that of Western civilization; he espouses a congeniality far more in keeping with the contemporary reality of a truly global culture.

Actually, the most singularly informative breakthrough in our recent understanding of the world is to be found in the works of cultural and social anthropologists. It is now obvious that the peoples of the world have been engaged in creating a dazzling array of formulations of what it is to be human. On a close, reflective, and patient look, it is apparent that novelty rather than similarity is the hallmark of human civilization. Following James, if we cast off our conceptual and habitual cultural predispositions, we find that ritual, dance, food, costume, language, myth, architecture, artifacts, and an original sense of space and time revel in as many rich subtleties as there are gatherings of people who trace themselves to a wide variety of ethnic, religious, and climatic origins. These subtleties are primarily relational, tied as they are to expectations, responses, and to a vast range of aesthetic manifestations. The traditional penchant for reducing differences to similarity and novelties to familiarity destroys the panoply of meanings that lurk in all of our observations, all of our listening, all of our touching—in short in all of our experiencing. In 1907, James tells us in his *Pragmatism:*

> There can *be* no difference anywhere that doesn't *make* a difference else-where—no difference in abstract truth that doesn't express itself in a difference in concrete fact and in conduct consequent upon that fact, imposed on some-body, somehow, somewhere, and somewhen.[5]

Fascination with these differences and respect for their messaging enables us to live and let live. More, such an attitude enables us, by contrast, to enrich the fabric of our own lives and to become more aware of the relationships at work in our own experience, especially those which disappear from our purview because they do not conform to the a priori range of accepted names for things and events undergone.

The interpersonal arena and the descriptions of social and cultural anthropology are not the only areas of human activity which sustain James's prescient judgment about the primary character of relations. Both modern art[6] and modern science have abandoned classical descriptive terms in favor of relational and process metaphors. This is especially true of modern painting, jazz music, modern dance, and modern physics, all of which stress happenings, events, and processes rather than objects or things. The influence of the thought of James on the physicist Niels Bohr and quantum mechanics is one powerful example of a twentieth-century realization of the significance of radical empiricism. A still more pervasive salutary fallout from James's doctrine of relations is his evocative description of our mental life as a "stream of consciousness," whereby we alternate between things and relatings, between perches and flights. Movement, change, and occasional moorings are the richer stuff of life than the time-honored boxes in which so many of us, lamentably, spend so much of our lives. James celebrates "streaming" and process as does much of the creative, imaginative, and frontier thinking of our century. The bequest of the philosophy of William James in this regard is the call to close the gap between the processive, dynamic way in which our life flows and the way in which we came to experience it, burdened by the closed concepts that often render our experiences as repetitive and even trite.

A second important contribution of William James to the life and thought of the twentieth century is his notion of pluralism. The generalized conclusion of James's statement on radical empiricism emphasized that he saw no need for any "extraneous trans-empirical connective support." James conceived this sense of openness as an antidote to both cosmological and theological closure. He also viewed this commitment to processive continuity rather than ontological unity as a counter to philosophical monism and closed systems of any kind. James had both a temperamental and philosophical aversion to finality, ultimate solutions, and any interpretation of our human situation which forbade loose ends, discontinuity, or embarrassing, unclassifiable remainders. As he put it in his 1909 work *A Pluralistic Universe:*

> Pragmatically interpreted, pluralism or the doctrine that it is many means only that the sundry parts of reality *may be externally related.* Everything you can think of, however vast or inclusive, has on the pluralistic view a genuinely 'external' environment of some sort or amount. Things are 'with' one another in many ways, but nothing includes everything, or dominates over everything. The word 'and' trails along after every sentence. Something always escapes. 'Ever not quite' has to be said of the best attempts made anywhere in the universe at attaining all-inclusiveness. The pluralistic world is thus more like a federal republic than like an empire or a kingdom. However much may be collected, however much may report itself as present at any effective centre of consciousness or action, something else is self-governed and absent and unreduced to unity.[7]

Pluralism is the pragmatic result of James's doctrine of relations. Things, events, hang together by relations, in a network which in the long run is empirically vague, no matter what proximate clarity we may attain. Nothing can be fully understood by itself, for every experience we have reaches, potentially, every other perceivable aspect of reality. Closure, names, and definitions are merely pragmatic strategies to construct a viable finite world in an infinite abyss. The perspective of other persons is partially constitutive of their reality and, therefore, by shared custom, partially constitutive of ours as well. If there is no single vantage point from which the world can be seen or interpreted or experientially had as whole, then every person makes his or her contribution to the ongoing statement as to how it is with the world, and how the world comes to be for me is in some way due to how the world has come to be for the other, for you.

In order to understand James's pluralism, it is crucial to realize that this multiplicity of interpretations, perspectives, and realizations is not a temporary fall from grace. James does not hold that pluralism is a waiting game, a temporary aberration until the archons of clarity—theological, scientific, or ideological—can rescue us from confusion. No, it is quite the opposite, for pluralism is the irreducible characteristic of not only the human presence but also of the evolutionary and developmental character of reality. In James's philosophy, closure and finality "violate the character with which life concretely comes . . . with an 'ever not quite' to all our formulas, and novelty and possibility forever leaking in."[8]

One could hardly overestimate the importance of James's pluralism as a basic strand of personal, social, political, and national policy on the contemporary world scene. Given the strident and long-standing homage to self-righteousness, along with the appropriate defensive propaganda, it would take a major change of heart for the present human community to take seriously even the possible plausibility of positions, claims, and attitudes to be inevitably pluralistic and therefore not subject to agreement in any form or for any reason. This situation leaves us in a serious quandary, for the absence of compromise seems to foretell a permanent and irresolute struggle on the one hand, or the demolishing of difference on the other hand. In this vein, recent events in both Vietnam and Afghanistan come all too readily to mind.

Relative to this thorny and inflammatory issue, the thought of William James can make a contribution. He offers us not the pragmatism identified with *Realpolitik,* but a pragmatism forged from his pluralism, his commitment to irreducible ambiguity and his conviction that the truth of the matter is not to be found in either a definition or in agreement between concepts and the alleged object. Rather the truth emerges from working out a hypothesis as subjected, tested, and revised in the light of ongoing experience. Pragmatic epistemology is a contextualism that not only brings to the fore the events before us but takes into consideration the possible future ramifications of the position taken.

If James is correct, as I think he is, that reality is evolutionary, developmental, and processive rather than static or complete in any way, then it is imperative to realize that positions taken by human diagnosis and human intervention are significantly, although partially, constitutive of the future course of events. Nowhere is this more apparent than in the activities of contemporary science and its application, contemporary technology. Classical realist epistemology held that the world exists as an object for us to "learn about." Once we knew the laws and principles governing reality, we could then follow them in a series of applied strategies, so as to effect salutary results. Recent science, however, is not simply realist or descriptive. To the contrary, it is intrusive and constructive, as is dramatically shown by modern medicine and modern physics. The principles behind the use of antibiotics, gene-splicing, pharmacology, and organ transplants take into account both the given stubbornness of nature and our capacity to effect the very laws which govern nature. Contemporary physics and chemistry provide similar examples of our capacity to transform reality, as witness the creation of artificial, "unnatural" entities such as plastics.

Unless we accept a retrograde, and politically unfeasible, Luddite position and abandon the march of modern technology, it is clear that we need a different epistemology than that of traditional realism. If science and technology continue to be intrusive, it is necessary that we include potential future ramifications as relevant to decision making. It is not sufficient to make a decision based on the simple face of the matter. Future implications must be taken into consideration. A baleful example of this warning is to be found in the use of therapeutic drugs and pesticides. Both strategies are for the purpose of alleviation or amelioration of an undesirable situation found either in human life or in nature. Both strategies, however, have spawned results often far more deleterious than the original object of concern; witness the responsibility of the drug thalidomide for massive birth defects, or the concentration of DDT in so many of the organisms of the world.

Although James had no such extensive crises in mind, his pragmatic and contextualist epistemology is of direct relevance. With James, we hold that all events, all decisions are pregnant with connections, many of which show themselves only subsequent to the human plan enacted. Granted that it is impossible to predict safely or accurately all of the implications of any decision, far greater attention must now be paid to future fallout from our attempt to "manage" nature. Truth as the mere correspondence between a concept and its object is far too narrow and inept when used as the method for evaluating the proper approach to the scale of problems now confronting world civilization. It would be far better if we were to develop an epistemology which accepted surprise, novelty, and potential mishap as permanent ingredients of human inquiry. In so doing, our decisions would be more tentative, less absolute, and consequently truer to the actual situation in which we find ourselves.

In addition to his doctrines of relations, pluralism, and pragmatic contextualism, James offers one further philosophical contribution to our effort at understanding and meliorating life in the twentieth century. James is a temporalist, by which I mean that he holds the affairs of time to be sacred. Further, according to James, the flow of historical experience is not tied to some fixed, determined master plan. The world is real and human intervention is real. The ultimate reach of reality may be infinite, but the human condition is clearly played out on a finite stage and all of its characteristics—theological, scientific, philosophical, and ideological—are finite in origin, intent, and significance. In his preface to a series of essays collected as *The Will to Believe,* James puts forth his unwavering commitment to his belief that the "crudity of experience remains an external element" of our experience of the world. He continues as follows:

> There is no possible point of view from which the world can appear an absolutely single fact. Real possibilities, real indeterminations, real beginnings, real ends, real evil, real crises, catastrophes, and escapes, a real God, and a real moral life, just as common-sense conceives these things, may remain in empiricism as conceptions which that philosophy gives up the attempt either to 'overcome' or to reinterpret in monistic form.[9]

The full meaning of this text is extremely instructive. If we are finite, if our experiences are finite, and if there is no higher meaning which transforms these experiences into something other than the way in which we undergo them, then the affairs of time, our things and events, are to be taken at face value. The flow of time is the only setting for judging the worth of human life and human activity. James reverses the assumptions of much of the history of religion and philosophy. The transcendent and infinite are abstractions, ways of compensating for the opacity and ambiguity in our human experience. Time is all we have and, as we know all

ULTIMATE SIN: TO WASTE PEOPLE'S TIME ...

too well, human time is finite, irreversible. Above all, time is terminal so far
as individual life is concerned.

From this metaphysical temporalism of James there proceed two radically different interpretations. The first holds that the necessarily terminal character of finitude—graphically spelled out by the words, organic
death—renders human life trivial and human activity absurd. The second
interpretation holds that the absence of a transcendent resolution of finitude, the absence of a transcendent principle of explanation, paradoxically
forces us to value the history of human life as the *only* source of the sacred.
Consistent with James's basic metaphysical position, this latter view regards the human affairs of time as worthy of total devotion on behalf of
amelioration and, where and when appropriate, celebration. Therefore,
starvation, interpersonal violence, and repression are not only morally
evil, but metaphysically evil as well, for they offend human life within the
fabric of time, knowing full well that there we have no future recourse to
any salvific resolution that transcends our human lives. In my judgment,
this second interpretation is an accurate diagnosis of our actual situation.
If we were to truly believe this, we would take vigorous steps to eradicate
the systemic evil which continues to plague global culture. Not only is this
evil harmful to human life and aspiration, it further mocks the only way we
have to account for why, in an infinite cosmological setting, the activities
of finite creatures have purpose.

For the most part, James was a nineteenth-century person and, as such,
he did not have access to the cataclysmic events of our own century, for
example, two world wars, the Holocaust, and Hiroshima. Had he experienced those events, he may have provided us with a more detailed and
rigorous application of his philosophical wisdom to concrete and massive
human disasters. Shortly before his death in 1910, he did write a suggestive
piece, which, despite its pre-World War I innocence, does provide us with
perhaps a viable approach to human violence. Entitled "The Moral Equivalent of War,"[10] it offers a pragmatic approach in which James contends
that the martial habituation of human nature has to be reoriented rather
than simply lamented, for the lamentation about the evil of war seems to
be followed, inevitably, by more war. The key word, of course, is "equivalent," and faced as we are with the specter of potential nuclear conflagration, we might well intensify our efforts to develop a globally applicable
equivalent. Surely, the energy, intelligence, vast economic resources, and
sophisticated systems of surveillance that have been marshalled to produce
a tenuous stalemate could be an extraordinary "weapon" for technologi-

cal and economic assistance to the millions of human beings for whom life is a bitter struggle against disease, poverty, and malnutrition.

No more than any other single source of philosophical wisdom is the thought of William James to be taken as a panacea. His approach, however, to the relationship between thought and action and his profound distrust of absolutes and final solutions are extremely significant for us in the twentieth century, since we have been seduced over and again by nostrums and dangerously false promises. James's pragmatic temper is the proper mood for contemporary society. His stress on the experience of relations and connections provides us with the metaphysical subtlety necessary as an antidote to the single vision which dominates so many of our endeavors. James's spiritual vision is also of note, for he insists that we celebrate the affairs of ordinary experience and that we realize it is we and we alone who are responsible for the course of human history. Due to the power of modern technology, we are now, for better or worse, the lords of history. If we have the "will to believe" in both our capacity to effect human healing of unnecessary suffering and in our responsibility to do so, then we shall, in time, create a human community worthy of the rich human tradition of hope, aspiration, and wisdom.

I turn now to the work of John Dewey and its significance for world culture. Dewey absorbed the basic assumptions and claims of William James, and, indeed, saw earlier and more perceptively than most that James's thought was the direction the future should take. In a 1931 essay, "The Development of American Pragmatism," Dewey affirms the stress on the future as found in James's thought.

> Pragmatism thus has a metaphysical implication. The doctrine of the value of consequences leads us to take the future into consideration. And this taking into consideration of the future takes us to the conception of a universe whose evolution is not finished, of a universe which is still, in James' term, "in the making," "in the process of becoming," of a universe up to a certain point still plastic.
>
> Consequently reason, or thought, in its more general sense, has a real, though limited, function, a creative, constructive function. If we form general ideas and if we put them in action, consequences are produced which could not be produced otherwise. Under these conditions the world will be different from what it would have been if thought had not intervened. This consideration confirms the human and moral importance of thought and of its reflective operation in experience. . . . One will understand the philosophy of James better if one considers it in its totality as a revision of English empiricism, a revision which replaces the value of past experience, of what is already given, by the future, by that which is as yet mere possibility.[11]

Dewey, however, differed from James in that he was neither a New England Brahmin nor a Europhile like James. To the contrary, long before it became either fashionable or necessary, Dewey was involved globally. His travels on educational matters took him to South Africa, Turkey, the Soviet Union, Japan, and China. In a venture that can be described as a one-person educational peace corps, Dewey realized the necessity of serious transactions with a world theretofore ignored or victimized by cultural imperialism. Dewey had nothing of the preacher or the vigilante in his makeup. He was careful to indulge the cultural priorities of his host country and merely suggested that democratic strategies could be developed as consonant with local prerogatives.[12] In retrospect, it is true that Dewey had none of the anthropological sophistication now available to us, yet he made an effort to reach out and test his educational and political theories and practices in some of the most volatile areas of the world between the two great wars.[13]

I have detailed the significance of James's contributions in the form of pluralism, pragmatic contextualism, and temporalism. Dewey continues these insights of James and attempts to build them into a social and political fabric in a far more extensive and sophisticated way than did James. Influenced in his early work by the sense of the social and the historical in the thought of Hegel, Dewey always demanded of himself that his judgments about personal possibility be realistic in the light of institutional limitations. Although he shared with James a life-long commitment to the need for individual and personal growth and for the necessity of liberation from false gods, Dewey also knew that the enemies of such growth were not simply errant or bad persons, but more often the very way in which we constructed our social, political and, above all, economic and educational institutions. His pragmatic temper was instinctual, as when he writes:

> To fill our heads like a scrapbook, with this and that item as a finished and done-for thing, is not to think. It is to turn ourselves into a piece of registering apparatus. To consider the *bearing* of the occurrence upon what may be, but is not yet, is to think.[14]

Dewey has in mind, here, an intellectual ingredient essential to a pragmatic epistemology, namely, the sharp sense of implicitness, which yields insight only to the alert. One has to keep a wary eye on the implication of decisions, warnings, and even suggestions. Both James and Dewey are chary of final solutions or a priori prognostications, both of which deny the inevitable role of chance in the human and natural equation of events. In this regard, Dewey is uncanny in his awareness that human plans for the future are necessarily fraught with obstacle, for any intrusion into the status quo generates responses and mishap precisely in proportion to the imaginative cast of the intention. For Dewey, as for James, neither optimism nor pessimism are the proper empirical response to the actual situation of the human condition. To be optimistic is to be potentially naive about the vagaries of natural forces which often presage disaster. It is also to be blithely unaware of the human capacity to act in a self-aggrandizing manner, even at the expense of the community or of those values which most of us cherish. On the other hand, to be systematically pessimistic is to draw the curtain on possibility, on growth, on novelty, and on the most indomitable characteristic of the human spirit, the ability to begin again, afresh, with hope for a better day.

Better than most major thinkers, Dewey understands the pitfalls of these two traditional options to the future of human activity. In response, he adopts the approach of James, which is also indicative of the American temperament when it is at its best, namely, meliorism. Put simply and etymologically, the attitude of meliorism is to *make things better*. At a deeper and more profound index of analysis, the attitude of meliorism acknowledges both sin and possibility. Dewey is adamant in his conviction that nothing will go totally right in either the short or the long run. He is equally convinced that all problems are malleable and functionally, although not ultimately, resolute, even if they are sure to appear in another guise at another time. I refer to this as a metaphysics of transiency, in which human life is seen as wandering, a traveling, a bemusement which rocks from side to side, comedy and tragedy, breakthrough and setback— yet, in all, a purposive, even progressive, trip in which the human endeavor makes its mark, sets its goals, and occasionally scores, an event which Dewey calls a consummatory experience, as in "that was *an* experience." Truly, then, meliorism is a salutary human approach, despite its lacking the drama of either pessimism or optimism. It takes no captives, makes no excessive claims, nor bows out in frustration at the opposition. Dewey evokes the deepest sentiments of human life, too often unsung and too often derided: that the nectar is in the journey, that ultimate goals may be illusory, nay, most likely are but a gossamer wing. Day by day, however, human life triumphs in its ineluctable capacity to hang in and make things better. Not perfect, simply better. Dewey has no illusions about the danger of this attempt to change institutions, habits, and attitudes. He is aware of the guarded response to *any* effort at change. In an affectionate and pre-scient text, Dewey confronts the opponent to change.

> Let us admit the case of the conservative; if we once start thinking no one can guarantee where we shall come out, except that many objects, ends, and institu-tions are surely doomed. Every thinker puts some portion of an apparently stable world in peril and no one can wholly predict what will emerge in its place.[15]

Dewey's awareness of the unpredictability of the future, especially when subject to human attempts at intervention, planning, or reconstruc-tion is refreshing in a period of time when we seem to replace one forecast with another without taking any responsibility for our role in the different and frequently contradictory results. We live in a time when futurology is in vogue and when the mighty forces of the computer and modern statistics combine to predict our future, day by day, detail by detail. That such pre-dictions often go awry does not seem either to deter our confidence or to chastise our arrogance. Dewey has a clue to these mishaps, for in true pragmatic style he is aware that to effect change in one area is to court disaster in another. Also, pragmatic sensibility has as a cardinal tenet that only consequences can effectively validate the truth or even the propitious-ness of a claim. Part of the disparateness in the relation between intention and realization has to do with the early abandonment of the quest in favor of some poor simulation. Dewey writes, "Men hoist the banner of the ideal, and then march in the direction that concrete conditions suggest and reward."[16]

Why is Dewey so tough on the viability of prediction and yet so san-guine on the possibility of human growth? My response is that Dewey has a doctrine of creative transiency, wherein the journey is its own mean and does not take its significance from a hoped-for, wished-for paradisaical future. In the language of medieval Christian theology, Dewey is clearly an incarnationalist and not an eschatologist. For him, the affairs of time are sacred, precisely because of human involvement, human care, and human intrusion.

Now, how does John Dewey set the stage for this creative transiency? At first blush, the context is quite straightforward. The human organism, embodied, transacts with the affairs of nature. This transaction is double-barrelled, for it is both a doing and an undergoing. As dramatically distinct as may be our personal experiencing, it is precisely the having of experience, each in our own way, which binds all of us together, no matter what our place on the planet earth.

> These commonplaces prove that experience is *of* as well as *in* nature. It is not experience which is experienced, but nature—stones, plants, animals, diseases, health, temperature, electricity, and so on. Things interacting in certain ways *are* experience; they are what is experienced. Linked in certain other ways with another natural object—the human organism—they are *how* things are experienced as well. Experience thus reaches down into nature; it has depth. It also has breadth and to an indefinitely elastic extent. It stretches. That stretch constitutes inference.[17]

The fascinating aspect of global culture is the dialectic in the life of each culture between *what* is experienced and *how* it is experienced. Dewey realizes that the differences in what we experience are clearly palpable as in the contrast between the *mountains* of mountain people and the *desert* of desert people. Similar palpability is available in the contrasts of rural-urban, coastal-plains, and frigid-torrid and other macroscopic matrices for undergoing experience. That palpability, however, only masks the deeper novelty, which emerges when we attempt to understand *how* others *have* their experiences, that is, *how* they do the world in which they find themselves and *how* that world, literally, does to them, better, does them. The master anthropologist of our time, Clifford Geertz, maps the perils and pitfalls of one of us seeking to know *how* another of us has his or her experience.

> The tension between the pull of this need to penetrate an unfamiliar universe of symbolic action and the requirements of technical advance in the theory of culture, between the need to grasp and the need to analyze, is, as a result, both necessarily great and essentially irremovable. Indeed, the further theoretical development goes, the deeper the tension gets. This is the first condition for cultural theory: it is not its own master. As it is unseverable from the immediacies thick description presents, its freedom to shape itself in terms of its internal logic is rather limited. What generality it contrives to achieve grows out of the delicacy of its distinctions, not the sweep of its abstractions.[18]

As Geertz notes, this obfuscation, which blocks our effort to understand another's experience, is heightened incomparably when we are involved in a different linguistic, environmental, and ritualistic setting—in short, in a distinctively different culture. Dewey's message is more general and more applicable to our present need to forge a genuinely global culture.

> Respect for experience is respect for its possibilities in thought and knowledge as well as an enforced attention to its joys and sorrows. Intellectual piety toward experience is a precondition of the direction of life and of tolerant and generous cooperation among men. Respect for the things of experience alone brings with it such a respect for others, the centres of experience, as is free from patronage, domination and the will to impose.[19]

There is clearly a deep sense of trust here in the quality in the experience of other persons and cultures. Dewey always invokes a sense of potential rejuvenation, despite the fact that he regards the transaction of the human organism and nature as necessarily and irreducibly problematic. The rejuvenation proceeds from the gains made in the fabric of time and is sullied by an indulgence of over-beliefs, pinings for immortality, and other assorted escapes from the grinding obviousness of our situation. Still, the will to adjudicate, heal, and advance the human cause in its temporal bind is not without celebratory occasions. Happiness in the Aristotelian sense is not hereby envisioned by Dewey, whose approach is more empirical, more realistic, and more attuned to the crushing sadness which visits most of our lives, most of the time. No, Dewey focuses rather on the occasional but crucial moments of celebration, joy, and the ability to break through the ersatz and the habitual. Dewey is cognizant of the surprises which lurk in everyday experience, but he also knows that we must be ever on the alert for these possibilities. Depressing though it be, most of us, the world over, spend days upon days simply fulfilling obligations of one kind or another, in a vast global fidelity to rote. Even the lives of the storied have such long patches of boredom, as witness the efforts of empresses and kings to entertain themselves, historically, with spectacles, usually of an inhumane and oppressive nature. Surely, their unhappiness, widely documented, does not trace to the absence of opportunity or of creature comforts, but rather to their inability to convert their experience to sufficient experiential nutrition for a human life.

In Dewey's metaphysics, the cognitive linchpin and the source of the major metaphors used to describe our place and activity in the world is the human body. Like James, Dewey paid close attention to the physiological process as a way of learning how we came to be in, of, and about nature. The alteration of nutrition and inanition is as true of our person as it is of our body. The respect for and piety toward experience, cited earlier, reveal that Dewey sees values and judgments as profoundly contexted by the variety of cultural experiences operative in the world. It is the liturgy, the celebration of these experiences, which hold his attention, for it is they that reveal the trust, the treasure, and the momentous in the lives of the participants. Dewey was not taken by either Plato or Aristotle, but he was enamored of the alleged lesser figures in the Greek philosophical pantheon, namely the sophists and the stoics. In fact, Dewey's thought is that of a latter-day stoic, for he believes that we are tied inextricably to the fabric and subject to the wiles of nature. Yet Dewey's stoicism is an American version rather than one of Greece or Rome. Consequently, it includes apertures of opportunity in a natural setting, which yield possibilities for the recreation of nature in the name of human needs.

The politics of managing these possibilities are fraught with danger, for historically the definition of human needs does not elicit wide agreement. The give and take in the scramble to both survive and celebrate constitutes a secular liturgy the world over. Dewey implores us to enter this fray alert and with our most formidable weapon, creative intelligence, which enables us to plot, to plan, to express opinions, and to reconstruct, always mindful of the twin obduracy of institutions and natural forces. The problems of food, population, sporadic regional violence, and the dark specter of nuclear obliteration demand of us that we invoke our creative intelligence on behalf of humane response. The first task is to learn from our past, for human history sets out the glories, the mishaps, the violence, and the achievements in our endeavor with a chilling accuracy. Better than most, Dewey knows of the wisdom of the past, for he converts it into currency for the future.

> Most mortals are conscious that a split often occurs between their present living and their past and future. Then the past hangs upon them as a burden; it invades the present with a sense of regret, or opportunities not used, and of consequences we wish undone. It rests upon the present as an oppression, instead of being a storehouse of resources by which to move confidently forward. But the live creature adopts its past; it can make friends with even its stupidities, using them as warnings that increase present wariness. Instead of trying to live upon whatever may have been achieved in the past, it uses past suc-

cesses to inform the present. Every living experience owes its richness to what Santayana well calls "hushed reverberations."[20]

The second task is to knit together those traditional opponents, education, politics, and aesthetic consciousness. Dewey has little patience with the compartmentalization of human activity into areas divined by a conceptual scheme rather than by the integral continuity of our experience as undergone. The baleful characteristic of our century is that, for the most part, the educational and political institutions of the planet do not meet the expectations or possibilities of the cultures which they control. Aesthetic sensibility and the engendered art forms are infinitely richer than the educational and political institutions through which they are filtered. Dewey's message is to return the educational and political processes and their institutions to a supportive relationship with the affective feelings, gestures, and aesthetic sensibilities of the culture in question. The separation of education and politics from the celebration of the everyday, an occurrence endemic to most of the cultures of the world, constitutes a blight on human feeling and on the conditions necessary for making human life tolerable. For Dewey, philosophy must insist on the renovation and celebration of those experiences which constitute the rhythm of our daily experience of the world. He insists that the alleged "commonplace" is a strategy devised by high culture to maintain an experiential caste and class system, one that perpetuates a hierarchy of values independent and ignorant of the richness found in our toil, our conversation, our gestures, and the happenstance of doing a day's work.

> I am loath to conclude without reference to the larger liberal humane value of philosophy when pursued with empirical method. The most serious indictment to be brought against non-empirical philosophies is that they have cast a cloud over the things of ordinary experience. They have not been content to rectify them. They have discredited them at large. In casting aspersion upon the things of everyday experience, the things of action and affection and social intercourse, they have done something worse than fail to give these affairs the intelligent direction they so much need. It would not matter much if philosophy had been reserved as a luxury of only a few thinkers. We endure many luxuries. The serious matter is that philosophies have denied that common experience is capable of developing from within itself methods which will secure direction for itself and will create inherent standards of judgment and value. No one knows how many of the evils and deficiencies that are pointed to as reasons for flight

from experience are themselves due to the disregard of experience shown by those peculiarly reflective. To waste of time and energy, to disillusionment with life that attends every deviation from concrete experience must be added the tragic failure to realize the value that intelligent search could reveal and mature among the things of ordinary experience. I cannot calculate how much of current cynicism, indifference and pessimism is due to these causes in the deflection of intelligence they have brought about.[21]

Global pedagogy must attend to affording us the ability to read the revelations of ordinary experience had in a ken, a clime, and a cultural setting diverse from our own. To be open to the experience of another is of double salutary significance. Not only do we apprise, learn, and participate in diversity but, perhaps paradoxically, we come to appreciate the novelty, singularity, and preciousness of our own experience. To participate in the plurality of experiences is personally explosive, for it trims our sails and curtails our arrogant provincialism while it widens our horizons and indirectly sanctions those experiences which are mundane to us, but exotic to others. Perhaps a global pedagogy should focus on precisely that relationship, namely, the shared experience of diverse experiences, such that the everyday would be experienced by others as exotic and therefore cast refreshing light on what we take to be routine.

There is nothing sentimental in these views of Dewey, for he regards them as essential to a democratic polity. On many occasions in his writing, Dewey stresses the relationship between a respect for ordinary experience, work, and the affairs of the everyday and the formulation of a society in which personal growth, dignity, and a creative advance become staples in the social fabric. For example, in *Democracy and Education,* in 1916, he writes, "Democracy cannot flourish where the chief influences in selecting subject matter of instruction are utilitarian ends narrowly conceived for the masses, and, for the higher education of the few, the traditions of a specialized cultivated class."[22] Dewey has in mind here the subtle but pervasive political management of curriculum, present in an obviously nefarious way in fascist states but operative as well in allegedly more enlightened nations. It is rare for a culture to sanction the quality of its ordinary experiences in a reenforcing curriculum structure. To the contrary, most cultures tend to ignore their own personal strengths and predilections in favor of a more embracing, yet inevitably more abstract, scholastic presentation. Nonetheless, unless we celebrate what each of us does, day by day, we run the risk of extensive cultural condescension. Furthermore, the efflorescence of artistic, literary, and scientific genius seems to always have its roots in the most apparently routine and mundane of cultural contexts. In his eightieth year, John Dewey points to the salutary effect of an environment in which each person can articulate his or her deepest feelings about experience. He writes that "a society of free individuals in which all, through their own work, contribute to the liberation and enrichment of the lives of others, is the only environment in which any individual can really grow normally to his own stature."[23]

Dewey was enamored of growth and perceptive about both the obstacles and the goals to its development. Although he had an irreducible commitment to the educability of all human beings, each to his or her potential ability, Dewey was aware also of the patterns of condescension and the class-oriented assumptions about human potential which so often scar an educational and social structure. He was convinced, as few before or since, that education, if structured in genuinely democratic ways, could overcome even the most oppressive and debilitating of regimes. In effect, with Dewey, we find a heightened version of the conflict between imposition, rote, and provincial, self-serving values and interpretations, as against free inquiry and the roaming of the unfettered mind, alert to its experiences, sensitive to its past, affectionate toward its future but distrustful of Draconian and magisterial pronouncements about the necessity of preserving the present.

Some think that our time on earth is but a vale of tears, and that we shall be healed only *sub specie aeternitatis*. In this regard, I report a moving allegory of the early third century A.D.—the tale of Perpetua, awaiting death as a Christian martyr.

> I had this vision: I saw Dinocratus coming out of a place of darkness, where he found himself in the midst of many others, all burning and parched with thirst, filthy and clad in rags, bearing on his face the sore that he had when he died. Dinocratus was my own brother. He died of illness at age seven, his face eaten away by a malignant canker, and his death repulsed everyone. I prayed for him: and between me and him the distance was so great that we could not touch. In the place where Dinocratus was there was a basin full of water, whose lip was too high for a small child. And Dinocratus stood on the tips of his toes, as though he wanted to drink. It caused me pain to see that there was water in the basin but that he could not drink because the lip was so high. I woke up with the knowledge that my brother was being tried. . . .

A few days later Perpetua has another vision:

> The day we were put in irons, this is what I saw: I saw the place that I had seen before, and Dinocratus, his body clean, well dressed, refreshed [refrigerantem], and where the sore had been I saw a scar; and the lip of the basin that I had seen had been lowered to the height of the child's navel, and water flowed out of it continuously. And above the lip there was a golden cup filled with water. Dinocratus drew near and began to drink from it, and the cup never emptied. Then, his thirst quenched, he began playing happily with the water, as children do. I awoke and I understood that his penalty had been lifted.[24]

Of such allegories was born the belief in purgatory, later so brilliantly detailed by Dante. Now neither John Dewey nor I believe in purgatory. Yet we both believe that the planet earth could become a *locus refrigerium,* a place of refreshment and healing, one in which the water of life might always run clear and sweet. Dinocratus is everywhere in our world, most often a victim of mindless internecine strife. A social philosophy, if it is to be truly helpful, must focus on the ways in which we can heal Dinocratus, face to face, during and in time.

Three

THE PRAGMATIC UPSHOT

Philosophical speculation is often regarded as above the battle, sheer folly, or at best distant from the problems and happenstance of the "real" world. In fact, no intellectual tradition has had such decisive influence on the way in which human beings have developed their system of values, especially as found in their religious, political, and social institutions, as has philosophy. The pervasive influence of Plato, Aristotle, Aquinas, Maimonides, Averroës, Descartes, Newton, Locke, Kant, Hegel, and Marx, among others, is extraordinary. It is well known that philosophy seeks to understand the *foundations* of judgments and beliefs. It is less well known that it is philosophy which most often is the *source* of the formulation of beliefs such that they become instantiated in social, political, and religious institutions.

Classical American philosophy is alone among the great philosophical clusters of the past in that it took as its mandate a conscious effort to press its philosophical claims into the tissue of experience for purpose of verification. Beginning with Emerson and on through the work of William James, Charles Peirce, Josiah Royce, John Dewey, and George Herbert Mead, the mission was to address concrete problems from a perspective which was both speculative and alert to the stubbornness of reality as actually experienced. The name given to this philosophical approach was pragmatism, although that is something of a historical misnomer. Actually, for Peirce, James, and Dewey, pragmatism was a method for resolving disputes over the deeply controverted questions concerning the meaning of truth. Further, they disagreed on the basic epistemological and metaphysical assumptions which gave rise to the pragmatic method. And although in his late period Josiah Royce took a pragmatic turn, his "pragmatism" was different from that of Peirce or James.

The classical American philosophers are more correctly understood as philosophers of experience, that is, as diagnosers of the flow of experience. They keep their eye on the irreducibly problematic character of our life in the world, and they attempt to float ideas which are assuaging and temporarily resolving. These philosophers are very chary of sheerly conceptual resolutions, demanding rather that their ideas "work," that is, are able to connect with the way in which experience is undergone and yet effect salutary change in the complex relationships between self and self, self and society, and self and nature. I call this the pragmatic upshot, by which I mean the detailing of the significance of imagination and speculation on the way in which we undergo our experiences.

If one believes, as I do, that the temporalistic, relational, pluralistic, melioristic metaphysics of James and Dewey is an accurate statement of how we should transact with the world, then the task is to apply these insights to the situations in which we find ourselves. The following essays pursue some of these living paths, for example: our experience of things, the education of our children, our experience of death, the quality of our cities, and the significance of being handicapped. Further work remains to be done with regard to our experience of the family, our bodies, sexuality, illness and disease, self-deception, hope, faith, joy, and despair.

I offer these essays as an effort to wander reflectively over our experience, with the perspective of classical American philosophy in the background and the intent to help make our situation "go better" in the foreground. To ask for more runs afoul of the finite and tentative character of being human.

8 *The Aesthetic Drama of the Ordinary*

I wish I could see what my eyes see.
VANILLA FUDGE

Traditionally, we think of ourselves as "in the world," as a button is in a box, a marble in a hole, a coin in a pocket, a spoon in a drawer; in, always in something or other. And yet, to the contrary, I seem to carry myself, to lead myself, to have myself hang around, furtive of nose, eye, and hand, all the while spending and wasting, eating and fouling, minding and drifting, engaging in activities more descriptive of a permeable membrane than of a box. To feel is to be felt. To be in the world is to "world" and to be "worlded." No doubt, the accepted language of expository prose severely limits us in this effort to describe our situation experientially. Were I to say, for example, my presence in the world or my being in the world, I would still fall prey to the container theory and once again be "in" as over against "out." Is this not why it is necessary to describe an unusual person, situation, or state of being as being "out of this world," or "spaced out" or simply "out of it." Why is it that ordinary language, or our language as used ordinarily, so often militates against the ways in which we actually have, that is, undergo, our experiencing? Why is it that we turn to the more specialized forms of discourse such as jokes, fiction, poetry, music, painting, sculpture, and dance, in order to say what we "really" mean? Does this situation entail the baleful judgment that the comparative bankruptcy of our ordinary language justly points to the comparable bankruptcy of our ordinary experience?

In gross and obvious empirical terms, it is difficult to say no to the necessity of this entailment. Surely it is true that we are surrounded by the banal, monumentalized in a miniature and trivial fashion by the American shopping center. And it is equally, yea, painfully true that the "things" of our everyday experience are increasingly de-aestheticized, not only by misuse and failure to maintain, but forebodingly in their very conception of design and choice of material, as witnessed by the recent national scandal in our urban bus fleet, when millions of dollars were spent on buses that were not built for city traffic, roads, or frequency of use. How striking, as well, is the contrast between those Americans at the turn of the century, who built the IRT subway in New York City, complete with a mosaic of inlaid tile, balustrades, and canopied entrances, over against their descendants, our peers, who seem not able to find a way to eradicate the stink and stain of human urine from those once proud and promising platforms and stairwells. So as not to contribute any further to the offensive and misleading assumption that our main aesthetic disasters are now found in the great urban centers of the Northeast, let us point to one closer to my home.

The city of Houston, in paying homage to a long outdated frontier myth of every "building" for itself, proceeds to construct an environment which buries an urban aesthetic in the wake of free enterprise. Houston gives rise to tall and imposing buildings whose eyes of window and light point to the surrounding plains, but whose feet are turned inward. These buildings do not open in a merry Maypole of neighborhood frolic and function. Houston buildings are truly sky-buildings, for they look up and out, leaving only the sneer of a curved lip to waft over the enervated neighborhoods below, most of them increasingly grimy and seedy. As an apparent favor to most of us, Houston provides a way for us to avoid these neighborhoods, allowing us to careen around the city, looking only at the bellies of the titans of glass and steel, astride the circular ribbon of concrete known appropriately as the beltway, marred only by the dead trees, broken car jacks, and the intrusive omnipresence of Texas-sized billboards. Perhaps it is just as well that we, too, rise above the madding crowd, for in that way we miss the awkwardness of wandering into one of those walled-off, sometimes covenanted and patrolled, fancy enclaves which make the city tolerable for the rich. And as we make our "beltway," we miss as well that strikingly sad experience of downtown Houston at 6 P.M. of a weekend evening, when the loneliness and shabbiness of the streets are cast into stark relief by the perimeter of empty skyscrapers and the hollow sounds of the feet of the occasional snow-belt emigre traveler, emerging from the Hyatt Regency in a futile search for action. What is startling and depressing about all of this is that the city of Houston is the nation's newest and allegedly most promising major city.

Actually, whether it is North, South, East, or West matters little, for in general the archons of aesthetic illiteracy have seen to it that on behalf of whatever other ideology they follow, the presence of aesthetic sensibility has been either ruled out or, where traditionally present, allowed to erode. Further, to the extent that we prehend ourselves as a thing among things or a functioning item in a box, then we get what we deserve. Supposing, however, we were to consider the major metaphorical versions of how we carry on our human experiencing and, in so doing, avoid using the imagery of the box. Instead, let us consider ourselves as being in a uterine situation, which binds us to nutrition in a distinctively organic way. James Marston Fitch, a premier architectural historian, writes about us as follows:

> Life is coexistent with the external natural environment in which the body is submerged. The body's dependence upon this external environment is absolute—in the fullest sense of the word—uterine.[1]

No box here. Rather we are floating, gestating organisms, transacting with our environment, eating all the while. The crucial ingredient in all uterine situations is the nutritional quality of the environment. If our immediate surroundings are foul, soiled, polluted harbors of disease and grime, ridden with alien organisms, then we falter and perish. The growth of the spirit is exactly analogous to the growth of the organism. It too must be fed and it must have the capacity to convert its experiences into a nutritious transaction. In short, the human organism has need of two livers. The one, traditional and omnipresent, transforms our blood among its 500 major functions and oversees the elimination from our body of ammonia, bacteria, and an assortment of debris, all of which would poison us. The second is more vague, having no physical analogue. But its function is similar and crucial. This second liver eats the sky and the earth, sorts out tones and colors, and provides a filter through which the experienced environment enters our consciousness. It is this spiritual liver which generates our feelings of queasiness, loneliness, surprise, and celebration. And it is this liver which monitors the tenuous relationship between expectations and anticipations on the one hand and realizations, disappointments, and failures on the other. We are not simply in the world so much as we are of and about the world. On behalf of this second type of livering, let us evoke the major metaphors of the fabric, of the uterus, through which we have our natal being. Our context for inquiry shall be the affairs of time and space, as well as the import of things, events, and relations. We shall avoid the heightened and intensified versions of these experiential filters and concentrate on the explosive and implosive drama of their ordinariness.

TIME

Time passing is a death knell. With the license of a paraphrase, I ask, For whom does the bell toll? It tolls for thee and me and for ours. We complain about the studied repetition, which striates our lives, and yet, in honesty, we indulge this repetition as a way of hiding from the inexorability of time passing, as a sign equivalent to the imminence of our self-eulogy. Time is a shroud, often opaque, infrequently diaphanous. Yet, from time to time, we are able to bring time into our own self-awareness and to bring time to its knees. On those rare occasions when time is ours rather than we being creatures of time, we feel a burst of singularity, of independence, even perhaps of the eternal import of our being present to ourselves. How has it happened that we have become slaves to time? Surely as children of Kant and Einstein, we should know better. For them and for modern physics, time is a mock-up, an earth phenomenon, no more relevant cosmically than the watches which watch time, supposedly passing. Still, Kant not withstanding, time is the name given to the process of our inevitable dissolution. On the morrow, our kidney is less quick, our liver less conscientious, our lung less pulsatile, and our brain less alert. Is it possible, without indulging ourselves in a Walter Mittyesque self-deception, to turn this erosive quality of time passing to our own advantage?

I suggest that we can beat time at its own game. Having created time, let us obviate it. Time, after all, rushes headlong into the future, oblivious to its damages, its obsoleting, and its imperviousness to the pain it often leaves in its wake. A contrary view is that in its passing, time heals. But it is not time which heals us, it is we who heal ourselves by our retroactive reconstruction of history. It is here that time is vulnerable, for it has no history, no past. Time is ever lurching into the future. We, however, can scavenge its remains and make them part of ourselves. For us, the past is existentially present if we have the will and the attentiveness to so arrange. I offer here that we recover the detritus of time passing and clot its flow with our freighted self-consciousness. We can become like the giant balloons in the Macy's Thanksgiving Day parade, thick with history and nostalgia, forcing time passing to snake around us, assuring that it be incapable of enervating our deepest feelings of continuity. What, for example, could time do to us if every time we met a person, or thought a thought, or dreamt a dream, we involved every person ever met, every thought ever thought, and every dream ever dreamt? What would happen if every event, every place, every thing experienced, resonated all the events, places, and things of our lives? What would happen if we generated a personal environment in which the nostalgic fed into the leads of the present, a self-created and sustained environment with implications fore and aft? In so doing, we would reduce time passing to scratching on the externals of our Promethean presence. Time would revolve around us rather than passng through us. Time would provide the playground for our activities rather than the graveyard of our hopes. We would time the world rather than having the world time us. And we would reverse the old adage, to wit, if you have the place, I have the time, for time is mine to keep and to give. And, in addition to telling our children now is your time, we would tell ourselves, no matter how old, now is our time.

SPACE

It is equally as difficult to extricate ourselves from the box of space as it is to escape from the penalties of time. Here too, we have failed to listen to Kant and Einstein, for space, just as time, has no existential reality other than our conception of it. Yet we allow the prepossessing character of space to dwarf us. Nowhere is this more apparent than in Texas, where the big sky of Montana is outdone by the scorching presence of a sun that seems never to set, frying our brains in the oven of its arrogance. In the spring of the year, the bluebonnets and Indian paintbrush state our position: fey, lovely, quiet, reserved, and delicate of manner. The Texas sun indulges this temporary human-scaled assertion while hovering in the background with vengeance on its mind. As the flowers fade, the horizon widens and the sun takes its place at the center of our lives, burning us with the downdraft of its rays. Listen to Larry King on the sun and sky in West Texas.

The land is stark and flat and treeless, altogether as bleak and spare as mood scenes in Russian literature, a great dry-docked ocean with small swells of hummocky tan sand dunes or humpbacked rocky knolls that change colors with the hour and the shadows: reddish brown, slate gray, bruise colored. But it is the sky—God-high and pale, like a blue chenille bedspread bleached by seasons in the sun—that dominates. There is simply *too much* sky. Men grow small in its presence and—perhaps feeling diminished—they sometimes are compelled to proclaim themselves in wild or berserk ways. Alone in those remote voids, one may suddenly half believe he is the last man on earth and go in frantic search of the tribe. Desert fever, the natives call it. . . . The summer sun is as merciless as a loan shark: a blinding, angry orange explosion baking the land's sparse grasses and quickly aging the skin.[2]

Texans pride themselves as being larger than life. But this is just a form of railing against the sun. The centuries-long exodus from the Northeast and the coastal cities was in part an escape from urban claustrophobia. In that regard, the escape was short-lived and self-deceptive, for it soon became apparent that the West presented a claustrophobia of another kind—paradoxically, that of open space. The box was larger, the horizon deeper, but the human self became even more trivialized than it was among the skyscrapers and the crowded alleyways and alcoves of the teeming urban centers. No, to the extent that we are overshadowed by an external overhang, be it artifact or natural, we cower in the presence of an *other* which is larger, more diffuse, still threatening and depersonalizing. In response, just as we must seize the time, so too must we seize the space, and turn it into a place, our place.

The placing of space is the creating of interior space, of personal space, of your space and my space, of our space. I am convinced, painful though it be, that we as human beings have no natural place. We are recombinant organisms in a cosmic DNA chain. Wrapped in the mystery of our origins, we moved from natural places to artifactual ones, from caves to ziggurats to the Eiffel tower. We moved from dunes to pyramids and then to the World Trade Center. The history of our architecture, big and small, functional and grandiloquent, lovely and grotesque, is the history of the extension of the human body into the abyss. We dig and we perch. We level and we raise. We make our places round and square and angular. We make them hard and soft and brittle. We take centuries to make them and we throw them up overnight. In modern America, the new Bedouins repeat the nomadic taste of old and carry their places with them as they plod the highway vascular system of the nation, hooking up here and there.

Some of our idiomatic questions and phrases tell us of our concern for being in place. Do you have a place? Set a place for me. This is my place. Why do we always go to your place? Would you care to place a bet? I have been to that place. Wow, this is *some* place. Win, place, show. The trouble with him is that he never went any place and the trouble with her is that she never got any place. How are you doing? How is it going? Fine, I am getting someplace. Not so well, I seem to be no place.

Recall that poignant scene in *Death of a Salesman* when Willy Loman asks Howard for a place in the showroom rather than on the road. In two lines, Howard tells Willy three times that he has no "spot" for him. I knew your father, Howard, and I knew you when you were an infant. Sorry, Willy! No spot, no place, for you. Pack it in. You are out of time and have no place.

Listen lady, clear out. But this is my place. No lady, this place is to be re-placed. The harrowing drama of eviction haunts all of us as we envision our future out of place and on the street.[3] Dorothy Day founded halfway houses, places somewhere between no place and my place, that is, at least, someplace. And, finally, they tell us that we are on the way to our resting place, a place from where there is no return.

These are only anecdotal bare bones, each of them selected from a myriad of other instances which point to our effort to overcome the onto-logical *angoisse* which accompanies our experience of *Unheimlichkeit*, a deep and pervasive sense of ultimate homelessness. We scratch out a place and we raise a wall. The windows look out but the doors open in. We hang a picture and stick a flower in a vase. We go from cradle and crib to a coffin, small boxes at the beginning and end of journeys through slightly larger boxes. Some of us find ourselves in boxes underneath and on top of other boxes in a form of apartmentalization. Some of our boxes are official boxes and we call them offices, slightly less prestigious than the advantage of a box seat. Everywhere in the nation, the majority of our houses are huddled together, sitting on stingy little pieces of ground, while we ogle the vast stretch of land held by absentees. One recalls here "Little Boxes," a folksong of the 1960s that excoriates the ticky-tacky boxes on the hillsides, as a preface to the yuppiedom of our own time. For the most part, our relation to external space is timid, even craven. From time to time, we send forth a camel, a schooner, a Conestoga wagon, or a space shuttle as probes into the outer reaches of our environ, on behalf of our collective body. Yet these geographical efforts to break out are more symbolic than real, for after our explorations we seem destined to repeat our limited variety of habitat.

The *locus classicus* for an explication of the mortal danger in a sheerly geographical response to space is found in a story by Franz Kafka, "The Burrow." In an effort to protect his food from an assumed intruder, the burrower walls off a series of mazes sure to confuse an opponent. This attempt is executed with such cunning and brilliance that his nonreflective anality is missed as a potential threat. The food is indeed walled off from the intruder—from the burrower as well. He dies of starvation, for he cannot find his own food.

The way out of the box is quite different, for it has to do not with the geography and physicality of space, but rather with our symbolic utilization of space for purposes of the human quest. We manage our ontological dwarfing and trivialization at the hands of infinite space, and the rush of time passing and obsoleting, by our construction, management, placing, and relating of *our* things. It is to our things, to creating our salvation in a world without guarantee of salvation, that we now turn.

THINGS

Thing, orthographically and pronouncedly, is one of the ugly words in contemporary American usage. Yet it is also, inferentially and historically, one of the most subtle and beautiful of our words. It is lamentable that we do not speak the way Chaucer spoke. From the year 1400 and a work of Lydgate, *Troy-Book*, the text reads: "That thei with Paris to Greece schulde wende, To Brynge this thynge to an ende." The Trojan war was a thing? Of course it was a thing, for thing means concern, assembly, and, above all, an affair. Thing is a woman's menses and a dispute in the town. Thing is a male sex organ and a form of prayer. (The continuity is not intended, although desirable.) Thing is what is to be done or its doing. I can't give you any thing but love, baby. That is the only thing, I have plenty of, baby. When you come, bring your things. I forgot to bring my things. My things are packed away. Everything will be all right. And by the way, I hope that things will be better.

What and who are these things to which we cling? An old pari-mutuel ticket, a stub for game seven of the World Series, a class ring, a mug, a dead Havana cigar, loved but unsmoked. My snuff box, my jewelry drawer, an album, a diary, a yearbook, all tumbled into the box of memories, but transcendent and assertive of me and mine. Do not throw out his things, they will be missed. Put her things in the attic, for someday she will want them as a form of reconnoitering her experienced past. Do you remember those things? I know that we had them. Where are they? They are in my consciousness. Can we find them? We didn't throw them out, did we? How could we?

The making, placing, and fondling of our things is equivalent to the making, placing, and fondling of our world. We are our things. They are personal intrusions into the vast, impersonal reach of space. They are functional clots in the flow of time. They are living memories of experiences had but still viable. They are memorials to experiences undergone and symbolically still present. The renewed handling of a doll, a ticket, a toy soldier, a childhood book, a tea cup, a bubble-gum wrapper, evokes the flood of experiences past but not forgotten.[4] How we strive to say hello, to say here I am, in a cosmos impervious, unfeeling, and dead to our plaintive cry of self-assertion. To make is to be made and to have is to be had. My thing is not anything or something. Your thing is not my thing but it could be our thing. The ancients had it right, bury the things with the person. We should do that again. Bury me with a copy of the *New York Times,* a Willie Mays baseball card, a bottle of Jameson, my William James book, a pipe, some matches, and a package of Seven-Seas tobacco.

The twentieth-century artist Alexander Calder once said that no one is truly human who has not made his or her own fork and knife. Homemade or not, do you have your own fork, your own knife, your own cup, your own bed, desk, chair? You must have your own things! They are you. You are they. As the poet Rilke tells us, "Being here amounts to so much."[5]

Our things are our things. They do not belong to the cosmos or to the gods. They can be had by others only in vicarious terms. Commendable though it may be for those of us who are collectors of other people's things, nonetheless, those who burn their papers or destroy their things just before they die are a testament to both the radical self-presence and transiency of human life. Those of us, myself included, who collect other people's things, are Texas turkey vultures, seizing upon the sacred moments hammered out by transients and eating them in an effort to taste the elixir of memory for our own vapid personal life. Ironically, for the most part their experience of their things were similar efforts, sadly redeemed more by us than by them. Now to the crux of the matter before us.

It is not, I contend, humanly significant to have the primary meaning of

one's life as posthumous. We and our things, I and my things, constitute
our world. The nectar of living, losing, loving, maintaining, and caring for
our things is for us, and for us alone. It is of time but not in time. It is
of space but not in space. We and our things make, constitute, arrange, and
determine space and time. The elixir garnered by the posthumous is for the
survivors. It cannot be of any biological significance to us, although many
of us have bartered our present for the ever absent lilt of being remem-
bered. St. Francis of Assisi and John Dewey both taught us the same *thing:*
time is sacred, live by the sacrament of the moment and listen to the
animals. We may have a future. It is barely conceivable, although I doubt
its existence. We do have, however, a present. It is the present, canopied by
our hopefully storied past, that spells the only meaning of our lives. Still,
the present would be empty without our things.

You, you out there, you have your things. Take note. Say hello, say
hello, things. They are your things. Nay, they are you. No things, no you,
or in correct grammar, you become no*thing*. So be it. Space and time are
simply vehicles for things, our things, your things, my things. These things
do not sit, however, in rows upon rows, like ducks in a shooting gallery.
These things make love, hate, and tire. Like us, they are involved. We consider now this involvement of persons, things, things and persons, all
struggling to time space and space time, namely, the emergence of events as
relations.

THINGS AS EVENTS AS AESTHETIC RELATIONS

We have been in a struggle to achieve nonderivative presence of ourselves
and our things over against the dominating worlds of space and time. Fortunately, for us, space and time do not necessarily speak to each other. Our
canniness can play them off, one against the other. The triumph is local,
never ultimate, although it does give us staying power in our attempt to say
I, me, you, we, us, and other asserted pronominal outrages against the
abyss.

A happy phenomenon for human life is that things not only are; they
also happen. I like to call these happenings events. The literal meaning of
event is intended: a coming out, a party, a debutante dance, a *bar mitzvah*,
a hooray for the time, given the circumstance. In my metaphysics, at least,
things are bundles of relations, snipped at the edges to be sure. Usually, we
give our things a name and this name takes the place of our experience of

NOT A COMPLETE ONTOLOGY THOUGH —
WHERE'S "WOUNDING" in
THIS MODEL...

the thing. It does not take long to teach a child a list of nouns, each bent on obviating and blocking the rich way in which the child first comes upon and undergoes things. It is difficult to overcome this prejudice of language, especially since row upon row of nouns, standing for things, makes perfectly good sense, if you believe that space is a container and time is the measure of external motion. If, however, you believe as I do, that space and time are human instincts, subject to the drama of our inner lives, then things lose their inert form. Emerson says this best when he claims that every fact and event in our private history shall astonish us by "soaring from our body into the empyrean."[6]

The clue here is the presence of a person. Quite aside from the geographical and physical relationships characteristic of things and creatures, we further endow a whole other set of relations, the aesthetic. I refer to the rhythm of how we experience *what we* experience. The most distinctive human activity is the potentially affective dimension of our experiencing ourself, experiencing the world. I say potentially, for some of us all of the time and most of us most of the time are dead to the possible rhythms of our experiences. We are ghouls. We look alive but we are dead, dead to our things and dead even to ourselves. As John Cage warned us, we experience the names of sounds and not the sounds themselves. It is not the things as names, nouns, which are rich. It is how the things do and how they are done to. It is how they marry and divorce, sidle and reject. The aesthetic drama of the ordinary plays itself out as a result of allowing all things to become events, namely, by allowing all things the full run of their implications. This run may fulfill our anticipations and our expectations. This run may disappoint us. This run may surprise us, or blow us out. Implicitness is everywhere and everywhen. Were we to experience an apparently single thing in its full implicitness as an event reaching out to all its potential relations, then, in fact, we would experience everything, for the leads and the hints would carry us into the nook and cranny of the implicitness of every experience.[7]

We are caught between a Scylla and Charybdis with regard to the drama of the ordinary. The scions of the bland and the anaesthetic convince us that nothing is happening, whereas the arbiters and self-announcers of high culture tell us that only a few can make it happen, so we are reduced to watching. My version is different. The world is already astir with happenings, had we the wit to let them enter our lives in their own way, so that we may press them backward and forward, gathering relations, novelties, all the while. Our affective presence converts the ordinary to the extraordinary. The world is made sacred by our *hand*ling of our things. We are the makers of our world. It is we who praise, lament, and celebrate. Out of the doom of obviousness and repetition shall come the light, a light lit by the fire of our eyes.

9 *Experience Grows by Its Edges* [1]

A PHENOMENOLOGY OF RELATIONS IN AN
AMERICAN PHILOSOPHICAL VEIN

All my knowledge of the world, even my scientific knowledge is gained from my own particular point of view, or from some experience of the world without which the symbols of science would be meaningless.

MAURICE MERLEAU-PONTY, *Phenomenology of Perception*

It is to take a precarious and even treacherous path to begin an essay on philosophy with an acknowledgment of one's "own particular view." Foundationalism, in either its Cartesian or contemporary analytic formulation, forbids such an allegedly subjective point of departure. Yet it is precisely here that phenomenology and classical American philosophy share both assumptions and endeavor. And both traditions can resonate to the description of phenomenology by Merleau-Ponty:

> The opinion of the responsible philosopher must be that *phenomenology can be practiced and identified as a manner or style of thinking, that it existed as a movement before arriving at complete awareness of itself as a philosophy.*[2]

Both American pragmatism and phenomenology have been called methods rather than philosophies. So be it. Practitioners of both know the differences which exist between pragmatism and phenomenology. Despite these acknowledged differences, some have made efforts to close the gap or at least to stress similarities.[3] My own predilection on this issue, if I can be forgiven a violation of the ostensible objectivity now required in philosophical discussion, comes to this. Phenomenology has taught me to take things, attitudes, ambience, and relations straight up, with no excuses. I pay little attention to the famous Husserlian bracket, which seeks for the pure essence of things, for I regard such efforts in his work and those of his followers as a form of epistemological self-deception, a result of the rigid science it deplores in a fruitless search for true objectivity. To the contrary, nothing, nothing, is ever totally bracketed, for leaks are everywhere.[4]

Yet the effort of phenomenology is salutary. Pay attention, says the phenomenologist. I listen to that warning. Intentionally, pay attention, says the phenomenologist. I listen more intently. This attending to the flow of experience is multisensorial, for it involves not only hearing but feeling, touching, seeking, smelling, and tasting as well. What, then, is it for a human being to be in the world?

I

Taken straight out, and day by night, to be in the world is not to be inert, a thing among things, a bump on a log. However surprising for the tradition of Aristotelian natural place and Newtonian mechanics, quantum physics merely confirms the multiple processing which is endemic to the activity of the human organism. Merleau-Ponty writes:

> Our own body is in the world as the heart is in the organism: it keeps the visible spectacle constantly alive, it breathes life into it and sustains it inwardly, and with it forms a system.[5]

We do not fit into the world as a Lego or a Lincoln Log. In fact, I believe that we have no *special* place in the organic constituency of nature. Our consciousness, so different, so extraordinary, so bizarre, especially in its dream state, is a marvelous and pockmarked perturbation of the eonic history of DNA. Following Dewey, we are in, of, and about nature. We are nature's creature, its consciousness, its conscience, however aberrant and quixotic; its organizer, namer, definer, and defiler; a transient in search of an implacable, probably unrealizable, final consummation. The human organism is surrounded, permeated, and contexted by both the natural and social environment. In speaking of William James's doctrine of the self as a relational manifold, John E. Smith writes, "Radical empiricism is a radically new account of how the self penetrates and is penetrated by the world."[6]

The way in which the human self abides in the world is an extraordinarily complex affair. The self projects itself into the world. The self constructs a personal world, a habitation. The self, when threatened, retreats, even attempts to eject from the world, a form of dropping out. The rhythm of these transactions is often lost in the macroscopic setting of getting through the day. The algorithmic subtleties of our movements, shifts in attitude, and construction, deconstruction, setting, shifting, and bypassing of barriers are often buried in the frequently graceless syntax of duties, obligations, and habituations. So typical are our routines that the virtually infinite number of plans, plots, and variations in the rhythm of our bodily movements are lost to our attention. Recent investigations in biochemistry, especially in the human liver and in cell surface and molecular biology, reveal an utterly extraordinary network. The electron microscope has revealed a dazzling array of complexity in an endless chain of relationships. The human skin is a battleground of bacteria colonies, symbiotic, voracious, and with long memories, as found in the unerring recurrence of dermatitis, repeatedly appearing on an isolated finger or toe, over and again.[7]

The phenomenological approach to the "lived body" has been an auspicious point of departure for philosophical speculation. The arrival of phenomenological and existentialist literature after the Second World War was a bracing antidote to the positivism and logical empiricism of the émigrés from the Vienna circle. As early as 1958, Rollo May and others introduced us to the empiricism of phenomenological psychiatry and existential analysis.[8] Following the path set by Ludwig Binswanger, Kurt Goldstein, and indirectly by Aron Gurwitsch, Richard Zaner correctly sees the medical model as the most propitious for understanding the activity of the human body, since it exaggerates medical case histories, which cast light on the hidden drama of simply being in the world as a body, as an organism, and as a conscious person.

For most of us, most of the time, being in the world has an obviousness to it. We move about, little aware of our gait, presence, and interruptive activities. From time to time an event, a startle, a happening, will jog us to immediate consciousness. A snake in the yard, a tarantula in the bathtub, or the rolling red neon lights of a police cruiser at our front door is required if we are to shake off our studied state of mesmerism, of ontological lethargy.

From 1916 until 1927, a pandemic swept the European continent. Technically called *Encephalitis lethargica,* it is known to us as sleeping sickness. Its victims numbered in the millions and very few avoided death. Those who did slumbered on, kinaesthetically anonymous, until the advent of the drug L-dopa, prescribed in the late 1960s. The subsequent "awakenings" have been described in a brilliant book by the neurologist Oliver Sacks.[9] In contrast to the way most of us are in the world, moving about in our unreflective, programmed way, I offer you, courtesy of Sacks, the movements of Lillian T., who, when she awoke, found her bodily movements, in an understatement, to be a chore. Burdened by violent "head movements" as a result of the pharmacological therapy, she was never in control of her body by instinct, only by detailed plotting. Sacks details her attempt to simply move from one place to another.

> One such patient had managed to maintain an independent life outside institutions for years, in face of almost incredible difficulties—difficulties which would instantly have broken a less determined or resourceful person. This patient—Lillian T.—had long since found that she could scarcely start, or stop, or change her direction of motion; that once she had been set in motion, she had no control. It was therefore necessary for her to plan all her motions in advance, with great precision. Thus, moving from her armchair to her divan-bed (a few feet to one side) could never be done *directly*—Miss T. would immediately be 'frozen' in transit, and perhaps stay frozen for half an hour or more. She therefore had to embark on one of two courses of action: in either case, she would rise to her feet, arrange her angle of direction exactly, and shout "Now!", whereupon she would break into an incontinent run, which could be neither stopped nor changed in direction. If the double doors between her living-room and the kitchen were open, she would rush through them, across the kitchen, round the back of the stove, across the other side of the kitchen, through the double doors—in a great figure-of-eight—until she hit her destination, her bed. If, however, the double doors were closed and secured, she would calculate her angle like a billiard-player, and then launch herself with great force against the doors, rebounding at the right angle to hit her bed. Miss T.'s apartment (and, to some extent, her mind) resembled the control room for the Apollo launchings, at Houston, Texas: all paths and trajectories pre-computed and compared, contingency plans and "fail-safes" prepared in advance. A good deal of Miss T.'s life, in short, was dependent on conscious taking-care and elaborate calculation—but this was the only way she could maintain her existence.[10]

Sacks also details the baleful motile effects of Parkinson's disease. The person afflicted with festination is subject to "forced hurrying of walking, talking, speech or thought" and takes steps which "tend to become smaller and smaller, until finally the patient is 'frozen'—stepping internally, but with no space to step in."[11]

A case history of a different kind is also illuminating. Reported by A. R. Luria, the distinguished Russian psychologist, it details the recovery efforts of a young soldier who was wounded with a bullet to the brain. He suffered "impairment of vision, loss of memory and the ability to speak, read and write."[12] This man, Zasetsky, made a heroic effort to retrieve his faculties. Over a twenty-five-year period, he wrote of his journey to possible recovery. The result is a 3,000-word document, or no more than 120 words per year, for twenty-five years. By contrast, the present chapter is 6,000 words and was written in four weeks, without either the human or clinical significance of that by Mr. Zasetsky. The space-time-place-object relationships that you and I take for granted were for our brain-wounded colleague a nightmare. Zasetsky reports on some disasters in doing the obvious:

> When the doctor learned what my first name was, he'd always address me that way and try to shake hands when he came over. But I couldn't manage to clasp his hand. He'd try it a second time, but as luck would have it, I'd forget I had a right hand since I couldn't see it. Suddenly I'd remember and try to shake hands again but would only manage to touch his fingers. He'd let go of my hand and try once more. But I still wasn't able to do it, so he'd take my hand and show me how.
>
> Ever since I was wounded I've had trouble sometimes sitting down in a chair or on a couch. I first look to see where the chair is, but when I try to sit down I suddenly make a grab for the chair since I'm afraid I'll land on the floor. Sometimes that happens because the chair turns out to be further to one side than I thought.

Luria comments:

> These "spatial peculiarities" were particularly distressing when he was sitting at a table. He'd try to write and be unable to control a pencil, not knowing how to hold it. He encountered similar problems in the hospital workshops where he went for occupational therapy, hoping he'd be given some work to do and thus convince himself he could be useful, fit for some kind of job. There, too, he was up against precisely the same difficulties.

Zasetsky continues:

> The instructor gave me a needle, spool of thread, some material with a pattern on it, and asked me to try to stitch the pattern. Then he went off to attend to other patients—people who'd had their arms or legs amputated after being wounded, or half their bodies paralyzed. Meanwhile, I just sat there with the

needle, thread, and material in my hands wondering why I'd been given these; I sat for a long time and did nothing. Suddenly the instructor came over and asked: "Why are you just sitting there? Go ahead and thread the needle!" I took the thread in one hand, the needle in the other, but couldn't understand what to do with them. How was I to thread the needle? I twisted it back and forth but hadn't the slightest idea what to do with any of these things.

When I first looked at those objects, but hadn't yet picked them up, they seemed perfectly familiar—there was no reason to think about them. But as soon as I had them in my hands, I was at a loss to figure out what they were for. I'd lapse into a kind of stupor and wouldn't be able to associate these two objects in my mind—it was as though I'd forgotten why they existed. I twisted the needle and thread in my hands but couldn't understand how to connect the two—how to fit the thread in the needle.

And then another annoying thing happened. By then I'd already learned what a needle, thread, thimble, and material were for and had some vague notion of how to use them. But I couldn't for the life of me think of the names for these or other objects people had pointed out to me. I'd sit there stitching the material with the needle, completely unable to remember what the very things I was using were called.

The first time I entered the shop and saw people working there, I noticed various things—a workbench, a slab of wood, a plane—and I thought I recognized these objects and knew what they were called. But when I was actually given a plane and a slab of wood, I fiddled with them for quite a while before some of the other patients showed me how to use these and other tools. I started to sand some wood but never learned to do it right, never did get it sanded. Each time I'd try, the surface would come out lopsided and crooked or had pits and bumps in it. And what's more, I got tired very quickly. While I was sanding the wood or looking at some of the other tools in the carpentry shop (a block of wood or a workbench) it was the same old story—I couldn't remember what any of these was used for.

When I went to a workshop to learn shoemaking, the instructor explained everything to me in great detail, since he was convinced I was very muddled and thick-headed and didn't know the first thing about making shoes. He showed me how to hold a hammer, drive nails in and pull them out, but all I learned to do was drive wooden nails into a board and pull them out again. And even then that was hard, because I couldn't see where the nails were supposed to go but kept missing the spot and banging my fingers until they bled. And I was very, very slow at it. So the only thing they let me do was bang nails into a board.[13]

Cases such as Lillian T. and Mr. Zasetsky abound in the literature and, tragically, in the everyday—our neighbors, friends, and family. They are a witness to the indolent response we have to our everyday movements, perfunctory and blind to the gift that a healthy DNA double helix awards to us, idiosyncratically. These extreme versions of what it takes to be in the world, versions which are extremely intensified by anyone who has had experience with the handicapped, are intensive role models for our untapped capacities and sensibilities. The richness of the everyday, had we the will to savor our possibilities, would far exceed our fantasies. Indeed, our penchant for the fantastic is but an indictment of how casual and unreflective has become our daily posture in a world which screeches at us, though we hear not.

Classical American philosophy, represented by James and Dewey, offers us some insight to the way in which we are in the world. James stresses human energy, human proclivity, and human daring. His self is Promethean: making, constructing, reconstructing, and bold in its effort to transcend the accepted conceptual frames of human experience, which often tie us down, and are often chary of suspension of disbelief. James invokes the "will to believe" as an antidote to our premature resignation to limits in the variety, reach, or implication of our experiences. Acceptance of the routine, the humdrum, and the obvious results in a flaccid, inert, and dull personal presence. James writes:

> Some men and women, indeed, there are who can live on smiles and the word "yes" forever. But for others (indeed for most), this is too tepid and relaxed a moral climate. Passive happiness is slack and insipid, and soon grows mawkish and intolerable. Some austerity and wintry negativity, some roughness, danger, stringency, and effort, some "no! no!" must be mixed in, to produce the sense of an existence with character and texture and power.[14]

As described by James, especially in his *Principles of Psychology,* the human self is Promethean and picaresque: a venturesome, risk-oriented, and experimental prober into the widest and furthest reaches of the flow of experience. John Dewey accepts this profile as an ideal. Dewey, for example, believes, "If it is better to travel than arrive, it is because traveling is a constant arriving, while arrival that precludes further traveling is most easily attained by going to sleep or dying."[15] Yet Dewey, a proletarian, in contrast to James, a New England Brahmin, realizes that the traveling is not done by an isolated self. To the contrary, Dewey's sense of a person being in the world is conflicted by the vagaries of natural forces and above all, by the bottom line admission that we are social selves, contexted, conditioned, herded, institutionalized, and tradition-laden. Despite the attraction of James's Promethean self, the cautions of Dewey with regard to the trappings that work on us as we confront the human condition must be taken with seriousness. One may lament the absence of an aboriginal approach to being in the world; but lamentation does not obviate the hard, irrepressible facticity of natural and social conditioning, a context provided throughout the work of John Dewey and George Herbert Mead.

One can posit still a third version of our being in the world, although the American intellectual scene pays little attention to it: that of the cosmological. In truth, James is right. We must seek to be prepossessive and creative in our dealings with the world in which we find ourselves. Yet Dewey is also correct in his stressing of the natural and social ambience which restricts our doings, limits our travelings, and short-circuits our desires. Still, not by the planet earth alone do we live. In our time, increasingly, the stellar has become accessible to us and the vaunted mystery of the moon, now an extended neighborhood. Contemporary astral physics has enhanced our reach a millionfold. Although our new and approximate knowledge of the age and extent of the universe has been dwarfing in the ultimate sense, nonetheless, paradoxically, the human odyssey takes on the hue of a remarkably novel and originally self-conscious presence in an otherwise vast, unfeeling, unknowing, and uncaring panoply of sheerly natural events. Extraterrestrial consciousness is a possibility, but we have no evidence. Until such appears, the universe is not aware of itself except for the activity of human life. Merleau-Ponty tells us that "because we are in the world, we are *condemned to meaning,* and we cannot do or say anything without its acquiring a name in history."[16]

The task of building a liberating human future, as I foresee it, assumes the Promethean self of James and the social sophistication of Dewey, Mead, the Marxists, and cultural anthropology, all rendered within a burgeoning social cosmology. That task, of course, remains to be done. For now, let us start at the beginning and discuss the lineaments of the potentially Promethean self and the dangers therein. The key to such a consideration is the understanding of relations, as first proposed by William James in his doctrine of radical empiricism.[17]

II

For James, and subsequently for Dewey, the human self is urged to build a personal world, although not as *ab ovo.* Rather this personal world is to be built in response to the "push and press of the cosmos," as James would have it, or, as Dewey suggested, a response to the irreducible and in-eluctable problematic which resides at the very point of transaction of the human organism with nature. Rather than there being one world, which we acknowledge from an alleged separately distant place, we have a series of worlds as constructs, as mock-ups. In the words of the neo-pragmatist Nelson Goodman, there are "ways of worldmaking" which he calls "ver-sions and visions."[18] Anticipating modern quantum physics, James sees the world as a relational webbing with objects as results of our conceptual intrusion, rather than as fixed givens in an already structured setting. Referring to essences as *"teleological weapons of the mind"*[19] and affirm-ing that *"there is no property* ABSOLUTELY *essential to any one thing,"*[20] James inverts the classical assumption that the world comes as given and need but be defined, denoted, and arranged. To the contrary, what we take to be objects in common parlance are bundles of relations, gathered first conceptually and then, by habit, perceptually. Speaking of the names of things—in this case, a painting—Michel Foucault criticizes the supposed one-to-one correspondence between our language and the object.

> And the proper name, in this context, is merely an artifice: it gives us a finger to point with, in other words, to pass surreptitiously from the space where one speaks to the space where one looks; in other words, to fold one over the other as if they were equivalents.[21]

In modern art, the names of the paintings are often but placeholders, vestibules for entry into a world of relations that prevent any denomina-tion or definition. If we could break the lock had on us by our inherited syntactical conceptual scheme, we could come to see, hear, feel, smell, and taste bundles of relations rather than objects, hardly more alive than the nouns used to name them. I believe that James is right. Aboriginally, the world is not made up of objects but rather is a continuum of concatenated relations. Scandalous though it may be to those for whom logic tells the only truth, if we were to focus on a single object and detail its relations, we would have access to a perceptual entailment which would involve us in everything that exists. Unfortunately, we do not even attempt this, for as James notes, "We actually ignore most of the things before us."[22] Far less do we follow the relational leads which spring from these linguistically ordained things. When alert, we do better. James describes our active sense life in the following way:

Out of what is in itself an undistinguishable, swarming *continuum*, devoid of distinction or emphasis, our senses make for us, by attending to this motion and ignoring that, a world full of contrasts, of sharp accents, of abrupt changes, of picturesque light and shade.[23]

The way in which an object is denoted on the macroscopic scale is due to one or more functional characteristics, for example, shape, size, texture, color, odor, place in space, or mobility. Once having been designated, except for occasional aesthetic considerations, the object falls into a class of conceptually identical companions: chair, glass, book. Thus we repress or ignore the relational run in every object, as in *this* book, with *that* kind of paper, smell, size, and as found on *this* table in *that* room in *this* house on *that* street in *this* neighborhood, county, state, region, country, hemisphere, planet, solar system, galaxy, and pluriverse. There is no doubt that we cut off the relations. The important question has to do with both *what* relations are cut and *how* we cut them. Who was the first human being to eat a lobster? Surely a more foreboding and less appetizing creature has not appeared to the culinary search. Yet, as with sheep brains, pigs' feet, and squid, the human being, here and there, follows a different relational trail. In those cases, relational plurality leads to delight and leaves the definition of pleasing as simply not sufficient for the longer reach.

If we were to follow each thing and event to its full perceptual implication, we would explode from experiential overload. James gives us a taste of this:

Only in some pitiful dreamer, some philosopher, poet, or romancer, or when the common practical man becomes a lover, does the hard externality give way, and a gleam of insight into the ejective world, as Clifford called it, the vast world of inner life beyond us, so different from that of outer seeming, illuminate our mind. Then the whole scheme of our customary values gets confounded, then our self is riven and its narrow interests fly to pieces, then a new centre and a new perspective must be found.[24]

Cutting off relations is therefore necessary for personal survival. But how do we cut? Do we snip and leave a small wound which heals in time? Do we hack and leave a gaping wound which festers and, when closed, leaves an unsightly scar? Do we fold over the rejected relation, biding time until we can recover and savor it? Do we let the relational lead or inference dangle, awaiting a propitious moment to reconnoiter and relive its possibility? Do we send the relation on a journey, hoping for a return? Or do we give it a one-way ticket? Finally, do we bury the relation, hoping for its continued interment, although worried about periodic reappearance through the cracks in our vulnerable psyche?

The world we build is exactly akin to the way we cut relations, indulge relations, and celebrate relations. More, our world takes off as novel and as distinctively ours precisely in response to how we make new relations of the relations already at work in the environ in which we find ourselves. It is clear, although not for the present setting, that the way we best understand this activity of making relations is to pursue the life of the young child. Genetic epistemology has much to teach us, for children naturally make their own relations until we teach them that the world has already been named and properly codified. Against their aboriginal bent, they are told to march in step, name by name, definition by definition, until they too see the world as an extension of local grammar and hidebound conceptual designations. The social and moral result of this aberrant pedagogy is dele-terious, as stressed, for example, by Merleau-Ponty in his discussion of the presence of "psychological rigidity" as a lamentable but typical charac-teristic of young children.[25] Yet for both young children and adults who are or who wish to become alive to possibilities heretofore undreamt, the making of relations is the way to build a distinctively personal world. I turn now to some of the obstacles to a salutary making of relations.

III

Being in the world is not a cakewalk. Our surroundings, personal, natural, and social are fraught with potential deception, actual invasion, and an omnipresent indifference. To make a world as distinctively ours by the making of relations is too often a rarity. The other-directedness made famous by David Riesman and his colleagues in *The Lonely Crowd*[26] can be raised to the status of an ontological category. In ideal terms, a person comes to consciousness and begins to work out one's place, one's version, and one's taste for this or that. Yet we now know that the burgeoning self is fraught with personal freight: genetic, familial, linguistic, bodily, clima-tic, ethnic, gender, racial, and even the subtleties of gait, weight, and smile. As I see it, the fundamental challenge is to convert the personal weaknesses into strengths and to drive our strengths into the teeth of a personally neutral but relatively pregnant world. The ancient philosophers, especially the Stoics and the Epicureans, offered sage advice on how to be in the world without getting maced. Taken overall, their warnings focused on the dangers of excess, indolence, and self-aggrandizement.[27] This was and is wise counsel. The intervening 2,000 years, however, have bequeathed a far more sophisticated environment as a setting for the constructing of a personal world. The dangers, the traps, and the obstacles are more subtle, more extensive, and more seductive than they were in antiquity.

The scriptural rhetorical question, Lord, what must I do to be saved? can be reinvoked by our children as follows: What shall I do to make a world which is personally mine, although it inheres, coheres, borrows, and lends to others who are making a world personally their own? Couched more indirectly, this is the question that our children and our students ask us. The initial response is obvious. Make relations! Build, relate, and then reflect. Reflect, relate, and then build. Seek novelty, leave no stone unturned. Fasten on colors, shapes, textures, sounds, odors, sights. Above all, never close down until the fat person sings. The only acceptable denouement is death. Until then all signs are go, that is, make relations until the maker is unmade. Still, in the making of relations, dangers lurk. We detail them as follows:

1) Relation starvation

Stinginess is omnipresent in the human condition, as anyone who has lived on tips will attest. The novel experience carries for some of us a warning signal. We are often suspicious of the new, an unfamiliar face, a turn in the road, a break from the routine. We tend to huddle with the familiar. Even the more flamboyant of us have our schedule, our pigeonhole for person and event. Novelty is unsettling. We prefer the familiar, the recognizable, the repetitive, for that awards personal control. In time, everything is forced to resemble something else, something prior, something already experienced. Have not I seen you before? Have not I heard you before? Repetition becomes so comforting that genuine novelty is reduced to prior experience. The width of our vision shrinks. We become more defensive about what we already know, less open to what we do not know.

Relation starvation is the incarnation of the a priori. All that happens has happened, for us, before. At least we think so. And that is because we focus only on famliarity, sameness. The novel is repressed, transformed into the familiar. We tend to chatter, over and over, about our experiences, warding off the novelty brought to us by others. We become monologic rather than open to dialogue and to those potentially liberating yet frightening and unfamiliar experiences out of our ken. We become shrill, repetitive, and overindulgent of the significance of our own past. Others' histories hold no interest for us, for they become indices of our deprivation rather than communal undergoings to share, however vicariously. The more committed we become to the significance of our own experiences, the less capacity we have to participate in the experiences of others. In time, the ultimate bane of human health emerges, jealousy. We soon become trapped in our own world, one which is shrinking, increasingly lonely and overesteemed. Relation-starved, we are less and less able to make relations, to break out, to build a world in which our personal style takes on meaning not by insularity but by contrast.

2) Relation amputation

In making relations, we run the risk of being strung out. Granted that shutting out relational possibilities leads to relation starvation and an encapsulated self, yet in our counter effort to reach out, we often fail to read the map of possibilities. Knowing when to desist, to withdraw, and to close down is very difficult. How much testing is enough testing? How much experimentation is enough experimentation? The explosive world of pharmacological nostrums is constantly blindsided by late appearing side effects. Pesticides, thalidomide, birth control pills, L-dopa, and countless other substances bequeath later "hits," events which are severely damaging to human life and which on retrospect call for earlier amputation.

On the one hand, risk is often avoided at the expense of possibility and breakthrough. The human odyssey is replete with stories of those courageous persons who defied the present data in favor of that which might emerge if one were to take the next step. One must never be cavalier. Nonetheless, surprise often awaits us as we forge a relationship heretofore banned or simply unthought. The burden is that we must learn to read the signs of implicitness. An early amputation of a lead will throw us back into the obvious. Persistence in following a relational possibility beyond its capacity to ameliorate and sustain the worth of the risk of the endeavor is foolhardy. We should not hang back and endorse the accepted slavishly. Premature amputation denies the long-standing historical message that taking a chance is usually fortuitous. Cut when necessary, but not out of fright or habit.

3) Relation saturation

There are those of us who get the message that the making of relations is liberating. For some, this awareness turns into a frenetic activity of multiple involvement, as though the quantity of experience was sure to ensure a significant life. We face here an overindulgence in the having of experiences, as though one need not bring to bear a reflective self in these transactions. Most often, those persons whose lives have been constricted by mores, repressions, and systemic habituation, upon the opportunity to break it open, respond with alacrity. New experiences are collected like hash marks. We become impervious to their significance, their dangers, their relationship to our past, our person, and our future. Unreflective in anticipation, undergoing and retrospection, these experiences follow one after the other into an unknowing bin, marked only—accomplishment. The relations, the potential implications, tumble about shy of significance and of no import to either our person or our prospects.

Relation saturation describes the fate of the person who eats without tasting. It is a relation-saturated person whose sexual activity is more characterized by a desire to do it again than to experience the doing of it in the first place. The depth of a single relation, the mastery of a technique or an instrument, as in the cello of Pablo Casals, is lost to the saturator. Endless variation replaces the nectar of a rich, single experience. The relation-saturator writes his or her autobiography at a tender age, failing to realize that it is subsequent personal history which casts genuine light on the relative importance of events once undergone without reflection. Sheer quantity of experience is misleading in its import. Following John Dewey, "Everything depends on the *quality* of the experience which is had."[28]

4) Relation seduction

William James was fond of urging us to live on the fringe, beyond the ken of normal, everyday experience. To that end, he experienced with hallucinogens and spent considerable time in pursuing investigation of the claims made on behalf of extrasensory perception. James was also fascinated by persons who claimed to attain extraordinary insight by virtue of religious, aesthetic, or even dietary experiences. He found saints, yogis, and clairvoyants of equal fascination. For James, the present reach of the normal consciousness was puerile when compared with what he regarded as possibilities as yet unseen except by a few unusually bold and gifted persons.

Actually, James points to a double fringe. The first we have discussed, for it refers to the implicitness hidden in every object, event, and situation. That fringe holds the ongoing relational leads which we too often prematurely cut in the name of obviousness and definition. The second fringe is more fascinating and more dangerous. Some persons are driven by the temptation to transcend the boundaries of common experience and belief. Through intense, single-minded commitment, they fasten on a vision of reality not given to the rest of us. Rooted in political or religious belief, this commitment can be liberating for others, but it can also be a snare of major self-deception. For every Abraham, Jesus, Mohammed, Marx, or Nietzsche, there are hundreds of self-benighted souls who become so enamored of their personal goal that they find themselves cut off from the stark claim of reality.

Still more dangerous is the fringe which is accessible by means of pharmacology. Mind-altering drugs are now a fact of public and familial life.[29] Yet the leap over the relational chain to experiences which are literally *de novo* and beyond normal capacity tends to freeze in a world of experience that has no connection with our body, our things, and our space-time relations normally undergone. I do not deny that the trip to the fringe is exhilarating. The question is whether one can ever return without experiencing severe depression in response to the comparative tawdriness of the everyday. The trouble with relation seduction, be it local fanaticism on behalf of a visionary goal or pharmacologically induced, is that it is addictive and therefore more manacling than liberating.

5) Relation repression

Often we have experiences which are potentially threatening to our well-being, at least as we conceive it to be so. Instead of allowing these experiences to play out their hand, we repress them. The relational implications of the experience cannot be severed once and for all. Rather they are shoved down into the labyrinth of our unconscious but nonetheless active self. We act as if we were in a World War I pillbox complete with flame-throwers, burning out the ground around us. Bunkered down, we seem to feel on top of things. And that is precisely the problem. The repressed experiences take on a life of their own, sifting their way up and into the nooks and crannies of our conscious life, designated here as our stomach, nervous system, dreams, tics, and temperament.

In the terminology of classical psychoanalysis, relation repression is often discussed under the rubric of trauma. Franz Kafka traces his comparative creative and interpersonal impotence to such an event. In a letter to his father, typically and fittingly not sent, Kafka tells of an event which set the stage for his life-long sense of alienation. As a very young child, Franz annoyed his father by constantly demanding attention while a guest was in the apartment. After repeated warnings, his father seized him and placed him outside on the *pavlatche,* the outside ledge, closing the doors on Franz in his pajamas. Locked out, cut off, and bewildered, Kafka concluded, "I was a mere nothing for him." This event, repressed and never worked out, did him "inner harm."[30] Even the final revealing of the event was posthumous and to an audience who knew neither Kafka nor his father. Such relation repression, repeated over and over in our own lives, is baleful and insidious.

I V

Being in the world is not a position of stasis. It is active, energizing, and potentially creative. Of course, it can also be enervating, treacherous, and self-deceiving. For those of us who wish to become persons, the world does not come ready-made. The doctrine of natural place was a provincial fall-out from the enclosed geography and cosmology of the Greek world of Aristotle, a point made in detail by Heidegger.[31] Our world is infinitely more expansive, more complex, more furtive, more demanding, and, if we have the will, more rewarding. The lattice-work of nature is intriguing. Still more intriguing is the set of relations which we ourselves fashion, knead, and impose.

Most of us have barely scratched the surface in our efforts to build a truly personal world. And few of us bequeath the ability to make relations to our children, choosing rather to pass on a shopworn box of maxims, shorn of relational excitement. On behalf of our possibilities, I tell you the story of the Polish mathematician. Our colleague, something of a dissident within the last decade, was arrested and placed in solitary confinement. He was left to himself with only a slop pail for company, having been refused his request for a pencil and paper. Seeking to keep personally alive, he did mathematical formulae in his head. Shorn of physical replication, he soon began to repeat the same mathematical relations, over and over, until they became frayed from repetition and lack of novelty. When released several years later, he said that he was about to eat his brain, for he had run out of relations and had no new formulae to revivify the inherited and so stalk out new ground. Surely, surrounded by the richest of novel possibilities, we can do as well. Or can we, oh we of little faith in the prevalence of surprise?

10   *The Inevitability of*
Our Own Death

THE CELEBRATION OF TIME AS A PRELUDE
TO DISASTER

Their foot shall slide in due time.
DEUTERONOMY 32:35

I. UNTIMELY MEDITATIONS

How strange, how singular, how unusual, is our understanding of death.
Each of us claims to know of death, yet our experience is necessarily indirect, vicarious, and at a distance. It is always someone else's death that
we experience. Yet the power of that experience of the death of the other is
such as to suffuse our very being with an intimacy of awareness, virtually
equivalent to our own death.

No reader of this chapter has died. Nonetheless, we speak of death as
though we knew of which we speak. I do not contravene or even doubt
such an assumption. Rather, I ask how it is possible that a vicarious experience can have such a direct hold on our deepest feelings and our most
intense of personal anticipations? My response to this question is unpleasant and unsettling, but it is true. In the test of time, we are all terminal.
And that fact, of which history, thus far, has allowed no exceptions, is the
most repressed and denied of all facts in the human condition. In turn, it is
this repression which makes the formal announcement that a person is

terminally ill so devastating. Such an announcement is unnecessarily vulgar, for it acts to separate some of us from others of us in a drastic and absolute way. Yet it is only time which is in question here, for to be terminal is the foreordained future of each of us.

Why have we allowed this situation to develop? The major reason is not cheering to those of us who seek to attribute the best motivations to the activities of human life. It is as though we lived our lives in the context of a global roulette wheel, so that the announcement of someone else's impending death somehow lessened the possibility of ours. David Cole Gordon writes:

> The thought of our finitude and ephemerality is so frightening that we run away from this basic fact of existence, consciously and unconsciously, and proceed through life as though we shall endure forever. When we recognize the inevitability of death by the making out of our wills and buying life insurance, it is as though the wills and the insurance related to someone other than ourselves, and we live our actual life as though death is not likely to touch *us*. Insofar as we consider the possibility of our own death at all, it is as an event that is as remote as the end of time, and so we tend unconsciously to repress the fear and the fact of our ultimate doom, or consciously to forget it.[1]

This foolhardy version of our own demise is verified by the habituation of our obituary reading. What, for example, are we to make of a recent story from the *Times Record* newspaper of Troy, New York?

> TROY, N.Y., Sept. 1 (AP) The switchboard at Times Record was flooded with calls this weekend, many of them from "really irate" citizens wondering what had become of the newspaper's obituaries.
>
> Not a single paid death notice or local obituary appeared in the paper Saturday.
>
> "Some people accused us of dropping the obituary page altogether," said Frank Dobisky the managing editor.
>
> "We haven't. Frankly, it never occurred to me that we should tell our readers that no one had died."

It *should* have occurred to the obituary editor to state publicly that no one had died. At a minimum, this would have brought reality to bear on the readers for whom only others die.

Irony aside, we have to face this peculiar masking of the inevitability of our own death. It is simply a matter of time passing before this inevitability emerges as personal, existential reality. In the opening lines of her brilliant essay *Illness as Metaphor*, Susan Sontag presents the irreducibility of our fundamental situation.

> Illness is the night-side of life, a more onerous citizenship. Everyone who is born holds dual citizenship, in the kingdom of the well and in the kingdom of the sick. Although we all prefer to use only the good passport, sooner or later each of us is obliged, at least for a spell, to identify ourselves as citizens of that other place.[2]

Sontag proceeds to discuss the metaphoric versions of two diseases, tuberculosis and cancer, as ones which have acquired the status of separating them from us, or us from them. Both diseases have been associated with death and a sense of fatalism in those who were afflicted. Yet tuberculosis is now curable and cancer is under medical siege, with the cure rate, depending on the bodily location, ranging from 1 to 90 percent. Sontag's point, however, and mine as well, is that century by century we seem to need a scapegoat, that is, a disease which, ostensibly at least, bears terminality for the rest of us. The invidious comparison between the terminally ill and the rest of the population, which is a temporary distinction at best, serves no legitimate purpose except to foster alienation on the one hand and self-indulgence on the other.

Let us pursue this question of terminality somewhat further. In addition to the contemporary classic case of terminal cancer, we have a series of euphemistic versions of terminality. No matter what the illness, the physician may say to family and friends that the patient "has no chance." In itself, this is an interesting phrase from the point of view of scientific, allopathic medicine. Or the statement may be that all potential remedies have been exhausted, which in turn leads to the comment that it is now in the hands of whomever or whatever. These last categories embrace religious overbelief, the salvific arm of divine providence, a brace of homeopathic nostrums, or the utilization of banned "miracle" drugs. Each of these in turn are desperate efforts to reverse or forestall the inevitable. With the exception of the occasional instance in which such efforts release hidden energies in the body, they are for the most part futile, although pursuing them is profoundly understandable. Even the slightest time gained in these approaches constitutes an important personal victory, for it is not death which is the opponent in these situations. Rather, it is the intrusive finality of the announcement of terminality that constitutes the offense against the person. Time gained is a profoundly human advantage set over against the obstreperously public announcement, which summarily and objectively curtails our right to live.

Similarly, I offer that it is precisely this presumptuous seizure of the natural flow of events that is the offensive strand in capital punishment, rather than the asking for death as compensation. Terminality is no more dramatically announced than when a person is sentenced to death at an appointed time and place. The nomenclature of the waiting space is even more vivid: death row. Literature, journalism, and film are especially interested in the event of capital punishment, for they act as our stand-in, enabling us to vicariously grab the power of awarding death from its more traditional sources—nature or, for some, God. Nowhere were the macabre dimensions of the death announcement more pronounced than in the city of Ossining, New York. Formerly, at that city's Sing Sing prison, the activating of the electric chair caused many of the lights in the city to dim, as if much of the citizenry had a hand in bringing about the final moment of a human life.[3]

Still other instances of terminality abound, some of them potential, as in entering a war combat zone or participation in daredevil sports. In such activities, the risk of death is an enlarged and even necessary specter which hovers over the event itself. The last days of the battles of Bataan and Stalingrad are grim reminders of the imminence of death. A German soldier, awaiting his fate at Stalingrad, writes as follows:

> Tomorrow I shall set foot on the last bridge. That is the literary way of saying "death," but as you know, I always liked to express things figuratively, because I took pleasure in words and sounds. Give me your hand, so that crossing it won't be so hard.[4]

In all of these instances of terminality, our death is due to forces outside of our control, even if we place ourselves in situations of jeopardy. One type of terminality, however, is of a decidedly different cast. I refer to that most prepossessing and intriguing of human acts, namely, the decision to commit suicide.[5] In so doing, it is we who announce to ourselves our own death. It is we who seize the time, the place, and the means. Modern Western civilization, especially in its Judeo-Christian version, has been largely unsympathetic with suicide and has placed negative religious and legal sanctions on it. We often work off the naive notion that the act of suicide entails some form of insanity, despite the fact that the certifiably insane rarely kill themselves.

One form of suicide that we tend to indulge somewhat is that of the person who responds to the announcement that he or she has a terminal disease. It is assumed that the reason for suicide in this case is due to the desire to avoid pain. To the contrary, I believe that this decision traces more to the refusal to have one's death announced by others, as though we were innocent bystanders to our own demise. More to the point of our present discussion are those suicides which are neither a response to impending death nor a result of temporary mental aberration. Consider those suicides which are self-conscious and self-possessed human acts designed to articulate a distinctive personal statement. Albert Camus once wrote, "There is but one truly serious philosophical problem, and that is suicide."[6] One can gainsay Camus's claim of singularity, but not of importance. Having played no role in our own coming into being, with all of its attendant cultural, familial, psychosocial, and genetic trappings, it should not strike us as perverse that we seek to preside over our own cessation from being. The most pessimistic version of the interval between our birth and our death is found in the writings of Sören Kierkegaard.

> What is reflection? Simply to reflect on these two questions: How did I get into this and how do I get out of it again, how does it end? What is thoughtlessness? To muster everything in order to drown all this about entrance and exit in forgetfulness, to muster everything to re-explain and explain away entrance and exit, simply lost in the interval between the birth-cry and the repetition of this cry when the one who is born expires in the death struggle.[7]

This description of the bare bones of our situation is accurate, but it need not be indulged. After all, we can go against the grain. Camus writes, "I want to know whether I can live with what I know and with that alone."[8] And, I argue, it is precisely the integrity of living within the boundaries of such knowledge that can occasion our decision to withdraw from the fray, in our own time and on our own terms. By this reasoning, and I emphasize reasoning, suicide becomes a rejection of a dehumanizing determinism, while simultaneously signaling an existential choice, a true act of human freedom. William James, for one, saw such a decision in precisely those terms. In the midst of a personal crisis at the age of twenty-eight, he wrote in his diary:

> Hitherto, when I have felt like taking a free initiative, like daring to act originally, without carefully waiting for contemplation of the external world to determine all for me, suicide seemed the most manly form to put my daring into. . . .[9]

Although many deeply reflective persons have committed suicide and are doing so at this moment, it is important to realize that neither Camus nor James did so. In fact, they developed imaginative and ameliorative strategies for coping with the stark reality of their own defense of the plausibility of suicide. I, too, have some suggestions for a human response to the avoidance of suicide and for dealing with the inevitability of our own death. Before turning to that discussion, however, we must consider a major way in which many persons shun the trauma of death—by belief in some form of salvation or immortality.

I do not refer here to a *hope* that somehow, somewhere, somewhen, all will go well for all of us who are, have been, or will be. Certainly, such a hope is a legitimate and understandable human aspiration. But to convert this hope into a commitment, a knowledge, a settled conviction, is to participate in an illegitimate move from possibility to actuality. It is understandable that we wish to escape from peril, but it is unacceptable to translate that desire into an assured belief that we have so escaped. The history of culture has presented many varieties of immortality. Perhaps the most ingenious, although the least plausible, is that of traditional Roman Catholicism, wherein each of us, *bodily,* is resurrected glorious and immortal or damned and immortal. The attraction here is that our eternal life will be affectively continuous with our mortal life. Other versions of the doctrine of immortality involve claims of reincarnation, metempsychosis, immersion, or absorption, each attempting to perpetuate the me which is me, in one form or another. Obviously, I have no final knowledge of these claims nor do I know of anyone who has. Evidence on their behalf is scanty, scattered, tentative, highly personal, and empirically dubious. Yet many of us cling to one or more of these solutions, as a redoubt, a trump card, or a last-minute reprieve from the overwhelming evidence that we are terminal.

Philosophical, political, and even religious thought of the last century and a half has been characterized by increasing dubiety about the possibility of immortality. Attention also has been given to the complex cultural reasons for the persistence in the belief in immortality, and the explanations are as varied as the doctrine in question. Marx, Freud, the existentialists, Dewey, and Norman O. Brown, among others, have all attempted to account for the persistence of this belief. Brown's version is especially fascinating, for in his judgment the quest for immortality is the *locus classicus* of the human disease. Following the Freud of *Civilization and its*

Discontents,[10] Brown contends that our refusal to face our own death (Thanatos) has led us to repress the life force (Eros) in favor of comparatively permanent civilizational monuments. In short, our greatest neurosis is history, through which we attempt to transcend the burdens of time and project ourselves as having meaning beyond our own lives. In this regard, the monument par excellence to our flight from temporality and from finitude is the "having" of children. By that means, we assert our transcendence from the sheerly local and death-bound character of our lives. In so doing, however, we abandon access to the nectar that comes to those who live the life of Eros, hear the call of immediacy, and, as such, for Brown, cease to be human organisms in any profound sense of that meaning. In his chapter "Death, Time and Eternity," he writes:

> If death gives life individuality and if man is the organism which represses death, then man is the organism which represses his own individuality. Then our proud views of humanity as a species endowed with an individuality denied to lower animals turns out to be wrong. The lilies of the field have it because they take no thought of the morrow, and we do not. Lower organisms live the life proper to their species; their individuality consists in their being concrete embodiments of the essence of their species in a particular life which ends in death.[11]

Here we have the height of irony, for in our effort to transcend the life of the lower organisms, we fail to realize even that level of Eros, wallowing rather in a self-deceptive flight from the burden of time passing.[12] Brown's prescription for overcoming this false transcendence, this escape into self-deception, is complex and personally radical. At this point, I bypass the details of his resolution in order to say, quite directly, that in my judgment he asks us to marry our own death. He cautions against a preening narcissism, in which we take ourselves too literally, as well as against the fruitless flight from the temporal, the immediate, and transient Eros. At some point in our life, the sooner the better, we should confront the inevitability of our own death and absorb this awareness into the most active forefront of our consciousness. The message is clear and twofold: avoid the temptation to invest in meaning which transcends our own experience of the life-cycle; and affirm the imminence of death as the gateway to an unrepressed life in which the moment sings its own song, in its own way, once and once only.

Although I regard Brown's critique of immortality as devastating, his resolution in *Life Against Death,* and again in *Love's Body*,[13] is beyond the pale of possibility for all but the heroic figure, the person who lives perpetually on the horizon, on the furthest edge of each and every experience. The fundamental question is whether there is a median way between the self-deception of personal immortality, on the one hand, and the radical commitment to the moment, on the other. If we live within the bowels of the temporal process, can we not have also a sense of the future, a sense which does not delude us into thinking that we have transcended time? Put directly, can we experience ourselves as terminal and yet live creative, probing, building lives which, nonetheless, ask for no guarantees and for no ultimate significance to be attributed to our endeavor? I, for one, believe that we can live this way; nay, I believe that it is only in this way that we live a distinctively human life. In fact, I offer that a life lived consciously in the shadow of our own death is one which can prehend the scents of the most subtle of messages, namely, those intended only for creatures who risk living within the rhythm of time. With such an attitude, categories basic to human life and understanding undergo a change in our experience of them. As our fundamental expectation for human life changes, so too does our perception of time, growth, history, and experience undergo comparative changes. Let us now map these developments in some detail.

II. THE LIFE OF THE LIVE CREATURE

I believe that we should experience our own lives in the context of being permanently afflicted, that is, of being terminal. This is not to propose a morbid personal style, but rather to ask that this attitude ride as an abiding presence in the active recesses of our conscious life. Surely the shift from ancient to contemporary cosmology has doomed the doctrine of the equivalence of cosmic space with human life. The unintelligible distances, activities, gestations, and denouements of contemporary cosmology have dwarfed us and rendered illusory any human effort at ultimate accountability by our appeal to our proper *place*. The place we claim in the infinite universe is precisely that, a claim, an assertion, a seizing, an activity unknown to and unfelt by infinite space. The cosmology of human life is scarcely more extensive than our sociology. We have domesticated one planet and one lunar satellite and have probed several other planets. Electronically and mathematically, we have extended ourselves somewhat further. Nonetheless, relative to galactic plurality, let alone infinite space, these extraordinary human efforts are scarcely more than explorations of one city block or of a fifty-acre farm. Further, we are told as one active possibility that cosmic reality itself is entropic, winding down on its inexorable way to nothing.[14] In short, whatever may be the long-range future of cosmology, I do not see any auspicious signs that it will provide a resolution of present personal plight.

Historically, a paradox emerges which is intriguing and instructive. When, in antique times, we held the universe to be finite, we also held that it was eternal. Human life had a fixed and natural place in this version of the world, and only *sub specie aeternitatis* could it play a permanently meaningful role in the cyclically repetitive flow of time. Modern cosmology, for the most part, holds reality[15] to be infinite and, on behalf of the doctrine of relativity, denies that we have a natural and fixed place. The paradox is that in the modern view time has no ultimate meaning, yet it does take on profound human meaning, for it is both unrepeatable and the distinctive way in which human life asserts its presence and significance in the context of infinite reality. Infinite space becomes increasingly domesticated by being subjected to human time.

Given this cosmological context, our fundamental situation is transiency. We are of the species *Homo viator*, persons on a journey, human travelers in a cosmic abyss. Actually, in my judgment, transients is a better word than travelers, for the latter often connotes a definite goal, an end in view, or at least a return home. A transient, however, is one who is passing through. The meaning of a transient's journey is precisely that: the journey itself. In transiency, paraphrasing John Dewey,[16] it is the *quality* of the journeying which counts, not the end in view and certainly not the claim that we have journeyed. The quality of transiency is achieved by passing through rather than by passing by. We should make our journey ever alert to our surroundings and to every perceivable sensorial nuance. Our journey is a kaleidoscope of alternating experiences, mishap, setback, celebrations, and eye-openers, all undergone on the *qui vive*.

I repeat that space becomes meaningful for us to the extent that, through time, we build ourselves into it and convert space to place, to our place. It is necessary for us to make a place, for I do not believe that we have any inherited or natural place, as awarded. Just as the bottom line of death is that we are not around and about anymore, so then does life mean to be in a place, from someplace, on the way to someplace. We cannot do this by ourselves, for to be in place is to be relative to some other place, someone else's place. Friendship, family, media all serve to context our place, as they set over against us another place. Our memories are thereby crucial to a human life, for they carry past places to a present place, enabling a single place to be laced with all of the places we have been. Memories save the loss of places and the loss of persons from total disappearance. Actually, our losses often become more intense aspects of our present experience than our present itself. In the flow of the journey we hook ourselves to persons, places, things, and events, allowing us to reconnoitre, while passing through. A classic and profound hook is that of our junk drawer. Scraps and pieces of memorabilia tumble over one another, unworthy aside from their endowed meanings, given in a prior experience. An opera ticket, a ring, a watch, a baseball, a rejection slip, a cancelled check, defy their ejection from our junk drawer, for they are laden with meaning and they act as personal clots in the onrushing flow of our lives.

Nonetheless, despite the richness of our memoried past, we cannot allow ourselves to be trapped in nostalgia. Following William James, life is as much in the transitions, as it is in the events we experience directly.[17]

No doubt our past experiences should remain alive in our consciousness and should be stirred and restirred so that they envelop and enrich our present experiences. But it is to the future that we wend. We cannot stand still. If we do, atrophy awaits us. Our deepest personal need, then, is to grow, for personal growth is the only sure sign that we are not yet dead. And by growth we mean here the capacity to convert our environment into sources of personal nutrition, to eat experience, as it were. The deeper meaning of growth is not an increase of size, length, height, or any other quantitative measure. Rather, it has to do with fructification, enriching, enhancing, and the pregnant provision for still further growth. Dewey's much maligned comment—"since in reality there is nothing to which growth is relative save more growth"—yields more than meets the eye.[18] In Dewey's understanding, growth is not characterized by a teleological movement to a final end. Rather, it is the quality of being humanly enriched by our experience, even if it be failure or loss. Further, growth is not simply an outcome or a result. It is the very nature of the live creature when participating in the flow of experience. In the following text, Dewey is referring to children, but he refers equally to all of us. "Where there is life, there are already eager and impassioned activities. Growth is not something done to them; it is something they do."[19] It is doing to the world and being done by the world which constitute the fundamental human transactions and allow for the possibility of growth. Hanging back while waiting to be rescued ultimately from the flow will not generate growth. Indulging and preening our ego, impervious to the messaging of the world, will not generate growth. In order to grow, that is, to live the life of a live creature rather than a life of second-handedness, we must forge a self-conscious relationship between our acceptance of our irreversible fragility and our creative energies. The most revealing focus of developing this relationship is our own version of the meaning of time and its attendant significance for the meaning of things, events, and history.

And now I come straight out and say where I stand on this issue. I believe that time is sacred. It is not sacred, however, because it has been so endowed by God, the gods, nature, or any other force. I believe that time is sacred because human history has endowed it with our meaning, our suffering, our commitments, and our anticipations. Can we sustain this position, if we place it over against our previous discussion of the inevitability of death? What can we say, for example, when faced with the following text from the ancient Roman philosopher, Marcus Aurelius: "And, to say all in a word, everything which belongs to the body is a stream, and what belongs to the soul is a dream and vapour, and life is a warfare and a stranger's sojourn, and after-fame is oblivion."[20]

The Aurelian text is candid and accurate. He resolves it by an appeal to the cycle of nature, which gives human explanation for the existence of the human organism. This resolution, however, does not remove the bite from the fact that we are born to live and destined to die. I contend that the utter frustration of this contradiction in our personal situation cannot be resolved. Rather, speaking for the living, I take my point of departure from a text by John Dewey.

> We always live at the time we live and not at some other time, and only by extracting at each present time the full meaning of each present experience are we prepared for doing the same thing in the future. This is the only preparation which in the long run amounts to anything.[21]

Here Dewey joins hands with the thought of Norman O. Brown and with the medieval tradition of the sacrament of the moment. Contrary to those positions, however, Dewey acknowledges no forces at work, neither Dionysian nor divine, other than the constitutive transactions of human life with the affairs of nature and the world. For better and for worse, we make the world and we endow nature with our presence, our values, our arrogance, and our fealty. You and I inherit thousands of years of human formulation, human judgment, human management, human violence, and human affection. Still, we come upon the world fresh, as if for the first time. The historically encrusted implications rush out at us as we seek to see, hear, touch anew. The novelty is not the world, for the world is tired, even jaded, with millennia of human hands and minds kneading it into a human image. No, the novelty, if it is to be at all, is found in us, in you, in me. It is not the monumental or the charismatic which provides the clue to the magnificence of being human. Rather, it is the celebration of the ordinary that enables us to make our way as truly human, avoiding the twin pitfalls of the humdrum, ennui, and boredom, and the equally dehumanizing attempt to escape from the rhythm of time on behalf of a sterile and probably self-deceptive eternal resolution. Most likely, we have no ultimate future. This should not keep us from participating in the explosive possibilities of our present, no matter what the situation. Setback enriches as well as breakthrough.

Our impending death is not the major obstacle to our becoming truly human. The obstacle is found in our running for cover on behalf of our escape from death. We sell ourselves short. We should listen to the poet Rainer Maria Rilke, who praises our very ephemerality.

> But because being here amounts to so much, because all
> this Here and Now, so fleeting, seems to require us and strangely
> concerns us. Us the most fleeting of all. Just once,
> everything, only for once. Once and no more. And we, too,
> once. And never again. But this
> having been once, though only once,
> having been once on earth—can it ever be cancelled?[22]

Indeed, can it, can we, ever be cancelled? I think not. Celebrate!

11 *Do Not Bequeath a Shamble*

THE CHILD IN THE TWENTY-FIRST CENTURY—INNOCENT HOSTAGE TO MINDLESS OPPRESSION OR CHILDREN AS MESSENGERS TO THE WORLD

What the best and wisest parent wants for his [her] own child, that must the community want for all of its children.
JOHN DEWEY, *The School and Society*

[We] will not be the victim of events, but will have the clarity of vision to direct and shape the future of human society.
MARIA MONTESSORI, *Education for a New World*

What could be more poignant and disturbing than the photographs of the faces of victimized children over the past fifty years. Beginning with the children of the Holocaust and on through the devastation of the Second World War, Biafra, Vietnam, Laos, until our own time in Cambodia, their blank, bewildered stares flare out from their gaunt, malnutritioned bodies. The ravages of global violence are especially addressed to the children. Their innocence in these conflicts is a stark reminder of the systematic madness that plagues all societies, which one by one, become self-righteous and oblivious to the nature of their victims as one cause or another is pursued. I would be more confident in the possibility of the praiseworthy movement for care of the unborn generations, if I were to see equal care for those who have just been born, the children of the world.

As we begin its penultimate decade, the twentieth century has been a tumultuous and inordinately complex century. We should remind ourselves that we not only approach the end of a century, but of a millennium as well. In that regard, the twentieth century brings to a head hundreds of years of yearning and cultural experiences, which yield a legacy that we avoid at deep peril. Some decades ago, we viewed the coming of the twenty-first century with considerable romantic optimism. The year 2001 connoted the marvels of space technology and liberation from the burdens of the industrial world. Recent events have rendered that version of our future unrealistic and, dare we say it, experientially shallow. I say shallow because the vision of the next century left out the gnawing problems of the planet earth, as though they could be transcended and thereby forgotten. This attitude, it now turns out, was vulgar naiveté. No, the legacy of the twentieth century is more sobering, although I do not gainsay the potential significance of its spiritual bequest. Let us examine this legacy in some detail.

As the inheritors of Western culture, we have witnessed a dramatic shift in our consciousness. We now think and feel in global terms. The Second World War signaled both the end of colonialism and the beginning of the full planetary consciousness. Those of us who were educated in the first fifty years of this century were introduced to a warped cultural map of the past. We were taught one version or another of a Euro-American provincialism, as though a majority of the world's population and their historical achievements were obsolete. Our strident refusal to learn the language of other lands was peculiarly coupled with our penchant for quick tours in which we gawked at the monuments of what we too often took to be a dead past. The splendid Cambodian monument of Angkor Wat attests to the majesty of a storied history but in our time, the photo-teletype sends us the pictures of hordes of deracinated and emaciated Cambodian children, victims of the power politics which rage around them, as indifferent to their future as to their past.

The last four decades of geopolitics have profoundly transformed our consciousness. Now, to be truly human, we must think in planetary, global terms. I remember vividly when this transformation began to take shape in my own mind. The year was 1954 and I read of the impending conference to be held at Bandung, Indonesia. It was announced that no "white" nations would be invited, and it was at that conference that the gathered nations described themselves as "the third world." The impact of that conference was obvious; East and West were no longer apt planetary divisions. Subsequent to the event, we have seen the reemergence of Africa, China, and the nations of Latin America as distinctive and distinguished forces on the world stage. Human culture is now truly world culture. Our experience of literature, religion, philosophy, dance, music, art, and costume have been immeasurably enriched. The only viable strategy for our global future is the adoption of a pluralism in which the angles of visions, styles, and beliefs of the world's cultures mesh in the creation of a genuinely egalitarian world society.

There is no question that this spiritual bequest of the twentieth century on behalf of global consciousness is salutary. Nonetheless, there is a dark side to our new-found awareness, for no sooner do we become aware of the riches of global culture than we realize the attendant problems which also emerge. In truth, the glaring fact of the matter is that we are now faced with a crisis of global proportions. This situation takes the form of a crisis in energy, food, ecology, and population, to which is added the ambivalence of high technology. We talk now about the world in which our children's children will come to consciousness.

However difficult it may be for us to comprehend existentially, it is necessary for us to project the future and to assess its viability by analysis of our present plight. Although I am not given to Cassandra-like prophecies of doom, we must face the fact, nonetheless, that we are witness to a planetary siege mentality.[1] Our most serious difficulty, despite its being hidden from most of the bourgeois world, is that of food. Despite the extraordinary advances of modern agricultural technology, the geometric increase in the world's population has raised the specter of widening human sectors in which future starvation is a high probability. It is a well-known paradox that the people who can least afford to have children have them, whereas the birth rate among the affluent, and especially among the middle class, has dropped. As contemporary anthropologists have detailed, the reasons for this are culturally complex and perhaps impervious to a solution. Yet, the brutal fact prevails; there exists an inverse ratio between those who have the resources and those who have the need. So serious is this matter that allegedly thoughtful people have introduced the notion of triage into the field of world hunger. Taken over from the language of the battlefield, the word triage refers to tripartite division of the wounded as found in the field hospital. The breakdown is as follows: those who will die even if treated; those who will live even if not treated; and those who will live only if treated. The first category is abandoned, the second is asked to suffer through to resolution, whereas the resources are given only to the last group. The analog to world hunger does not hold, for all, if fed, could live. But food triage, depressingly, has been considered as a serious option on the ground that, in time, there will be enough food for some but not for all. The question facing our children is who gets the food? Or is the question different, that is, who among the next generations will be willing to cut their consumption drastically, so that all may eat? Of course, the true doomsday prophet foresees a solution to world starvation and overpopulation (the latter estimated conservatively at 7 billion people forty years from now): nuclear conflagration.

To the twin problems of food and population, we now add the depletion of nonrenewable resources, known in the jargon as the energy crisis. In addition to the obvious economic hardships this crisis can generate, we should focus also on the deeply personal disadvantages which will accrue. The key word here is inaccessibility, namely, the denial of the possibility of visiting the distant environs which surround us and, still more crucial, the denial of the possibility of visiting each other. We face a social impacting and a loss of national, let alone global, consciousness. We must implore our children to search for viable alternatives so that this crisis will be averted, else they will plunge backward into the provincial limitations of centuries past.

The irony of the above difficulties is that a resolution would be forthcoming if it were not for the emergence of still another world problem, that of ecological trashing. Symbolically, this is the most unsettling of all of our problems, for it results from the fallout of some of our most successful endeavors. John Dewey, in *Experience and Nature,* long ago told us that we were in an irresolute struggle with the affairs of nature and that nature, if abused, would strike back.

Time is brief, and this statement must stand instead of the discourse which the subject deserves. Man finds himself living in an aleatory world; his existence involves, to put it baldly, a gamble. The world is a scene of risk; it is uncertain, unstable, uncannily unstable. Its dangers are irregular, inconstant, not to be counted upon as to their times and seasons. Although persistent, they are sporadic, episodic. It is darkest just before dawn; pride goes before a fall; the moment of greatest prosperity is the moment most charged with ill-omen, most opportune for the evil eye. Plague, famine, failure of crops, disease, death, defeat in battle, are always just around the corner, and so are abundance, strength, victory, festival and song. Luck is proverbially both good and bad in its distributions. The sacred and the accursed are potentialities of the same situation; and there is no category of things which has not embodied the sacred and accursed: persons, words, places, times, directions in space, stones, winds, animals, stars.[2]

Surely, the warning is clear; "the world is a scene of risk." The solution of those problems most bothersome to one generation, often become irresolute difficulties of a subsequent generation. Time extracts its price. We and our children are inheriting polluted oceans, rivers, lakes, streams, and air. Some of us live on top of Love Canals, obviously inappropriately named as their noxious fumes and chemicals penetrate our deepest genetic structure. We, in our generation, have committed the cardinal sin. Instead of bequeathing a "leg up," a better world, or whatever cliché comes to mind, we have passed on a time bomb. Our children's ecological future is fraught with the residue of chemical seedings, poisonous in the long run. Our present generation is trapped in a classic case of Catch-22. The energy crisis threatens our economic stability, our social patterns, and even penetrates to our long held image of ourselves as a necessarily mobile people. Yet, our potential resolutions of this problem are foreboding in their own right. If we reopen our massive coal reserves, we heighten our pollution level and expand the deadly presence of acid rain, which has already deadened hundreds of lakes and thousands of fish in upper New York State. The turn to nuclear power is even more frightening, as the events of Three Mile Island graphically attest. The genius of high technology is necessary to resolve the world's problems just detailed. Yet, it is that same high technology which has so threatened the delicate balance of the world's ecosystem, especially in its biochemical arrangements.

The rights and needs of the present generations must be set over against the rights and needs of unborn generations, worldwide. Our children will have to be the generation which effects the transition from the present-mindedness which has dominated the recent centuries to a forward-looking care for future generations by assuring a perpetuity of resources and by a resisting of the short-run exploitation of nature. Further, although not sufficient for a resolution of these perplexing and abiding problems, it would be symbolically significant if the present generation would begin a concerted effort to stop trashing our environment. And, on this behalf, the messages of ecologists should be built into every curriculum, from the teaching of preschool children on to university life and adult education. As we know, there is considerable religious fervor loose in the world. I, for one, am not very impressed by its ideological self-righteousness and its abandonment of the problems most pressing to most of us. Better if that energy were addressed to what is truly sacred in our lives, our land, our things and living space and, above all, our ability to provide for a creative future for our children.

What we must avoid is the increasing sense of our haplessness in the face of these difficulties. Many of us feel dwarfed or even trivialized by the events of this century. Too often, then, our tendency is to abandon our best instincts for amelioration and to dilute our energies in favor of either a laissez-faire attitude or some form of extra-terrestrial resolution. This will not do, for the forces of exploitation and manipulation do not so sleep or become seduced by nostrums of an otherworldly cast. Rather, we must begin and, where begun, intensify a reeducation of our attitudes toward the future and especially toward our use of the planet earth.

II

Obviously, it is beyond the scope of this paper and, more tellingly, beyond my competence, to offer technical and specific resolutions of these difficulties. Fortunately, we have a different task at hand, namely, our educational bequest, such that our children and their children will be better prepared for the next century than we seem to be. And, in this context, the backdrop of our consideration is the work of Maria Montessori. Her explicit contributions to our discussion are threefold. First, she is the first and, in fact, the only truly global educator. Second, however unwitting it may have been, she has anticipated the decline of the nuclear family as the primary source of preschool education. In this regard, she has been especially acute in helping us to cut between the twin pitfalls of sentimentality and indifference in our relationship to children. Third, we can learn from her notion of the prepared environment and her structuring of the attitudes of care for that environment on the part of participating children. Her work in this area could become an important strand in rebuilding our care for the earth. Let us examine these contributions, *seriatim,* in an effort to forge a pedagogy more sensitive to our actual situation than is the haphazard methodology of most of our peers.

Initially, the most striking feature of Montessori's work is that her method, her teachers, and her learning children in her programs are to be found throughout the world. No other educator has such global influence, for although Pestalozzi, Rousseau, Herbart, and Piaget have each made their contributions, they are restricted for the most part to Western culture. John Dewey, it is true, has had enormous influence in the Orient but not in Western Europe nor the third world. Montessori, to the contrary, has struck a universal chord in the lives of children wherever they are found. I trace this important fact to three sources. First, she wisely believed that children of very early age had abilities to learn, independent of their peer group cultures, which were rarely tapped in any formal way. Second, it was not necessary to import teachers who had a secret message to deliver. Indeed, teachers in the usual sense were not part of the Montessori picture. Rather, Montessori directresses and later directors could be either imported or homegrown, so long as they honored the autodidactic activities of the children. It was the children, after all, who taught themselves, so long as the environment was prepared, the materials utilized, and the goals or directions made clear. In very young children this could and has taken place in a wide variety of cultures throughout the world. Third, the Montessori children were not class structured. From the first days of the Casa dei Bambini, Montessori was convinced that children of all backgrounds and all cultural limitations were capable of self-learning.[3] Indeed, it is often characteristic of a Montessori program that the children are representative of a far wider range of cultural and economic advantages than the more traditional programs.

The global influence of Montessori was not an accident of history. Long before our own awareness of the inextricability of our lives on this planet, she saw the need for the recognition and development of the abilities of children throughout the world. As early as 1910, she resigned her lectureship at the University of Rome and struck her name from the list of practicing physicians, and committed herself to "all the children in the world, born and as yet unborn."[4] She then began a lifelong journey on behalf of children's rights and of their liberation from the darkness of unknowing. Her work was to take her beyond Italy to the United States, Latin America, India, Ceylon, France, Germany, Holland, Ireland, Spain, Austria, and Pakistan. UNESCO had its spiritual if unsung founder and the global consciousness of our time can look back now on its remarkable anticipation by this remarkable woman educator.

I turn now to Montessori's second contribution to our time and its significance for the future, namely, her contributions to the potential independence of young children from parental structures for the purpose of learning. Allow me to be frank at this point. I do not believe that preschool programs or day-care centers are the optimum environment for young children. In that regard, I am an unabashed believer, only so far as children are concerned, in the structure of the nuclear family. Increasingly, for a wide variety of reasons, this belief is out of step with the social realities of our present situation in America, to say nothing of cultures distant from us. Speaking only of our own American culture, the signs are telling for the growing irrelevance of my point of view. Soaring divorce rates, single parents, homosexual marriages and, most of all, the tremendous increase of women's participation in the public economic sector, all point to the need for an extraordinary increase in the care of preschool children. And these developments, of course, are in addition to the always shocking displacement of children in various countries due to war, famine, or one or another lethal political dispute.

I do not see Montessori's approach to the education of young children as a panacea, any more than could that of any single perspective. Yet, in these troubled times, which point to still more vast difficulties, her philosophy of the child takes on increased meaning. Of special importance is her insistence that we have both a deep and abiding care for the child and a firm commitment to the independence and irrevocable liberty of the child. It is the persistent transaction of these two attitudes, situation by situation, which gives the wisdom to Montessori's educational practice. As parents and teachers, we are often vulnerable to the children in our care, such that out of a sense of our own inadequacy, or frustration at their inadequacy, we either indulge them or lose confidence in their ability and thereby shut them down.

Montessori teaches us that young children are more capable than we assume, but she also stresses that they need more shepherding than we are often willing to give. For those who came to consciousness under the influence of Freud, there seems to be something irreducibly simplistic about Montessori's version of the child, to say nothing of her ineptitude on the crucial problem of sexual development. Yet as we develop global consciousness and take into our purview the lives of children around the world, the high bourgeois ethos of Freud and other practitioners of our assorted neuroses, despite its intrinsic fascination, seems to fade in the order of relevance. So too with the much ballyhooed electronic revolution that we were told was imminent. An occasional child may have an

"R2D2" as a companion, but the more likely future will be characterized by the struggle for physical sustenance and for a place rather than a room of one's own. If we truly believe in the future of our children, we shall teach them to care about the world in which they are going to find themselves, a world notably more recalcitrant than the one in which we live. And this leads us to Montessori's third contribution to life in the twenty-first century, her notion of a prepared environment and her doctrine of things.[5]

In speaking of the prepared environment and the didactic materials, I have no intention of returning to the earlier internecine struggles among Montessorians as to whether the environment and the materials were either impervious to innovation or in desperate need of innovation. Twenty years ago I wrote on this issue as follows:[6] The notion of structure, so central to Montessori's thought, does not of itself preclude the variety of experiences that is indispensable for learning. The entire criticism of her approach is rendered ineffectual by Montessori's explicit remarks in *Spontaneous Activity in Education,* relative to novelty. She writes, "As a fact, every object may have infinite attributes; and if, as often happens in object-lessons, the origins and ultimate ends of the object itself are included among these attributes, the mind has literally to range throughout the universe."[7] It is not simply a question of quantity that is at stake here; rather the relationship between the potentialities of the child and the *kind* of experiences offered. It is not the number of options that constitutes novelty, for as Montessori states, "It is the qualities of the objects, not the objects themselves which are important."[8]

With this important caveat of Montessori in mind, and in the light of our present discussion, let us consider the significance of the prepared environment and of the didactic materials. The Montessori environment is prepared in that certain materials are to be used, and used in an orderly way. It is, however, just as much a preparing environment, for the child must come to grips with its structure, its advantages, and its limitations. The Montessori child is not a robot who is slotted into a tight, rigid, and programmed environment. Rather, the key to Montessori's philosophy of education is that the child is a potentially explosive organism who will respond to the proper tactile stimuli. The prepared environment is an open-ended nest in which feeding, growth, and finally maturation beyond its bounds takes place. The most creative and seminal characteristic of the prepared environment is that the children take responsibility for it and for their relationship to it. In a word, they care. Further, they care about each other, for each is dependent on the rest, if the environment is to be truly seminal for the awakening of each child's ability. The entire endeavor is shared, although each child has his or her distinct personal process under-way, as is symbolized in the periodic experience of silence undergone by the children.[9] Even more significant for our present discussion is that the children, when finished with the materials, return them to their proper resting place where they can be used by another child. This use of the materials is analogous to our deep need in the next generations to arrive at a state wherein we do not plunder, that is, do not go beyond the fixed limits of the nonrenewable resource. How different would be our situation if the present generation were taught as children the existential reality that others follow us and must subsequently use the things that we use.

We have still one more dimension of Montessori's use of materials. She has a superb sense of their tactility and the way in which children are pro-foundly informed and conceptually transformed by the activities of their bodies, especially their hands. The intimacy of the child to the world is thereby not limited to the affairs of nature. Indeed, things, artifacts, are neither neutral nor inert, but carry with them the capacity to stir and pro-voke the sensorial foundations for learning which each of us carries deep within our nascent person. To learn to read with the hands as well as with the eyes is a marvelous melding of mind and body, concept and percept, in a pedagogical strategy that is worthy of the fact that such dualisms are not experientially separate in the first place. For Montessori, to touch is to be touched. She places herself in that long tradition of thought which holds that the world and all of its doings speak to us out of the very depth of being and meaning.

Montessori has offered us a first step in understanding the power of our things. Her materials, sparse in number and comparatively simple, are but an opening wedge into the vast range of possibilities upon which we can call to educate our children. Modern technology has made available an endless range of materials, each different in shape, composition, surface, and function. Children throughout the world should place their hands on samples of all of them and so learn of their viability, their use, their fragility and, above all, their danger. In the context of classical Montessori educa-tion, allow me to introduce just three new ways of dealing with the en-vironment, all of which are essential to education in the twenty-first cen-tury. In addition to the classical materials, I would introduce materials that are highly desirable, but not enough of them to go around, rather just enough to be frustrating. This situation would introduce the children to a structural sense of scarcity. Other materials would be introduced, but when used, would be consumed and nonrenewable. The question is, Who gets to use them? Finally, I would introduce materials which not only corrode themselves, but corrode the other materials as well. And here we have the experience of pollution. Unpleasant pedagogy? Yes, decidedly so, but a necessary pedagogy, nonetheless.

I, for one, take the message of the ecologists seriously. In my judgment, the classroom should be structured as a miniature ecosystem. What better than a Montessori approach as suitable for this pedagogical move to the twenty-first century? Combined with the best implications of the revolution in the arts and the revolution in design, we could encourage our children to begin, from their beginning, to participate in and slowly develop on their own terms an environment which is aesthetically alive, pedagogically responsive, and ecologically responsible. I offer that it is our responsibility on behalf of succeeding generations that we forge this new, creative, and fail-safe pedagogy, one that will develop a cultural and civilizational literacy.

Finally, what after all are our options, our alternatives? One is the voice of the doomsday squad, who divide over two equally reprehensible and unacceptable alternatives: nuclear conflagration and worldwide starvation. At the opposite pole, we have the Pollyanna optimists, combined with science fiction, who see half of the world relocating to outer space by the twenty-second century. If the first alternative is unacceptable, the second is unlikely. Do we have a third alternative? I believe that we do, although it is neither as foreboding nor as dramatic as the first two options. Let us own up to our situation, honestly and without illusion. We must remake the earth in the image of our best qualities. We must dilute and even topple the forces of aggrandizement and exploitation. Nothing will rescue us except ourselves. Neither the gods nor the forces of nature are on our side. We must reconstitute the awe and the reverence of the earliest people in our quest for a new relationship with the world in which we find ourselves. We are the enemy and we are the saviors. The planet awaits our decision. Which shall it be? This is the message I tell my children and I suggest that it is the message you tell your children and that they should tell their children. Shall our children be innocent hostages to mindless oppression and ecological disaster, or shall they be in fact, in deed, and in imagination, messengers to the building of a truly human world?

12 Cultural Literacy

A TIME FOR A NEW CURRICULUM

In our time and in our nation, public precollegiate education is in serious disarray. It is now a nationally observed phenomenon that despite good intentions on the part of teachers and despite generally intelligent students, even those students who proceed to colleges and universities seem culturally deprived. They exhibit a staggering ignorance of history and letters, and their symbolic resources for imaginative reconstruction seem bankrupt. It is as if the soul has disappeared, leaving only a more or less satisfactory standardized test as the approach to learning.

The reasons for this state of affairs are complex and obviously not amenable to easy solutions. This is not the place to probe the educational politics of the situation, although they are decidedly relevant, as the Conant report[1] attested decades ago. We are faced with something of an institutional fait accompli, in that colleges of education prepare most of our teachers in a decidedly nonhumanistic[2] and nonspeculative framework. It should not come as surprising that these teachers then teach our children in a similar vein. Nothing less than a radical transformation of the curriculum in teacher education programs, a transformation long overdue, can resolve that dilemma.[3]

It is now obvious that many students with high test scores and class rank are nonetheless unaware of even the preeminent events in the history of

Western civilization, and totally innocent of the very existence of major cultural traditions other than their own. In a recent effort to assess the knowledge of highly qualified and academically successful juniors and seniors in a major American university, I was startled to learn that thirty of forty students could not identify Socrates, the Roman Empire, the Protestant Reformation, Newton, or Beethoven. In fact, of the thirty simple identifications requested, the average score for the forty students was six correct. Despite the fact that we now live in a truly global culture, requests for information or insight about Oriental, Indian, African, or Islamic cultures are met with utter bewilderment.

Still more serious than this appalling absence of awareness of our historical and cultural past is the spiritual context of contemporary public education. Although exceptions exist, it is a safe generalization to describe the ambience of "being in school" as an alternation between boredom and violence. The major escapees from these nefarious poles are those children, due to family or occasionally ethnic pressure, who concentrate on "making it" and see one or more careers as the delineation of their human future. These judgments as to the plight of our schools are not novel. In fact, ample literature, both popular and scholarly, details this situation on a regular basis.

Admittedly, the critique of the studied emptiness of middle-class education and the warnings about the baleful future of those children who know only a career as the meaning of education are comparatively subtle in a nation that is increasingly characterized by the quick, the shallow, and the ersatz. Not so subtle, however, is the diagnosis of the school systems of our great urban centers. In such settings, involving millions of children, historical and cultural illiteracy is not, alas, the primary concern. Rather, we face dramatically high rates of absenteeism and adolescent dropouts. We face strife, social disorder, and plummeting scores in basic verbal and mathematical skills. Administrators, teachers, and community leaders are often called upon for heroic efforts in their attempt to structure a meaningful educational environment. Despite their efforts, increasingly, even liberal and pluralistically oriented parents are choosing to squirrel their children away in one of the urban private schools which now multiply like mushrooms after a constant rain. When added to the postwar flight of the self-announced gentry to the suburbs, the rise of urban private schools leaves the urban public school something of an embattled redoubt, an abandoned but peopled bunker, left behind.

In America, historically and morally committed to a democratic polity, it is essential that we continue, generation by generation, to educate all of our children in the best of our warranted wisdom so that they may take their rightful and necessary place in the ongoing presentation and continuance of our attempt to build a truly human future. The erosion of humanistic sensibility, awareness of the past, and basic competency in literacy and science, as often found in contemporary public education, constitutes a major threat to this essential national endeavor. Granted the occasional worthiness and even curricular imagination of private education, we must acknowledge that it is the quality of public school education which holds the key to the spiritual future of this republic. Therefore, we cannot be sanguine, for it is precisely public school education that mirrors the deepest crisis in contemporary America: the economic and social bifurcation between a struggling and cynical lumpenproletariat confined to poor rural and inner urban schools, and an affluent, morally laissez-faire middle class, making their way through private or suburban educational institutions. The separation of blacks and Hispanics from whites is, of course, a looming factor in this division, but it is not the decisive source of the division. Looming larger is the gap between the poor and the affluent, for that gap, regrettably and undemocratically, constitutes the major reason for the double standard as to what constitutes acceptable education for an American child. Despite the penchant for crisis management in American society, the crisis in American public school education remains obdurate and discussed only *sotto voce*. Highways, potholes, prisons, illegal aliens, and interest rates rank far ahead of the debilitation of millions of our children. The politics of this situation seem impervious to resolution, short of revolution, which, in this century, seems to bring only repression under a different rubric.

Given the skepticism about the salutary effect of recent federal programs for the solution of problems besetting the public schools, and given the economic climate of America in this decade, it is very unlikely that we will witness the appearance of an educational Marshall Plan in the near future. Consequently, the finances, the neighborhoods, and the clientele of the public schools will remain basically the same in this decade. The curriculum, however, need not remain the same. And we can move in the direction of a significant shift in the focus of the teaching process. I now offer some suggestions as to the ingredients necessary for a transformation of public education. Parenthetically, I do not have in mind the simplistic resolution, often put forth by university faculty, of adding materials and subject matter in the earlier years. As one who has taught Latin and English in secondary school, I can attest that this would only introduce increased confusion to the current curricular bedlam. Adolescent students who now take six, seven, and even eight different subjects a day in short time snatches are in no position to have more subject matter added. Although it is generally lamentable that such areas of important intellectual endeavor as philosophy, sociology, psychology, anthropology, the history of religion, and the history of science are not staples in a typical secondary school curriculum, I see no possible way in which they could become so except by ousting equally important concerns or by making the curriculum more of a patchwork quilt than at present. No, the needed change is in a different direction entirely. We must demythologize the discipline structure of our approach to education.

I believe that humanistic learning is present in every endeavor and that it is dramatically present in the traditional endeavors of precollegiate education. How did it happen that the discipline known as history became responsible for the history of everything, such that other disciplines became ahistorical? If I am teaching physics to secondary school students, is it not germane to the discussion that for more than 2,000 years physics and philosophy were identical? Is it not significant that the ancient philosopher Democritus anticipated modern atomic theory? Should not these students be told that the history of science is pockmarked with errors, many of them propagated far beyond the time of exposure because of political or ideological reasons? Would not the teaching of science be served well if we were to introduce the students to the contrasting conflicts found in the life and work of Galileo and Lysenko? In this way, the teaching of science might involve not only history but ethics and biography as well. A further example from the sciences pertains to biology. In Western civilization, biology was founded by Aristotle, and the phyla are his creation. Could there be a better model for students to emulate for developing the power of observation? And would it not be a contribution to these students for them to know that while learning Aristotle's approach to biology, they were also learning his method of philosophy, a method which infused Western culture until the late nineteenth century? Similar examples from the sciences can be multiplied indefinitely, and the historical dimension of every discipline should be an integral aspect of its presentation.

We do not quarrel with the fact that it is necessary and salutary that precollegiate education spend time on mathematics, and on reading, writing, and speaking English and at least one other language, all taught very early in the schooling process. And, whenever possible, computer assisted instruction should be utilized. But for the rest of the curriculum, at the outset for some years and then periodically thereafter, we should concentrate on autobiography/biography, the science of living things (that is, botany and physiology), sculpture, and theater. These suggestions are neither final nor definitive, although their interdisciplinary width makes them especially attractive. Properly structured and taught, they would be the filter through which all of the "subjects" now in the curriculum would be introduced. Before I attempt to justify the significance of these approaches to a new curriculum, I offer the following commentary on the importance of a cultural pedagogy, by which I mean the common source of our personal expectations, sensibilities, and evaluations.

Pedagogy is hapless and empty if it does not face directly the deep and pervasive dialectic between the historical and genetic conditioning of the person on the one hand and the impress of the novelties of the physical and social world on the other hand. This confrontation between our human heritage and the world in which we find ourselves is the stuff out of which we weave that fragile creature we call our very own self. The key to a successful mapping of this conflictual terrain is the making of relations, that is, the forging of a distinctively personal presence in the doings and undergoings which constitute our experience. The making of relations is a lifelong endeavor, but it is especially crucial in the lives of children, as they struggle to achieve self-consciousness in a vast, complex, and initially undefined environment. Helping our children to learn how to make relations is the central and most important task of pedagogy. To the extent that they do not learn to make their own relations, children are doomed to living secondhand lives. They become creatures of habituation who merely follow out the already programmed versions of their experience as inherited from parents, older siblings, and self-appointed definers of reality such as teachers. Ironically, a child who knows how to make relations can convert even authoritarian and repressive treatment into paths of personal liberation, whereas a child who does not make relations converts invitations to free inquiry into derivative and bland repetition. This irony is made vivid for us when we realize that most often the lives of those whom we regard as "great" are characterized by affliction, suffering, and frequent rejection. In the hands of those who can make and remake relations, even negative events become the nutrition for a creative life.

Just what is it for a child to make relations and why do I regard it as crucial to a humanistic pedagogy? First, we must dispel any naiveté about the allegedly virginal character of the emerging self. The profound and complex preconscious conditioning of the self is a fact of our time. Modern sociology, with its roots in the thought of George Herbert Mead, stresses the social origins of the self, holding that without the me, the socially derived "generalized other," there would be no I. Modern psychology, with its roots in Freud and Jung, stresses the irreducible presence and power of our unconscious. Or conversely, modern psychology, here following B. F. Skinner, holds that we are totally conditioned by the operant impress of external stimuli. The sociology of knowledge founded by Karl Marx contends that our consciousness, far from being original, is derivative of institutions. For Marx, "institutions" referred to church, state, family, and money, whereas recent thought adds gender, race, ethnicity, language, climate, and region as initiating boxes from which we never really escape.

It is now culturally obvious that as we come to self-consciousness in our early years we are playing out our inherited genetic and social trappings. None of us can ignore the conditioning power of this inheritance. The existence of a pristine self, free of the entangling alliances of one's genetic and social past, is a myth. To be born white or black, male or female, Irish or Jewish, is an inherited context as thick as the earth itself. To experience one's postnatal years in the city or on a farm, in the snow or in the desert, is an informing crucible that our consciousness can repress but never totally dismiss. One could multiply these inheritances indefinitely, and a diagnosis of their significance in the lives of children could become a rich source of self-awareness as well as of awareness of others by contrast. In fact, these diagnoses would be the beginning of the child's self-understanding and the beginning of the child's attempt to build a new, distinctively personal world.

My point here is that the only way to obviate the deleterious second-handedness of our inherited trappings is to bring them to the fore and diagnose them as to their richness, their narrowness, and the role they play in our assumptions. Under careful and probing guidance, even very young children are capable of fleshing out their distinctive sense of time, space, place, size, color, tone, and ever more subtle ambiences of the world in which they "find" themselves. In this way, the inheritances are transformed from conceptual boxes, in which the child is unknowingly encased, to perceptual fields fit for romping and reconstructing in the light of present experiences. This is precisely what I mean by the making of relations, namely, taking these inherited conditionings and turning them from conceptual rocks into something more diaphanous, crossed and recrossed with variant images, attitudes, and styles. There is nothing arcane in this, for children, despite their inheritances, seek novelty naturally, unless they are prevented by a pedagogy which attempts to reduce all of their experiences to a common denominator. For example, just recently, a teacher was queried in a newspaper article as to how she would begin her teaching after the children returned from their Hanukkah/Christmas holiday. She replied that if they insisted, they could take a "few minutes" to say what they did during that time, but then it would be "back to the routine." One can hardly dignify this approach as educational, for the classroom is a morgue and the children are cadavers, passive witnesses to an anatomical dissection on behalf of a fixed curriculum.

Is not this the time to assist in the conversion of the children's ordinary reportage of these remarkable events, celebrated for two millennia, into something extraordinary and within their reach? Is not this the time to read them O. Henry's "Gift of the Magi" and appropriate selections from the *Diary of Anne Frank*? Is not this the time to introduce them to Ramadan, the holy period of Islam, and then to contrast Judaism, Christianity, and Islam with Buddhism and Hinduism? Is not this the time to assist the children in leaping upon an experience about to be had and/or undergone so that they may open it up and reach out to neighboring experiences, both similar and starkly different? It is necessary for one to have experience if one is to make relations and create a personal world, tied to others, but yet distinctive. To have experience without making relations, especially of dissimilarity, is to be left with the inert, repetitious, and routine.

Like William James, I too believe that experience grows by its edges.[4] By nature, the child comes into the world on edge, on the *qui vive,* with a penchant for making relations. Traditional education, however, seems perversely determined to block this run of the imagination, opting rather for a world made up of boxes, separate one from the other, each defined and named, impervious to the rash of potential relations that yield themselves only to the reflection born of experienced perception. Is it not long overdue that contemporary educational practices integrate the accrued wisdom of this century and come to realize that names, categories, schema, and definitions are but functional placeholders in our experiencing the flow of events, linked to each other in a myriad of ways? With the exception of speculative mathematics and formal logic, percepts should reign over concepts. Definitions should never be taken to exhaust the meaning, texture, tone, or implication of that defined. Ambiguity should be restored to its proper place as the proper response in direct proportion to the importance of the experience undergone. Love and loyalty, for example, are exquisitely ambiguous; no amount of quantitative social science methodology can clarify them sufficiently, such that they become fully understood or manipulable.

I have no objection to the proper utilization of quantitative methodology, and I am aware of the necessity of scientific rigor. Similarly, I endorse the importance of high technology and the utilization of the computer in the attainment of ever more sophisticated and accurate access to data. No, my concern is quite different. I lament the suffusion of the elementary and secondary school curriculum with disciplines and approaches whose major task is to prepare students for successful functioning in an ostensibly high-tech future, as though such activity was to be the primary activity of a human life. If we are to survive as an originating human culture, we cannot view the reflective awareness of our past, the extensive knowledge of other cultures and other languages, literature, the arts, and speculative science as activities merely desirable but actually peripheral to the more important task of "getting along" in the future. This approach may enable us to survive as a nation, that is, as the saying goes, to hold our own. On the other hand, we shall become spiritually bankrupt.

As an antidote to the drift away from having the humanities as the centerpiece of public elementary and secondary school education, I offer that we should make use of four curricular modules: autobiography/biography, the science of living things (botany and physiology), sculpture, and theater. My justification is as follows:

AUTOBIOGRAPHY/BIOGRAPHY

How are young persons to find a wedge into the tissue of experience in a way which transcends the narrowness of their own ego development? One way, of course, is to be driven by an event, either magnificent or disastrous. Such events are rare in our lives and even they become meaningful only in proportion to our reflective awareness of their significance. A second possibility exists, less intense but more available. I refer here to the way in which we can be carried beyond our immediate ken by participating in the recorded lives of the many startling and creative persons in our collective lineage. Think, for example, how extraordinarily rich is the prose and the historical content of the life and death of Socrates, as written by Plato. Here we introduce the student to a raft of central concerns: classical Greek culture, philosophy, religion, ethics, politics, and finally the important and profound question of our death, as raised in the discussion as to whether Socrates committed suicide. Equal wisdom is to be gained from the life of Thomas Jefferson, who also introduces us to architecture and to his deep feeling for the land, on behalf of an agrarian ethic. The meaning of courage and indomitability in the face of adversity is brought to our consciousness by the study of the lives of Queen Elizabeth or Joan of Arc. Virtually every human characteristic and every cultural and intellectual movement is represented by one or more biographies and autobiographies. Through this medium, we have access to the achievements and the plight of every race, region, ethnic group, religion, and cultural persuasion. And we need not confine our materials to happy endings, for we have much more to learn from the slave narratives and from the stories of survivors of the Holocaust, the Gulag, and Hiroshima. I do not see the study of biography and autobiography as a replacement for systematic study. Rather I view it as propaedeutic and an accompaniment. The plaintive cry "Why do I have to study physics?" is not well met by the stock reply "Someday you will use it." Far better to study the life of Newton and Heisenberg and develop a hunger for the activities of physics.

The biographies of the famous, the great, and the notorious are an obvious way to have students begin to understand the multiplicity of cultures and life experiences, which then cast light on their own lives. Equally important are the reported lives of those persons who are comparatively unsung or known only for their prowess in a limited area or for a single accomplishment. Their stories do not have a fabled backdrop, but the human quotient may be even closer to the experiences of the students. Of special value may be the lives of the totally unknown, as pieced together from diaries and letters found posthumously. In 1963 and 1967, I traveled with our five children across America, some 40,000 miles in and out of every continental state. One of the most moving sets of experiences resulted from our indefatigable effort to stop at hundreds of local museums throughout the country. In those modest buildings, on those modest streets, we found the letters and diaries of the founders: men, women, and children. Beautifully written both in prose and in penmanship, belying the fact that their formal education, mostly in the nineteenth century, was limited in scope and time, these documents evoked a sense of the past, of human misery and triumph equal to the legendary figures we celebrate. It is of importance to note that the beauty of the style and the depth of feeling in these documents is accompanied by a simplicity of access. They can be read by children without difficulty. I think of the letters of the people of the former whaling communities of Sag Harbor and Cold Spring Harbor on Long Island. I think of the letters of the settlers in Texas and Minnesota and Colorado. For every Lewis and Clark, for every Daniel Boone, there are hundreds of people like you and me who wrote of their experience in a moving and telling way.

In addition to the students bathing in the reflective waters of the experience of others, ordinary as well as extraordinary, the pedagogical task is to urge them to keep their own diaries and to save their letters. The suggestion of keeping a diary at a young age is often met with an embarrassed incredulity. The responsive refrain is often in the plaintive vein of "Who, me?" or "Who would care?" Perhaps no one would care. Perhaps someone would care. Perhaps many would care. The significance of the diary does not depend on these future possibilities. Rather, the writing of a diary, influenced by the reading of others' lives, provides the student with a private landscape for self-diagnosis and for the integration of the past with the present. The diary will provide the glare of self-examination. The prose will improve and the life of the student will be privately exposed to the twin canons of evaluation: the niggardliness of the everyday and the occasional breakthrough or conquest. The personal importance of the student's diary will not achieve the significance of the spotlight cast upon the *Meditations* of Marcus Aurelius, but the rhythm of a life will be notably similar.

THE SCIENCE OF LIVING THINGS

Despite our many differences, one from the other, creature from creature, we share a rich and incontrovertible common bequest, that of being a live creature. The plants, the animals, and human beings are living things. (Some say the stars are as well, but we shall leave that discussion for another time.) With the exception of those few who believe in pan-psychism, an intriguing although as yet unverified hypothesis, most people accept the distinction between the organic and the inorganic as funda-mental to any understanding of reality. The science of living things would introduce the student to the life and death cycles of plants, vegetation, insects, animals, and human beings. Ideally, this should involve both lab-oratory and field work. The task here is not only to introduce the student to the names and functions of organisms, but also to stress the dramatic sharing and conflict that is a permanent characteristic of living. It is easy to replicate the life and death cycle of vegetation, plants, insects, and small animals in a classroom setting. Objections to the existence of these living things in the classroom are often bureaucratically self-serving, because of alleged inconvenience. The death of a geranium or a hamster, especially one giving birth, provides an unending and, ironically, fertile source for the exploration of the most important event in our lives, our own death.

Moving to the human organism, considerable time should be given to the liver and the brain, organs which are masterpieces of perturbation, consummation, and messaging. The rhythms of setback and recovery are salient characteristics of these organs. The liver, for example, nicely and appropriately named in English, has as its obligation the managing of more than 500 activities, each essential not only to human well-being, but to life itself.[5] I am reminded of the ancient text from the Book of Ezekiel (21:21): "For the King of Babylon stood at the parting of the way, at the head of the two ways, to use divination: he made his arrows bright, he con-sulted with images, he looked in the liver." And from the Greek doctrine of the four humors, through the medieval period and into Shakespeare's time, the amount of liver bile was thought to have a direct bearing on a person's temperament. Modern medical science has abandoned these anthropomorphic versions of the liver, yet the urgency and centrality of its function still hold. A biochemical marvel, the human liver is a sorter, a dis-patcher, a condemner, a welcomer, and the arbiter of what stays in our body and what leaves. In short, the human liver is a supreme maker of rela-tions, our biological brain. Its malfunction is our serious illness. Its death is our death. For the children, the obvious fallout of this study of the liver, as well as of the brain and of the kidneys, each a maker of relations, is an awareness of the simultaneous power and fragility of the human body, a dialectic which is repeated in our religious, ethical, social, psychological, and imaginative transaction with the world.

SCULPTURE

What the liver is to the inner world of our bodies, the hands are to the outer world in which we live out our lives. Different from fish and from snakes, we are prehensile creatures. With our hands we touch, we grab, we hold, we push, and we pull. More subtly we caress, we knead, we feel, and with our hands, we make sounds and things and signs. Our hands are the major way in which we penetrate the world, seeking to learn its texture and occasionally seeking to remake the world in our image, be it a representation, fantasy, or an original construct. It is with our hands that we touch and care for the most intimate and private parts of our bodies and, as adults, care for the bodies of those we love. Our hands enable the violin and the piano to yield their enchanting sounds. Our hands enable us to write and type the messagings of our person. Our hands go still only in our sleep or at our death. It is well known that the most human and "living" aspect of a human cadaver is the hand; the fingers are crooked over the palms, seemingly clinging to life when all else has failed.

In this vast variety of activities of the hand, the most distinctive and powerful version is to be found when we sculpt. In so doing, we render the external world in our own image. No matter what the material, we can fashion it into shapes and contours which bespeak the press of our desire to build a world that is singular and original. Pedagogically, the intention is to have the student create his or her own imaginative image of the world, experiencing deeply the extension of human intimacy, the hands, into the obduracy of materials. Accompanying this creative and managing activity would be research into the textual makeup and history of the materials utilized. Each student would provide analysis of the materials to be used, and share this information with the others; the result would be a common apprisal of the history and texture of cloth, paper, clay, plastics, woods, and metals. Shared too would be the range of skills necessary to an effective managing of these materials, such as carpentry, welding, the use of a kiln, and an array of decorative abilities. Salutary as well would be the collapsing of the pernicious distinctions between the fine arts, the practical arts, and the industrial arts. Sculpture is remarkable precisely for its capacity to integrate every conceivable human way that we have to effect a change in the nature of the material before us, in effect, to make something undreamt of in nature.

In addition to the mastery of technique and the understanding of the potentialities and limitations in the nature of materials, the making of sculpture offers students an excellent opportunity to forge relationships between themselves and the world in a personal and imaginative medium. On the basis of my experience with this approach to learning, I have no doubt that the results will range from the obvious to the surreal and from the beautiful to the grotesque, thus bequeathing a mirror image of the dazzling, albeit too often hidden, plurality as potential to human creative activity. In time, these sculptures will be in every classroom, in homes, and perhaps even in public places. In this way, the community will relive its own fantasies, histories, and personal perspectives through the hands of its children.

THEATER

The last of our suggested curricular modules is that of theater. Of all the ways to educate, theater is the most demanding and complex, both in preparation and execution. The rewards in learning and experience, however, more than justify the effort. Basically, we can either select our source of theater as pedagogy from plays already written and performed, or we can have the writing of the play as part of the activity.[6] Each option has its advantages. The former provides the students with a play that has been evaluated and represents approved wisdom, style, and dramatic effect. All of the details necessary to staging are provided, so that the students can concentrate on effecting a successful production. I would suggest several attempts at utilizing already written and produced plays before trying to write an original script, since starting from scratch would probably not produce the quality of plays already extant. Still, the advantages here are considerable. Learning to write dialogue, developing a plot, generating believable characters, and setting out the specifications for stage directions are all extraordinarily valuable in teaching students how to write and how to set up a human world. It would be especially valuable if the development of the script could be done in concert, thereby introducing the students to an ongoing and shared community of inquiry by which they as generational peers would evolve their view of the world, its values, and its pitfalls.

Whichever of the above two methods is followed, the pedagogical rewards are considerable. First, theater is contextual; it is set somewhere. The setting may be ancient Greece as in the *Agamemnon* of Aeschylus or in

England during the late medieval age of the history plays of Shakespeare. Or, the setting could be more modest, say Willy Loman's unbecoming home in New York and a small hotel room in Boston, as found in Arthur Miller's *Death of a Salesman*. Additional sites abound: airplanes, farms, ghettoes, ships, war sites, mountains, and even totally imaginative sites such as alien planets. Whatever the site, the pedagogical bequest is that the students must enter a world other than their own. Costume, jargon, climate, and an endless set of cultural assumptions will differ from theirs. By virtue of participating in a theatrical presentation of this other world, they would be forced, by contrast, to sharpen their experience of their own world while avoiding the subtle danger of habituation and repetition.

A second positive result of the pedagogy of theater results from the preparation of the play. Ideally, all of the ingredients necessary to the production should be made by the students. Lighting, costumes, scenery, and other appurtenances also should be the responsibility of the students. As with sculpture, this responsibility will bring together the fine arts and the applied arts. As an example of this merging of disciplines and technical skill, take the problem of costumes. They should not be obtained ready-made but rather should be made by the students. What, then, is a toga? Of what material was it made? How did it fit? Were they all identical? What of those worn by a male, female, slave, free person, citizen, or child? And did the dress differ by the time of the day, the year, the season, or cere-monial occasion? Equally tantalizing is the nature and history of footwear, undergarments, and personal weaponry. This historical research is only the first step, for when the knowledge of "what" was worn "when" and "why" is attained, the students must then attend to "how" it was made and make it themselves.

One could go further and have the students make the technology, how-ever primitive, which made the clothing and utensils of other, earlier cul-tures. Not only will this provide a deep and lasting insight to the ingenuity and steadfastness of the children's forebears, it also will cast a light of appreciation and even marvel on the achievements of contemporary tech-nology. Two anecdotes will illustrate this point. At the end of the nine-teenth century, John and Alice Dewey founded a laboratory school for children. One of the exercises was to bring in a bushel of raw cotton plants and have the children pick the cotton and prepare it for processing. After a day of this, they barely had enough cotton for a pair of socks, and their untutored hands were sore and abrased. The children were then introduced to Eli Whitney and the invention of the cotton gin. The second anecdote comes firsthand. When our son Brian was in the fourth grade, his public school teacher devoted a major part of the year to having the class build a replica of the Mercury capsule, launched just a year earlier. The children read articles on aerodynamics, the mysteries of space, and were taught the elementary physics of this astonishing phenomenon. They did all the carpentry and other material preparation. The capsule grew, imposing, dazzling, and mysterious, although accessible to its creators. It stood in the center of the classroom and each day took on portentous stature as it neared completion. For our son, now a secondary school teacher of the industrial arts and a master carpenter, the experience in the fourth grade was incomparably the richest of his eighteen years of schooling. Depressingly, although not surprisingly, this story has a bitter ending. Despite the protests of irate parents, our fourth-grade teacher was fired at the end of that memorable year. It seems that he did not complete the fourth-grade syllabus.

A third reason for introducing the pedagogy of theater as a central module in our curriculum is the reenforcement of effort and experience by doing the play for an audience, either student peers or perhaps parents and relatives. The best of these dramatic productions could even be shared with the community at large. As a medium, theater surpasses the symphonic concert and even cinema in its ability to draw the audience out of its consciousness and into a different and often novel setting. The legendary excitement of the "opening" is deserved, for the footlights are just that, lights which illuminate the walking of an audience into the lives of others. Theater is rhetorically and scenically embracing. Song and dance are infinitely more alive and captivating when they are aspects of theater; hence the power of opera and ballet. The most ordinary of plots and banal of prose turn into excitement in the context of music and song, as when the libretto of *La Bohème* is rendered operatically by Puccini. The simplest of tales rise from their obviousness when Tchaikovsky offers us the ballets *Swan Lake* and *The Sleeping Beauty*. Even the dramatic starkness of Thornton Wilder's *Our Town* draws the audience into its environment and then back again to their own consciousness for a nostalgic rumination on their childhood. To create theater is not only to create a human world. It is to create so that others, the audience, can participate, can share, and can enter into the process. No other medium, no other art form, no other human activity, can make relations in so many ways, so expansively, so extensively, so multiple in style and theory and artifact, so subtle, so explosive, so clear, so ambiguous, so deft, so explicit, and so rich in implication. If I am correct in this assessment, then our children must have the opportunity to develop these theatrical skills, attitudes, abilities, failures, and successes from their preschool years through their adult life.

I do not have an idée fixe on these four modules for a revised precollegiate curriculum. Other possibilities come to mind: archaeology, pathology, dance, and comparative anthropology, to cite some of many. Frankly, they and others seem absorbable and able to be taught within the imaginative pedagogical approach to autobiography/biography, the science of living things, sculpture, and theater. Actually, adjustments to these curricular suggestions and even replacements are not destructive to the above discussion, so long as we remember that the irreducible task of pedagogy is to help others to make relations, such that the deepest recesses of personal privacy transact with human others, with an external world, and with the images gleaned from a storied and even repressed past. In this way we build our world. It is a world borrowed, stolen, hidden from others, shared, lamented, celebrated, and occasionally a result of personal triumph.

Surely in a nation ostensibly committed to excellence and to equality, we cannot afford to deprive our children of access to the wisdom of the past and to the stirring and value-laden modalities and media of the arts and the humanities. They have every right to be taught how to write, listen, read, and speak with a deep understanding of our full cultural heritage. The computer, in the end, will be only as meaningful as the quality of our input. If we render generation after generation culturally deaf and dumb, the rising spires of high technology will be but a contemporary parallel to the Tower of Babel.

13 Glass without Feet

DIMENSIONS OF URBAN AESTHETICS

Some time last year I made my way to the area adjoining the Galleria in the imposing new outer city of Houston. Entering one of the more formidable glass towers so as to experience its inside, I was stopped by a security guard who asked me if I had an appointment with anyone in the building. I replied that my appointment was with the building—to see if it had a soul and was open to the presence of personal space. He tossed me out. I went looking for a newspaper, a sandwich, a personal opening to these jutting edifices of technological supremacy. No luck! No kiosk! No paper! No sandwich! No body! No place! Just a marvel of impersonal use of space. Consequently, no personscape.

I. COMING TO CONSCIOUSNESS

Far from offering solid, impermeable barriers to the natural environment, [the building's] outer surfaces come more and more closely to resemble permeable membranes which can accept or reject any environmental force. Again, the uterine analogy; and not accidentally, for with such convertibility in the container's walls, man can modulate the play of environmental forces upon himself and his processes, to guarantee their uninterrupted development, in very much the same way as the mother's body protects the embryo. . . .

JAMES MARSTON FITCH [1]

The human body is neither a container nor a box in a world of boxes. To the contrary, our bodies are present in the world as diaphanous and permeable. The world, in its activity as the affairs of nature and the affairs of things, penetrates us by flooding our consciousness, our skin, and our liver with the press of the environment. We respond with our marvelous capacity to arrange, relate, reject and, above all, symbolize these transactions. In effect, we as humans, and only we, give the world its meaning. Even as embryos in the comparatively closed environment of our mother's womb, we are open to the experience of the other. The quality of the other and how we transact with the other constitutes our very being as human. Let us diagnose some of these transactions in general terms and then specify our relationship to the world as natural and to the world as artifact, as human-made, that is, as urban.

For the human organism, coming to full consciousness is an exquisitely subtle phenomenon. We are always enveloped by the climate, known in America as "the weather." We weather the world and the world weathers us. Except for the occasional outrageous performances of nature such as typhoons, hurricanes, earthquakes, and tornadoes, our experience of the weather is largely inchoate, that is, subliminally conscious. Unfortunately, inchoate also is our experience of most things, doings, happenings, events, and even creatures. I say that this is unfortunate because our tendency to categorize, name, and box the affairs of the world signifies a drastic decline from the alert consciousness of environment which characterized our young childhood.

The most telling way to realize how little we actually experience that which takes place within the range of our bodies is to focus on the very young child. For children, the world comes, as William James suggests, as a buzzing and blooming continuity. The nefarious dualisms between color and shape, past and present, even between organic and inorganic, are foreign to the child, who has an extraordinary capacity to experience relations, that webbing which holds the multiple messages of the environment in an organic whole.[2] Despite the ongoing richness of the child's experience of the world, adults quickly strike back. They have long been conditioned to see the world as disparate, each thing and event complete unto itself, each with an appropriate name tag courtesy of the fixed categories of Aristotle, Euclid, and linguistic syntax. The children soon yield and, like the rest of us, sink into the oblivion of the obvious. The occasional poets rise above this sameness of description, but their special place only reenforces the jejune character of how we feel and describe the world in which we find ourselves.

Allow me to offer a way out of this Platonic cave, in which we so often languish, cut off from the teeming richness so potentially present in our experience. Returning to the uterine analogy, I prefer us to experience the world as if we were in a permeable sheath rather than trapped in a linguistic condom. If we listen to the wisdom of the Greek and Roman stoic philosophers, then we know that the world speaks to us from the very depths of being. The *logos*, the word, the utterance, is meant for us if we but listen, feel, touch, see, and allow ourselves to be open to the novelty, originality, and freshness that is endemic to experience. Openness to experience is crucial, by which I mean that we allow our perceptions a full run before we slap on the defining, naming, locating tags of place, thing, and object. Coming to consciousness in this way allows us to be bathed by a myriad of impressions, each of them too rich for the task of organization, a task which should follow far behind, gathering only the husks, the leftover from what we have undergone in a personal and symbolic way.

All experience counts and counts to the end of our days. This includes the salamander who lives on my porch and dazzles me with its change of skin color; the forgotten rake which leaps up in the melting of an April snow; those lovely Georgian doors that front the row houses in Dublin city; Brahman bulls with human visage; the Irish setter on its haunches, nose poised to spring in response to the advance of an impinging world; the great Gretzky streaking the ice and the soaring of the marvelous Dr. J.; or, more profoundly and demanding, the crippled seventy-year-old mother who, upon learning of the impending death of her incontinent, cystic fibrosis, totally retarded forty-eight-year-old daughter, cries out in anguish, "Not my baby, not my baby!"

Boredom and ennui are signs of a living death. In that the only time we have is the time we have, they are inexcusable faults. Sadness and even alienation, given our personal and collective miseries, are proper responses, especially attenuated as they can be by occasional joy and celebration. Coming to consciousness has nothing to do with the traditional pursuit of happiness, an attempt illusory and self-deceiving for a human organism whose denouement is the inevitability of death without redemption. Rather, the signal importance of how we come to consciousness is precisely that such a process is all we are, all we have, and all we shall ever be.

The world appears to us as given, yet we knead it to our own image, for better and for worse. As we slowly awake to our environment, to our cosmic and planetary womb, we soon find that the more local arrangements are the ones which formulate how we come to know and feel ourselves. In American culture, one of the most prepossessing of these local contexts for consciousness is the dialectic between nature, on the one hand, and artifacts, especially those supreme artifacts, cities, on the other hand. Two hands, but one consciousness. Two hands, but one nation. For Americans, the experience of nature and city has been both actual and mythic, depending on the site in which a person came to consciousness. The difference between the experience of nature as primary and the experience of city as primary is not one between good and bad or positive and negative. It is, however, a difference which has important ramifications for our evaluation of the kind of environment we should seek to build and for a host of allied personal concerns, values, preferences, and attitudes. If nature is the environment we inherit and city is the environment we build, what then is the ideal relationship between them? What does nature teach us that we need to maintain if we are to remain human as we make an abode, a human place in which many of us live together? Further, what does the history of cities teach us about what we have discovered to be distinctively human and propitious in that which we have made for ourselves, undreamt by nature or by the animals or by the insects?

II. NATURE AND CITY

As in all such general terms of description, nature and city[3] are herein used with a specific cultural context in mind: that of North America. We have before our consciousness Boston and the Berkshire mountains; Chicago and Lake Michigan; Denver and the Rocky mountains; San Francisco and its Bay; Miami and the Everglades; Missoula and the Lolo Pass; Houston and West Texas; the ocean cities, the river cities, the cities of the plains; and, of course, those dots of nostalgia from the event-saturated past as we traversed the land—North Zulch, Snook, and Old Dime Box, those representative Texas fables.

In American terms, nature was always writ large. The history of the meaning of nature for America is as old as our first settlements and as central to the meaning of America as is our vaunted political history. The stark generalization is that nature took the place of the Bible as the script by which Americans searched for the signs of conversion. How shall we know when we have been saved? This was the plaintive and genuine question most prominent on the lips and in the heart of the early American Puritans. Faced as they were, however, with an environment deeply forbidding and foreboding, as well as lushly promising, they soon began to equate their

justification with their ability to bring nature to its knees and celebrate Zion in the Wilderness. Witness this revealing 1697 text from the
"Phaenomena" of Samuel Sewall:

> As long as nature shall not grow old and dote but shall constantly remember to
> give the rows of Indian Corn their education, by Pairs: So long shall Christians
> be born there; and being first made meet, shall from thence be Translated, to be
> made partakers of the Inheritance of the Saints in Light.[4]

As the American eighteenth century opened, the fixed meeting houses of
the Congregationalists and Presbyterians were slowly but inevitably being
replaced by the itinerant preaching of the Baptists and the Methodists.
America was on the move! Nature was calling; the West was calling. First,
the Berkshires, then the Alleghenies, the Appalachians, western Connecti-
cut, western Virginia, Kentucky, the Northwest Territory, the Mississippi,
the pony express to California, the Mormon trek, Texas, and—as late as
1907—the emergence of Oklahoma. This 200-year history of frontier conflict, frontier conquest, and frontier failure became the central theme of
American consciousness, lived in the "West" in nature, and vicariously
lived in the "East" in the cities which always "trailed" behind, as redoubts,
points of departure. It is essential to realize that the public story of the
American odyssey was played out in the clutches of nature, at war with
nature's children, the American Indians, and at war, internally, on the
land, about the land, for the control of the land.

To the West they wend. To the West is to be free. To the West meant
simply to leave the city, wherever it might be, and chase the setting of the
sun. This is why California, despite its protracted adolescence, symbolizes
the end of continental America.[5] And this also is why Texas still retains its
mythic value, for Texas is endless, large, vast, and still provides the scape
for disappearance into the land and the chance to start over. Further, this is
why Americans are wary of cities, often seeing them as vulgar necessities
and as interruptions in the natural flow of persons in nature. The public
voice of America tells us that cities are places to go, to sin, to buy, to
sell—in short, to visit. The utter unreality of this judgment, given that 90
percent of all Americans live on but 10 percent of the land, points to the inordinate power of our long-standing romance with nature, especially as it
is biblically sanctioned and artistically recreated in story and film. This
tradition confirms our indigenous belief that mobility, exodus, change of

place, are necessary for salvation. Is it any wonder, then, that despite the presence of historical monuments and grandiloquent architectural sorties, we build our cities not as habitats for persons but rather as pens for those waiting to leave, to leave for the land where, allegedly, human beings truly belong.

III. THE SPACE AND TIME OF NATURE AND CITY

The most dramatic and long-lasting influences on a person coming to consciousness are their senses of space and of time. What could be more different for me as a person, than if I came to believe that I was in space as one creature among others, all of us with space to spare, rather than if I came to believe that no space was present for me unless I seized it and made it my own space, that is, my place? What could be more different for me as a person, than if I believed that time was seasonal, repetitive, and allowed for reconnoitering over the same experienced ground again and again, rather than if I believed that time was by the clock, measured in hours, minutes, and even in rapidly disappearing seconds? The difference between the space and time of nature and the space and time of cities has its most important impact on our perceptions of the environment, sufficient to generate a very different experience of ourselves, our bodies, our memory, and our creative life.

The affairs of nature are inexorable. Even the intrusions, such as drought and tornadoes, follow the larger natural forces. Although spawned elsewhere, they occur periodically, loyal to conditions routinely present in nature. Cities, however, have no correlate to the seventeen-year cycle of the appearance of the cicada. Nature space is spacious, with room for recovery, for redemption, for second and third chances. Vision in the space of nature is predominately horizontal, as though a person were on permanent lookout. The plains and the desert afford us an extraordinary visual reach, a field for our eyes to play upon, as in an endless cavorting through space with nothing definite, no things to obtrude. Still more powerful is the heightened sense of distance given to us from our mountain perch. This horizontality passes over the billions upon billions of individual items present in nature space, those of the flora, the fauna, and the living creatures of the soil and sky. But the very vastness of nature space requires a special attention, a special ability to grasp and relate the presence of the particulars. Thus, persons of nature space are homemade botanists, entomologists, ichthyologists, and animal scientists, constantly aware of variations which await the patient observer of what only seems to be stretches of sameness. For city dwellers, this potential richness of nature space is missed, for they have been schooled to confront the obvious in their experience, multiple sounds, objects, things, and events—all up front and requiring no search. Actually, persons of city consciousness often find the virtually endless sky of nature space, as in Montana and Texas, to be claustrophobic. This situation is obviously paradoxical but it is instructive. When a person experiences so vast a distance, a sky so wide that the eye reaches out endlessly with no end in sight and no grasp of the subtle particulars of shadow, cloud, and terrain, then that person shrinks back in an introverted, hovering manner, alone and fearful. The claustrophobia of open space for the person of urban consciousness is precisely the opposite of the experience of persons of nature consciousness, whose claustrophobia erupts when they first find themselves adrift in a teeming city street, cut off from sky and horizon by glass canyons.

The time of nature space is likewise special. I call it fat time, for it is measurable by seasons, even by decades. The shortest time in nature time is that of sun time and moon time, both of which are larger by far than the hurried ticks of clock time, so omnipresent in cities. Nature time is also consonant with body time, a rhythm akin to the natural processes of the physiology of the human organism. This rhythm is present in the daily transformation of night into day and then into night once more, just as our bodies sleep, wake, and sleep once more. These events mirror exactly the nutrition cycle in our bodies and more poignantly, more naturally, they are microcosmic instances of the life and death of crops, insects, the leaves of the trees and, on a larger scale, our own life, whose rhythm, like that of nature, turns over in a century.

If we are properly attuned, nature time, like nature space, affords an abode for a distinctively human marriage between the body and the affairs of the environment. Being in and of nature, then, seems to make sense. Yet not by matched rhythm alone doth we live. The human organism, on an even deeper personal terrain, historically and culturally has expressed a need to develop an interior life, singular and independent of the external world. For the most part, this possibility is absent in the time and space framework of nature. I see the result of this absence as twofold; first, a quiet yet present sense of personal loneliness and even alienation pervades much of the lives of nature persons; second, in response to that situation, from the beginning of humankind, we have abandoned the rightness of nature for us and huddled together by building cities. The great American philosopher Ralph Waldo Emerson, no lover of cities and a master delineator of the majesty of nature, writes:

> We learn nothing rightly until we learn the symbolical character of life. Day creeps after day, each full of facts, dull, strange, despised things, that we cannot enough despise—call heavy, prosaic and desert. The time we seek to kill: the attention it is elegant to divert from things around us. And presently the aroused intellect finds gold and gems in one of these scorned facts—then finds that the day of facts is a rock of diamonds; that a fact is an Epiphany of God.[6]

It is this "aroused intellect" which is at work in the building and maintaining of cities, a homemade environment which demands human symbolization for purposes of survival. The space of city space is vertical rather than horizontal. The sky fades into anonymity, replaced by the artifactual materials of wood, concrete, mortar, steel, and glass, each married to the other in an upward spiral of massive presence and extensive height. Yet the massiveness and the height, even in the great towers of the John Hancock building in Boston, the Sears Tower in Chicago, and the twins of the World Trade Center in New York City, are human scale, for by our hands and by the technological extension of our hands we built them. They belong to us, they are our creation. The mountains, the great lakes, the rivers, the desert, belong to someone, somewhere, somehow, someway, somewhen else. They have mystery and distance from our hands. City space is not found space nor space in which we wander. Nor is it space that fulfills the needs of our body, understood physiologically. Those, rather, are the conditions of the space of nature. Quite to the contrary, city space is space seized, made space, wrestled to a place, our place, a human place. A building is a clot, a clamp, a signature in the otherwise awesome, endless reach of nature space. City space as human place is rife with alcoves, alleys, streets, corners, backs and fronts, basements, tunnels, bridges, and millions of windows which look out on other windows. This introverting character of city space is the source of human interiority. The reach of vision is short-circuited by the obtrusion of objects, impermeable, stolid, and in need of symbolic regathering. Bus stations, train stations, cafeterias, urban department stores, pawnbrokers, betting parlors, Ticketrons, stadia, bars, courthouses, jails, hospitals, and innumerable other "places" gather us in a riot of interpersonal intensity. These spaces, once they become places, colonize space with an intensity and a personal messaging which defy their comparatively small size, for they multiply meaning independent of both physics and geometry. These city places are spiritual places, transcending the body as a thing in space. City space is person-centered and symbolically rich. The accusation of anonymity as lodged against urban life is a myth of nature dwellers. Cities are fabrics, woven neighborhoods, woven covenants, each integral and thick in personal exchange, yet each siding up to the other, so as to knit a concatenated, webbed, seamed, and organic whole. If the truth be told, the capacity of genuine urban dwellers—as distinct from visitors, transients, or those on the make so they can return to the land—constitutes a most remarkable phenomenon in human history. The history of the city is a history of human organisms, ostensibly fit for nature, rendering the artifactual affectionate, sentimental, warm, and symbolically pregnant.

The mountains, rivers, streams, lakes, oceans, insects, animals, plants, stars all belong to nature. But the buildings, trolleys, depots, museums, and Hyatt Regencies belong to us. They are human versions of nature, found, so far as we know, in no other planet, in no other place, for there is no other place which is human place, our place. Emerson praises this human capacity to render the activities and things of the world as more than they be, as simply taken or simply had. With Emerson the task is to use our "power of imagination" so as to clothe the world of the everyday with immortality, else we become dead to ourselves.[7]

The activities which make a city out of nature, converting it to artifacts with distinctive human significance, function, and symbol, are characteristic of a millennia-long effort at transubstantiation, the effort to render nature an abode for human life in its liturgy, its interpersonal transactions, and its artistic creations. The space of nature is aesthetically rich but it is never art unless rendered so by human ways. City space is artifact supreme, the most extensive, detailed, multimedia human creation in the history of what we do to nature, rather than our simply being in nature.

The time of city time also reverses that of nature. City time is thin time, transparent time, the experience of virtual instantaneity. Ruled by the clock rather than by the sun, city time measures out our experience in short bursts, such that we place ourselves under enormous pressure to make every minute count. City time seems to have no attendant space, no room to move around and idly look ahead. To exist sanely in city time requires that we build an inner life, an introspective fortress in which we can reflectively lounge impervious to the din accompanying rapid time passing. Despite the rush of events and the multiplicity of persons transacting in an infinite number of ways, city persons soon develop a sense of privacy which they carry deep within them, even in the midst of public urban clamor. It is not ironic but rather fitting that America's most distinctive game, baseball, is usually played on a sylvan field smack in the middle of the city. It is a nature game, defying time, which has no permanent role to play, for a baseball game can be tied to infinity. Sitting in the afternoon sun in Wrigley Field in Chicago, where night baseball is forbidden, provides the urban dweller a natural cranny, nestled among the tenements and elevated trains, a space in which time is defeated, halted and sent scurrying.[8] This contrasts with the clock games, hockey, basketball, and football which are so driven by time that they attempt to cheat its passing by asking for overtime.

The great Hawaiian sailors who, without instruments, charted the Pacific Ocean, seemingly had sun dials for souls. City persons hide their souls and chart their way with urban clocks, that is, watches, which they wear everywhere, even to bed. Analog, digital, bells, songs, faces of every kind; each way a way to tell the time and in so telling, tell ourselves where we are, how we are, and how much time we have left. Although for most of the past decade, I have been a resident of that recent category of the amorphous, a Small Metropolitan Statistical Area (SMSA), having a teeny population of only 100,000 people, I am by consciousness still an urban person. Consequently, when someone asks if they can see me, I respond, seriously and with conscious intent, that "I have a minute." What an extraordinary statement, and still more extraordinary that increasingly, even in an SMSA, people are not offended. Orthodox psychoanalysis, an urban phenomenon to be sure, features a couch with a large clock visible to the patient so that the hour of soul-searching wears down publicly. The urban factory introduced the tradition of punching the clock. If one were late, the clock would punch this out and you would be docked. Urban time has a fixed and narrow memory. It exacts its price twenty-four hours a day, seven days a week, year in and year out. This is wearing and therefore urban persons hurry by you without a howdy, for they are carrying on a conversation with themselves, a dialogue that protects them spiritually from the ravages of urban time.

In this contrast between nature and city, one further contrast should prove helpful, that of the presence of nature in the city. I do not refer to the greening of the city, too often a euphemism for planting shrubs around ugly buildings. Rather, I mean those times when nature shouts at the top of its voice and does so in the confines of a city. Some years ago, with family, while traveling across the horizontal state of Kansas we came upon, in the distance, a magnificent tornado. It soaked up the sky and drew all of the horizon to its center. I subsequently learned that aside from some ranch fences and an errant cow, it played itself out without causing damage. The people of the city of Wichita Falls, Texas, have no such romantic memories. When a tornado visited their city, it cut a violent swath, scattering bodies, homes, and automobiles, and left a calling card of disaster. These comparisons are apt, for they provide insight to the relative imperviousness of nature as contrasted with the awkward vulnerability of the city when nature strikes. Two further examples will assist us here. A massive snowstorm on the plains is troublesome and causes some disarray, even death here and there. Yet, by contrast, the endless snow dumped on the city of Buffalo some years back created such havoc that the competition for scarce resources brought the viability of social cohesion into serious question. And a hurricane which dances its wild dance off the Gulf Coast is far different from the hurricane which visits Galveston Island or, as recently happened, has the temerity to blow out those archetypes of high technology, the windows of the Houston skyscrapers.

This contrast, however, need not always be frightening or deleterious to urban life. Fog in a woodland is eerie and moving. It takes a back seat, however, to the late summer fog which cascades in glorious tufts across the boulevards of the city of San Francisco, washing and whitening, along the way, those lovely row houses which face the Pacific Ocean. And few events can match the fall of a gentle and wet snow on a late-night city street, providing a white comforter for the sleepers and a glistening cover for the nocturnal walkers. One could replicate these appearances of nature in cities around the world: the overcast, icebound streets of a December Moscow; the gentle Irish rain on a pedestrian overlooking the River Liffey in Dublin; the London fog; and the rising sun over the River Ulna in the Prague of Franz Kafka, heightening the twin spires of the castle and the cathedral, church and state, yin and yang, the glory of medieval Christendom.

When cities intrude upon nature, it is an assault. When nature intrudes upon cities, it is a challenge, a transformation of urban life into still more imaginative forms.

IV. PERSONSCAPE: "BUILDING" THE FUTURE

It is now clear that the older cities of America are in serious trouble. The reasons for the decay of the inner city and the rise of anomie is now well documented. Despite the many discussions as to how to heal this situation, the problem remains critical, although glimmers of hope poke through, as for example in the exciting revitalization of the city of Baltimore. The financial recovery of the incomparable city of New York is also a cause for cheer and efforts to transform Detroit, Philadelphia, and St. Louis are welcome. In this essay, however, the issue is quite different. What of the "new" southwestern cities like Houston, Dallas, and Tucson? Have they learned anything from the relative demise of their older peers? I think not.

The older American cities long ago learned from their European forebears that the most crucial characteristic of a viable city was human scale. I call this the presence of "personscape," by which I mean the urban ambience which affords the city dweller the same bodily continuity with the environment as that found in nature. Even New York City, despite its overwhelming population and the dominating presence of its huge buildings, has preserved the sense of neighborhood, intimacy, and personal accessibility. Until recently, the city of Los Angeles, a comparatively new city, failed in precisely the way that Boston, New York, and Chicago succeeded, namely, to be a resource for ordinary and local experience as well as for the glitter of being on the town. Los Angeles, in its reworking of downtown, has attempted to address that lack and become a city in reality as well as in claim.

Traditionally, our great cities have been water cities, adjacent either to oceans, to lakes, or to rivers. Water has the capacity to bathe the soul and to provide a stimulus for the symbolization of the environment. Water yields depth, fog, mist, the reflection of sun and moon, and especially the possibility of escape, by boat, by reverie, and by suicide. Many of our new cities, however, are land cities; these include Denver, Tucson, Phoenix, Dallas, and even Houston, despite its ship channel and occasional bayou. Land cities as prepossessing and powerful constitute a new event for America. The city of Dallas is the *locus classicus* for this development. Deeply symbolic of the state of Texas, Dallas, like an oil well, erupts from the land rather than slowly oozing from the water. At the top of the hotel in the Dallas-Fort Worth Airport, there is a lounge surrounded by enormous picture windows. One can look out, as one does in many other similar settings in this nation. In this case, one sees nothing, nothing. Yet catching the cityscape of Dallas by air is an unusual experience. No matter how one approaches Dallas, its appearance is shocking, arising as if out of nowhere. Dallas is a land city, an urban bequest to the interior of America. It defied the loneliness of the plains and seeks to celebrate the land in a way different than ever before. Although water dominates the origin of American cities, it is intriguing to contemplate the metaphors which will feed the land cities, for the earth, the dirt, the plains, hold their share of mysteries as well. And the sky, the sky of the land cities, is visible. Despite the reach of the new buildings, the Dallas, Houston, and Tucson sky holds its own. The old cities have no sky. Their citizens are introverted cellar dwellers, looking down and in, or when up, no further than the tops of closely packed buildings. It is novel and exhilarating to be in a major city and still be able to reach for the sky. Still more inviting are the cities of Austin and San Antonio, river cities yet surrounded by land, by vast stretches of openness. In those cities, the river, the sky, and the new buildings make for a scape original in America, powerful and rich in potential poetry.

So much for the possibilities. The actuality is troublesome. Only a few years ago, I was staying at a motel adjacent to the University of Arizona. I asked the bellman directions for visiting the city of Tucson. He warned me, gravely and sternly, of the dangers in such a trip. Rejecting those warnings as endemic to the long-standing myth about cities, I walked a gentle, suburban three miles into the city of Tucson, arriving at 9 P.M. This city of some half-million people was closed; not a light, not a joint, not a person. Stopping a police patrol car, I asked where was it happening? Answer; no happening, no shopping, no action, no nothing. I returned to the dreaded anonymity of my tacky suburban motel.

I close as I open, on the theme of glass without feet. A city, to be a city, *must* have a downtown. A city, to be a city, must have a residential downtown, a walking place. Pretentious buildings without arcades, without accessibility to the wanderer, the stroller, stifle the very meaning of a city. The contrast between the foreboding office buildings open only from eight to five, and the fancy hotels with their lineup of limousines and airport taxis, on the one hand, and the urine-stained bus stations on the other, has become an unpleasant reality in the new cities. It is not that we are without historical wisdom. One of the truly great cities of the world, Rome, can teach us how to build a human city. In Rome, the old and the new, the elegant and the proletariat, the monumental and the occasional, are married day by day as people of every persuasion, of every ability and every desire, mingle in a quest for the good life. The warning is clear, for those American cities which have abandoned their downtown areas for the ubiquitous external mall have become faceless, soulless blots on the landscape. Neither city nor nature, they are witnesses to the emptiness of contemporary American life. Heed the message; cities are for people, ordinary people who move through both the day and night in the search for nutrition, spiritual and aesthetic nutrition.

It would be ironic folly if the new land cities were to repeat the disasters of the older urban areas. Annexation of suburban land does not resolve the fundamental question as to how to build a city. The inner city, downtown, is still the irreplaceable soul of urban life. The city of Houston, a masterpiece of transportation madness, seduced by glass towers dotting the sides of its ugly freeways, sprawling, struggling for identity, has recently looked within. Downtown Houston, as pathetic an area as can be found in a major American city, has become a cause for concern. Houston, alert to its major symbolic role in the new America, now has thoughts about invigorating its inner city. This is encouraging news, and it is to be hoped that the potential success of the city of Houston will be a model for new cities throughout the land. We come to consciousness in the grip of space, time, and touch. Nowhere is this more crucial than in the quality of urban life, where, it turns out, even in the Southwest, even in Texas, most of us live. Let us give the glass towers some feet, so that we may walk about in a genuinely human home, our city.[9]

14 *Isolation as Starvation*

JOHN DEWEY AND A PHILOSOPHY
OF THE HANDICAPPED

It is not enough to insist upon the necessity of experience, nor even of activity in experience. Everything depends upon the *quality* of the experience which is had.
JOHN DEWEY, *Experience and Education*

As to the word "handicapped," never has a historical definition, as found in our great dictionaries,[1] been so out of touch with the contemporary meaning. Originally defined as a "capping of the hands" that would provide equity between the superior and inferior in sport and games, the word only later became associated with disabilities, physical and emotional. In our time, however, the word has undergone a profound transformation. It now refers to a situation different but not necessarily inferior. Indeed, there is now a political aura to the term "handicapped," one which connotes growing power and respect. This development is a far cry from the condescension and ignorance characteristic of the public's reaction to the handicapped only two decades ago. Witness the following statement in the litigation between Ms. Lori Case and the State of California, which occurred as recently as 1973.

> With minor exceptions, mankind's attitudes toward its handicapped population can be characterized by overwhelming prejudice. [The handicapped are systematically isolated from] the mainstream of society. From ancient to modern times, the physically, mentally or emotionally disabled have been

alternatively viewed by the majority as dangers to be destroyed, as nuisances to be driven out, or as burdens to be confined. . . . (T)reatment resulting from a tradition of isolation has been invariably unequal and has operated to prejudice the interests of the handicapped as a minority group. (Lori Case *v.* State of California, 1973, p. 2a)[2]

After an extended series of court cases, this prejudice was finally overcome, at least in the legal sense. In the following comment, the importance of the Public Act of 1975 is detailed.

The Education for All Handicapped Children Act of 1975, Public Law (P. L.) 94–142, is not revolutionary in terms of a role for the federal government. P. L. 94–142 represents the standards that have over the past eight years been laid down by the courts, legislatures, and other policy bodies of our country. Further, it represents a continued evolution of the federal role in the education of children who had handicaps. For example, much of what is required in P. L. 94–142 was set forth in P. L. 93–380, the Education Amendments of 1974.

Most importantly, P. L. 94–142 reflects the dream of special educators and others concerned about the education of children with handicaps, for it has been the hope of our field that we as special educators would one day be able to assure every child who has a handicap an opportunity for an education, that we would be free to advocate for appropriate educational services for these children, that we would be unfettered by inappropriate administrative constraints, and that we would not always have to temper critical decisions about chidren's lives by the inadequacy of public resources. In this sense, P. L. 94–142 becomes the national vehicle whereby the promise of state and local policy that we have heard for so long, and the dreams that we in the profession have hoped for, for so long, may become a reality.[3]

Although this public act is directed at children, it sets a tone for all handicapped people in the United States, now a considerable portion of the population. In fact, to refer to the handicapped as a minority may well be a euphemism, for the figures are quite staggering. Ranging from a low of 13 million handicapped, as provided by the Urban Mass Transportation Administration, to a high of 41 million, as provided by the Department of Health, Education and Welfare, the cautious mean indicates that American society is characterized by a substantial number of citizens with operative disabilities.[4] As a nation we face a social, political, psychological, and moral problem of sizable proportion and of existential exigency.

It may be of assistance to our understanding of the meaning of handicapped if we were to make a distinction between the temporarily and the permanently handicapped. Many of us, at one time or another, have suffered a severe disability. Nonetheless, despite the pain, the inconvenience, and loss of personal power in our activities, we were buoyed by its transiency. The assumption that we would get better, be healed, and get back to normal carried us through our temporary plight. Lurking in the background, although functionally repressed, was the specter of permanence, and a foreboding that we would not get better and that our condition was here to stay. The difference between a transient disability, no matter its length of time, and a permanent disability is akin to the immeasurable and qualitative difference between the finite and the eternal. The difference between the *healing* of a smashed and severely damaged human limb, on the one hand, and an amputation, on the other hand, is incomparable.

As human beings we fear closure not only in its ultimate sense, as in our own death, but in any number of proximate senses, as in the permanent inability to perform in a way considered natural to human life. Looked at objectively, to be permanently blind, deaf, or crippled in some form is to be denied an avenue of access to the world. Some activities, some experiences, are thereby simply not possible. Despite our previous sufferings and disabilities, those of us who are not permanently handicapped actually have no experience of the dramatic force of closure which permeates permanent disability. Nonetheless, as found in those isolated heroic figures of the past and now, in startling numbers, those so handicapped have been able to overcome in such a way as to magnify the alternative avenues of experience. Indeed, so extraordinary has been this development in the activities of the handicapped that it is legitimate to see them as performing in a way superior to those of us for whom our sense life is desultory, haphazard, and taken for granted. Paradoxically, it is the nonhandicapped who often face closure, albeit of another, more subtle kind. It is they who have eyes but do not see, ears but do not hear, for they have taken their bodies for granted. The handicapped, to the contrary, although ostensibly they do not see, or hear, or walk, do each, in their own way, for their bodies are supremely sensitized to the slightest sensorial nuance. In Dewey's sense, it is they who are "live creatures." Significantly, the new education of the handicapped mirrors Dewey's philosophy in an accurate and creative way. Indeed, it realizes Dewey's vision more than most other contemporary forms of education. Two primary reasons for this relationship between Dewey's philosophy and the education of the handicapped can be cited. First, Dewey's diagnosis of the human condition is to see us all as continuous with nature and therefore, in general, "handicapped" in the attempted resolution of our problems, because nature gives no quarter and often demands of us a response that is not humanly possible. Second, he sees education as a form of deep "coping," problem-solving, and assisting, rather than as any final solution to the irreducibly problematic situation of being in the world. I shall consider these two aspects of Dewey's thought in turn.

II

This is neither the time nor the place to undo the many gratuitous misinterpretations of the philosophy of John Dewey. One such mistaken view of Dewey, however, has to be opposed straight out. I refer to the view of Dewey's thought as a Pollyanna vision, innocent of mishap and evil and too trusting in human ingenuity. Not only is this view unfair to Dewey's thought, it actually reverses his fundamental position. For Dewey, existence involves risk and chance and is indeed an ontological gamble. He writes that "luck is proverbially both good and bad in its distributions," for "the sacred and the accursed are potentialities of the same situation."[5]

Dewey, then, proceeds to detail the deleterious effects of a long-standing philosophical tradition which divides the experience of reality into higher and lower orders of experience, thus emptying out the complex content of our actual situation. By defining reality as that which we wish existence to be, we render defect as unnatural and "render search and struggle unnecessary."[6] The higher order, which remains only in philosophical imagination, yields perfection. Of this unreal turn of events, Dewey writes:

> What is left over, (and since trouble, struggle, conflict, and error still empirically exist, something *is* left over) being excluded by definition from full reality is assigned to a grade or order of being which is asserted to be metaphysically inferior; an order variously called appearance, illusion, mortal mind, or the merely empirical, against what really and truly is.[7]

In so proposing, philosophy has abandoned its task, namely, a description of the generic traits of existence as undergone, empirically, by human life. For Dewey, when so undergone, the most primitive of these generic traits show themselves to be a "mixture of the precarious and the problematic with the assured and the complete."[8] The point is clear; all human experience is riven with the presence of a dialectic between the stable and the precarious; no existence, event, or quality escapes this dialectic. In effect, at every moment of our lives we alternate between being free to do and being handicapped, each in our own way. Called in to map our way through this thicket, Dewey laments the frequent effort of philosophy to bypass it.

> Under such circumstances there is danger that the philosophy which tries to escape the form of generation by taking refuge under the form of eternity will only come under the form of a bygone generation. To try to escape from the snares and pitfalls of time by recourse to traditional problems and interests:—rather than that let the dead bury their own dead. Better it is for philosophy to err in active participation in the living struggles and issues of its own age and times than to maintain an immune monastic impeccability, without relevancy and bearing in the generating ideas of its contemporary present.[9]

For Dewey, to the contrary, the method of philosophy must confront the "teachings of sad experience."[10] The most dramatic upshot of such teachings is the irrational and inequitable distribution of suffering among human lives. The following text from Dewey can be read as a direct response to the existence of the handicapped.

> There is no need to expatiate upon the risk which attends overt action. . . . Fortune rather than our own intent and act determines eventual success and failure. The pathos of unfulfilled expectation, the tragedy of defeated purpose and ideals, the catastrophes of accident, are the commonplaces of all comment on the human scene.[11]

Further, we should avoid any "doctrine of escape from the vicissitudes of existence by means of measures which do not demand an active coping with conditions."[12] The stark realism of Dewey, which owns up to our human plight, does not presage a drift to pessimism. In fact, it is precisely the nature of the difficulties that we face which leads him to develop a doctrine of coping and healing. Like Emerson before him, Dewey stresses the doctrine of possibility. Setback and mishap are unavoidable, yet they set the stage for growth and human activity. The crucial factor in the assessment of the quality of human life is the affective quality of the transaction. It is *how* we undergo the necessary alternations between the stable and the precarious which reveals the quality of our lives. Perfection or consummation is rarely attained, but the rhythm of the human struggle carries with it deep moral and aesthetic significance. The "live creature" even makes friends with its stupidities, "using them as warnings that increase present wariness."[13] Indeed, at one point, Dewey even states that periodic alienation is necessary if genuine growth is to occur.

> Life itself consists of phases in which the organism falls out of step with the march of surrounding things and then recovers unison with it—either through effort or by some happy chance. And, in a growing life, the recovery is never mere return to a prior state, for it is enriched by the state of disparity and resistance through which it has successfully passed. If the gap between organism and environment is too wide, the creature dies. If its activity is not enhanced by the temporary alienation, it merely subsists. Life grows when a temporary falling out is a transition to a more extensive balance of the energies of the organism with those of the conditions under which it lives.[14]

It is important to notice that the most severe difficulty encountered by a human being is that of isolation from the flow of events. This isolation prevents the making of relations and prevents recoveries and consequently growth. Periodic alienation enhances the rhythm of our transactions with nature and the world of experience, but isolation drops us out and away from the very leads and implications which the flow of experience harbors for our needs. The historical isolation of the handicapped from the flow of events resulted in precisely this devolutionary situation, wherein the actual handicap became a minor and subsidiary problem in comparison to being cut off from the avenues and possibilities of future experience. Following Dewey's basic metaphysical scenario, the pedagogy of the handicapped, above all, must be a pedagogy of involvement and not one of isolation.

The variant ways, then, of managing these phases of alienation and growth in human life give rise to the multiple approaches of Dewey relative to the classic methods and fields of inquiry. The fundamental setting is the transaction of the human organism with nature or with the environment. Nature has a life of its own, undergoing its own relatings, which in turn become what we experience. Our own transaction with the affairs of nature cuts across the givenness of nature and our ways of relating. This is *how* we experience *what* we experience. Dewey was a realist in the sense that the world exists independent of our thought of it, but the meaning *of* the world is inseparable from our *meaning* the world.

Experience, therefore, is not headless, for it teems with relational leads, inferences, implications, comparisons, retrospections, directions, warnings, and so on. The rhythm of *how* we experience is an aesthetic process, having as its major characteristic the relationship between anticipation and consummation, yet having other perturbations such as mishap, loss, boredom, and listlessness. Pedagogy becomes then the twin effort to integrate the directions of experience with the total needs of the person and to cultivate the ability of an individual to generate new potentialities in his experiencing and to make new relationships so as to foster patterns of growth. And politics is the struggle to construct an optimum environment for the realizing and sanctioning of the aesthetic processes of living. Finally, the entire human endeavor should be an effort to apply the method of creative intelligence in order to achieve optimum possibilities in the never ending moral struggle to harmonize the means-end relationship for the purpose of enhancing human life and achieving growth.

I turn now to the ways in which Dewey developed the method of creative intelligence with regard to the problem of education. In my judgment, both his theoretical underpinnings and his concrete suggestions for practice are both germane and viable for our time. In addition, although he did not develop his philosophy of education with the handicapped specifically in mind, Dewey's position, as we have just hinted, is remarkably apropos for any formulation of a pedagogy for the handicapped.

III

In Dewey's thought all experiencing, except the inchoate, is a knowing of some kind. To be in the world is to be in a learning situation or, to coin a phrase for Dewey, experience is pedagogical. Of this contention, Dewey writes:

> Now, old experience is used to suggest aims and methods for developing a new and improved experience. Consequently experience becomes in so far constructively self-regulative. What Shakespeare so pregnantly said of nature, it is "made better by no mean, but nature makes that mean," becomes true of experience. We do not merely have to repeat the past, or wait for accidents to force change upon us. We *use* our past experiences to construct new and better ones in the future. The very fact of experience thus includes the process by which it directs itself in its own betterment.[15]

The fact that for Dewey experience is pedagogical does not account for the specificity or distinctive importance of pedagogy, although it does provide the setting for the task of pedagogy. The human organism transacts with nature, with the environment, and thereby finds itself in a situation which is problematic. Relative to the interests and goals of the organism, the task is to make one's way through the flow of experience while attempting resolutions of the obstacles to human growth. If philosophy is called upon to map the terrain of this transaction, pedagogy seeks to forge a mutuality between the possibilities active in experience and the strengths and predispositions of the person in question. When teaching takes place, it takes place. It does not have as its justification some future time. "Education, therefore, is a process of living and not a preparation for future living."[16] Dewey unites the process and the goal of learning. The nectar of awareness and accomplishment does not await an ultimate future, for it is gathered on the way, as a testament to the richness and finitude of experience. Learning for Dewey is not an epiphenomenon, tacked onto a regimen of mental flagellation. Rather it is a process, yielding its rewards enroute and from time to time, consummating in an insight, a skill, a breakthrough to the mastery of a handicap or even, occasionally, a mastery of a discipline, an activity, or an area of vital concern. Attention to detail and rigor of method are not separated in Dewey's purview from the joy and celebration that accompany the process of learning. The worse things are, the more dramatic is the need for a creative pedagogy. "The intellectual function of trouble is to lead [us] to think."[17]

Long before the work of Maria Montessori and Martin Buber, John Dewey, with the imaginative assistance of his wife, Alice Chipman, rejected the view of children as but small adults. He had an uncanny sense of the spatial and emotional aesthetics necessary to creative learning. The classrooms of the Deweys' laboratory school at the University of Chicago were furnished for the physical needs and abilities of children. The Deweys provided classrooms for children which responded to both their emotional and physical needs, thereby formulating an optimum environment for learning and for interpersonal transaction of the most fruitful kind. Dewey would have strongly approved of the recent movement to arrange for access to buildings and for appropriate materials for study on behalf of the handicapped.

And he would have realized both the advantages and the disadvantages to "mainstreaming" handicapped children in traditional settings. I believe that Dewey, facing today's problems, would opt for functional "mainstreaming" in which handicapped children would be integrated into the emotional and social life of the school and yet would have access to the distinctive pedagogical and physical strategies necessary to their educational well-being. Dewey had a life-long commitment to opposing artificial and economic obstacles to the learning process, especially on behalf of those to whom unhappy chance had dealt a debilitating injury.

In Dewey's philosophy, growth is relative to the situation in which one finds oneself. Growth is not a linear notion but rather signifies the transaction with nature as problematic. Also, it connotes the ability to resolve, if only contextually, to overcome and, above all, to recover from loss. Growth is an "on the way" fruit of experiencing as subject to intelligence and purpose. It is not solely dependent on habitual responses, accepted customs, or on reaching preconceived goals, especially those determined by persons who do not have the experiences, difficulties, or strengths of those undergoing the transaction.

Although subject to critical and often unreflective abuse, Dewey's position on the importance and nature of growth is quite clear.

> Since in reality there is nothing to which growth is relative save more growth, there is nothing to which education is subordinate save more education. It is commonplace to say that education should not cease when one leaves school. The point of this commonplace is that the purpose of school education is to insure the continuance of education by organizing the powers that insure growth. The inclination to learn from life itself and to make the conditions of life such that all will learn in the process of living is the finest product of schooling.[18]

Learning from life connotes a fidelity to the situation, capacities, and limitations of the learner. Each of us brings anticipations, possibilities, and relative abilities to the learning process. Such a context is always complicated and that of the handicapped more so. But the basic process holds, nonetheless. Relative to our possibilities, we seek achievements. Dewey's warning in the headnote to this chapter is a telling one. "Everything depends upon the *quality* of the experience which is had."[19] The achievement of quality is inseparable from the making of relations and from seizing the implications of what we are doing. The learner, in Dewey's understanding of education, is neither a mere spectator nor a listener. Learning is by doing, mastering, managing as well as by losing and failing. Setback, mishap, and even failure are not disasters. Rather, they can serve as creative wedges back into the tissue of experience, prophesying a renewed effort to attend, assist, or perhaps even resolve the problem in question. Surely, the handicapped understand and welcome this approach to the practice of education.

Dewey's stress on activity and the making of relations as central to the process of education has been known as the project method, that is, one in which we propel ourselves into the environment and make a distinctively personal version out of its givenness. It has been alleged that this approach of Dewey is overly experiential and lacks the intellectual character necessary to a proper educational experience. This judgment is wrong on two accounts. First, consistent with Dewey's total philosophical outlook, the undergoing of experience is itself a learning experience. He writes that "there is, apparently, no conscious experience without inference; reflection is native and constant."[20] Second, Dewey is aware of the strategic character of reflection when brought to bear on an organized set of experiences as found in the educational process. It is in the reflective relating of doing to undergoing that the person has a genuinely educational experience.

> Mere activity does not constitute experience. It is dispersive, centrifugal, dissipating. Experience as trying involves change, but change is meaningless transition unless it is consciously connected with the return wave of consequences which flow from it. When an activity is continued *into* the undergoing of consequences, when the change made by action is reflected back into a change made in us, the mere flux is loaded with significance. We learn something.[21]

Dewey, however, does warn us against the reverse error, namely, one in which theory floats loose, innocent of the experience from which it is to proceed and to which it is to point. Such self-aggrandizing theoretical activity is the bane of genuine education, for it renders tawdry the activities which actually make up our life situation and casts dubiety on the importance of our ordinary activities. On this matter, Dewey counsels wisely:

> An experience, a very humble experience, is capable of generating and carrying any amount of theory (or intellectual content), but a theory apart from an experience cannot be definitely grasped even as theory. It tends to become a mere verbal formula, a set of catchwords used to render thinking, or genuine theorizing, unnecessary and impossible. Because of our education we use words, thinking they are ideas, to dispose of questions, the disposal being in reality simply such an obscuring of perception as prevents us from seeing any longer the difficulty.[22]

If Dewey's philosophy of education makes as much obvious sense as I think it does, why is it not more influential in our own time? Dewey would not be surprised at this neglect, for he believed always that the political and sociological structures were more determinant of institutional life than were philosophical ideas, no matter how perceptive. The key resolution of that disproportion, of course, was to develop a doctrine of political and social life which would find its way into influence and perhaps even power. Dewey made efforts in this direction, especially in the second, third, and fourth decades of our century. In that some of these efforts have significance for his philosophy of education, I shall consider them at this time.

IV

Although public consciousness of the needs and rights of the handicapped has been raised considerably, the level is not yet sufficient to ensure the social, economic, and political breakthroughs necessary to a national program of amelioration and personal adjudication. The final report of the now moribund Carnegie Council on Children makes this clear. The report is entitled "The Unexpected Minority: Handicapped Children in America." A *New York Times* commentary on this document reads as follows:

> [The report] cites the disabled child as the most oppressed member of contemporary American society and advocates a new civil rights movement to create major social changes in public institutions and in attitudes about handicapped children.
> Among its recommendations: that parents—not teachers, doctors, or counselors—exercise final authority over disabled offspring; that the handicapped organize into political groups; that the Federal Government help integrate these children into the educational and social mainstream by redistributing existing public funds and creating new ones.[23]

The classic paradox in American life—the tension between the rights of the individual and the often necessary intervention of the federal government to insure those rights—clearly surfaces here. It is laudable to insist that parents have ultimate authority over the education of their disabled children, but local bureaucracies often act as an insuperable obstacle in this regard. The major difficulty is that these parents are too often regarded by the rest of the community as adversaries, as competitors for tax revenues. This view of the community is atomistic and its only future is strife. The handicapped children are the inevitable losers. Dewey, no stranger to this development, urged a far more expansive communal attitude toward the education of children. "What the best and wisest parent wants for his [her] own child, that must the community want for all of its children. Any other ideal for our schools is narrow and unlovely; acted upon, it destroys our democracy."[24]

The educational rights of children, handicapped or not, do not constitute, in Dewey's view, a special interest group. Rather, the education of all of our children to their fullest capacity is an irreducible necessity if we are to survive as a nation and as a people. Long ago, our great Puritan forebear John Winthrop warned us that unless we be knit together, we shall be shipwrecked. The obstacles to such community sensibility are considerable, and Dewey was deeply cognizant of them. He was especially concerned with the deleterious and self-deceiving effects of a nostalgia for a form of "bootstrap" individualism. Although he had great confidence in the capacity of the individual to overcome obstacles, he deplored the naiveté that ignored the vast social, political, and economic forces which contrived to hinder and even prevent personal growth. Dewey held that "the educational task cannot be accomplished merely by working upon men's minds, without action that effects actual changes in institutions."[25] Yet attempts to bring about institutional change run afoul of the deepest special interest in American life, that of those who control the economic sector.

> The notion that men are equally free to act if only the same legal arrangements apply equally to all—irrespective of differences in education, in command of capital, and the control of the social environment which is furnished by the institution of property—is a pure absurdity, as facts have demonstrated.[26]

Not surprisingly, then, we are faced with two major problems in our effort to forge a new, equitable, and viable philosophy of education for the handicapped: namely, the need for a public consciousness raising and a transformation of institutional priorities. These two needs are of a piece, neither taking political precedence, for they are mutually necessary. Dewey's strategy is based on neither charity nor revolutionary fervor. Rather, he sees the need for social action on behalf of those who need ameliorative efforts as precisely a reflection of the democratic ethos. He writes that "to cooperate by giving differences a chance to show themselves because of the belief that the expression of difference is not only a right of the other persons but is a means of enriching one's own life-experience, is inherent in the democratic personal way of life."[27]

Only when we as a people take on seriously the obligations attendant upon the democratic ethos shall we have the will to effect the necessary transformations of our educational, social, political, and economic structures sufficient to a provision for the needs of the handicapped. No worse fate can befall a self-conscious human being than to be regarded as a pariah in his or her own culture. Isolation from the flow of experience is a fate worse than death, for it mocks the potentialities, expectations, and yearnings of the live creature. In Dewey's philosophy, "A true wisdom, . . . discovers in thoughtful observation and experiment the method of administering the unfinished processes of existence so that frail goods shall be substantiated, secure goods be extended, and the precarious promises of good that haunt experienced things be more liberally fulfilled."[28]

Unless we move expeditiously and imaginatively in the direction of a systematic response to the needs and rights of the handicapped, it is we, as a nation, as a people, and as individuals, who shall in the eyes of subsequent history be judged as morally handicapped. To be physically and emotionally handicapped is to be a luckless victim of the roulette wheel of natural history. To be morally handicapped is a result of self-indulgence, arrogance, and a blindness to the plight of others. Those of us who have been fortunate to be spared severe physical and emotional disability have an obligation to assure that we avoid collective moral turpitude by building a world fit only for ourselves. On behalf of John Dewey, and in my judgment as well, we have no other moral choice than to build a world in which the apertures of accessibility are as wide and as many as the variant styles and abilities of each and every one of us. To do less is to abandon the human quest.

APPENDIX: THE RENASCENCE OF CLASSICAL AMERICAN PHILOSOPHY

I believe that philosophy in America will be lost between chewing a historic cud long since reduced to woody fiber, or an apologetics for lost causes (lost to natural science), or a scholastic, schematic formalism, unless it can somehow bring to consciousness America's own needs and its own implicit principle of successful action.

JOHN DEWEY, "The Need for a Recovery of Philosophy"

Descriptive terms such as German philosophy, French philosophy, and American philosophy carry with them some intrinsic difficulties. Some commentators object to this national adjectival approach to philosophy as necessarily narrowing or even chauvinistic. From their perspective, philosophy has universal significance and should not be identified with the cultural life of a single people, region, or historical period. On behalf of this position, it must be agreed that efforts to confine philosophy to the interests and language of a single cultural tradition are inevitably procrustean and even counter to the long-standing mission of philosophical inquiry to seek the truth however and wherever that journey takes us. Consequently, no philosophical position is to be ruled out of consideration simply because its origins are antique or because it proceeds from a tradition and a language different from the one native to the philosopher in question.

The above strictures are to be taken as a caveat to those who believe that philosophic inquiry can be restricted by historical, linguistic, or even naturalistic confines. This is a method which is at best reductionistic and at worst propagandistic. These strictures, however, do not preclude the significance of the historical and cultural contextuality which attends all philosophical activity. The history of philosophy over and again attests to the presence of a historical matrix from which the philosophers formulate their version of the world, a version as culturally idiosyncratic as it is profound. Can one conceive of Plato and Aristotle as other than Greek philosophers; of Anselm as other than a medieval monk; of Descartes as other than a protégé of the new mathematics and science of the seventeenth century; of Hegel as other than a realization of German *Systemphilosophie*? The point here is not that these philosophers are reduced to their cultural contexts, or even that their respective contexts are able to account for the distinctive quality of their work. Rather, our intention is to indicate that the great philosophers proceed from their inherited linguistic, cultural, and historical settings in a way that enables them to feed off those settings and yet transcend them. It is both a paradox and a truism that those thinkers who attempt to ignore their inherited setting and thereby issue "universal" truths, *ab ovo*, inevitably find their work to be of significance to very few. With creative and seminal philosophers, their own cultural setting accounts for the origin of their work. It does not, however, account for its extensive influence. That influence is due rather to their ability to understand and transform their situation in a way which has distinctive meaning for world culture. In that vein, for example, Aristotle, Augustine, Leibniz, and Marx take their place alongside Lao Tzu, Buddha, and Jesus as profound articulators of their own experience as well as harbingers of the possible experiences of others in distant cultures.

The above comments are a backdrop to an examination of the thorny question of the relationship between American philosophy and philosophy in America. A full-scale analysis of this relationship would require nothing less than a focused survey of the history of American culture, a project far outdistancing the scope of the present essay. Nonetheless, some clarifying remarks are in order. The prepossessing character of America on the world scene tends to cloud from view the fact that for more than one and a half centuries America was a colony of England. Furthermore, given geographical range, America most often followed the cultural proprieties of Spain and France as well as those of England. In short, with regard to the affairs of high culture, the arts, literature, and philosophy, American achievements were thought to be secondhand. Whatever may have been the actual aesthetic achievements of American vernacular culture during the colonial period, the fact remains that American self-consciousness as to the worth of its cultural activities was dependent on evaluation from abroad.

The first public salvo against this cultural self-denigration was the prophetic utterance of Emerson in his preface to his essay "Nature": "The foregoing generations beheld God and nature face to face; we, through their eyes. Why should not we also enjoy an original relation to the universe?"[1]

Partially in response to the call of Emerson and others of his time, and partially in response to the explosive implications of the publication of Darwin's *The Origin of Species,* American thought in the last decades of the nineteenth century took the direction of originality. Led by Chauncey Wright (1830–75) and the young Charles Sanders Peirce (1839–1914), the distinctive interests and persuasions of American philosophy began to develop. If previous centuries had shown America to be derivative (an arguable contention), the last four decades of the nineteenth century revealed American intellectual and philosophical thought to be both original and substantial in influence. Indeed, no less than "Charles Darwin is reported to have observed that there were enough brilliant minds at the American Cambridge in the 1860s to furnish all the universities of England."[2] In quick succession, each with a distinctive flair and contribution, American philosophy of that period was graced with the appearance of William James (1842–1910), Josiah Royce (1855–1916), John Dewey (1859–1952), George Herbert Mead (1863–1931), and George Santayana (1863–1952), as well as other, less well-known thinkers such as G. H. Howison (1834–1916), W. T. Harris (1835–1909), and Thomas Davidson (1840–1900). This period came to be known as the golden age of American philosophy or, more modestly, as the classical age. Whatever nomenclature one wishes to append to this period, there is no doubt as to its unusual importance in the history of American culture nor, above all, to its singular importance in the history of American philosophy.

This is not to say, of course, that significant philosophers and philosophical developments did not take place after the classical period. A "second generation" of important philosophers was led by C. I. Lewis (1883–1964), Brand Blanshard (1892–), and the coming in 1924 of Alfred North Whitehead (1861–1947) to Harvard University.[3]

Appropriately, it was Harvard that extended the invitation to Whitehead, for although John Dewey was an extremely notable exception, the entire classical period, from Peirce to Whitehead, was dominated by

Harvard, either on behalf of its teachers or on behalf of its graduate students of philosophy, many of whom became the premier teachers of the succeeding generation.[4] This contention is not in any way to be taken as a denigration of the important philosophical work found at the University of Chicago at the turn of the century or the subsequent significance of Columbia University's development of pragmatic and historical naturalism which flourished in the second, third, and fourth decades of this century—traditions largely due to the influence of John Dewey. Rather, it is simply a matter of fact that Harvard had the edge.

After the Second World War, the philosophical situation in America took on a very different cast. The political upheaval in continental Europe caused many outstanding philosophers to emigrate to the United States. During the decade of the 1930s, America received Herbert Feigl, Herbert Marcuse, Rudolph Carnap, Carl Hempel, Hans Reichenbach, and Alfred Tarski, among others. Further, as is well known, the war forced Bertrand Russell to stay in America from 1938 until 1944. As a result of these events, the positivism of the Vienna circle, sophisticated Hegelian-Marxism of the Frankfurt School, and the Russellian approach to philosophy all gained a foothold on the American scene. After the Second World War, these influences were joined by the flood of writings from France and Germany on behalf of phenomenology and existentialism. Many American students once again returned to England for their philosophical education and brought back the early messages of logical empiricism, ordinary language, and linguistic analysis—varieties of what came to be known subsequently by the generic term "analytic philosophy."

From 1950 until 1965, the student of philosophy in America, a term now used advisedly, was confronted with a bewildering array of philosophical materials from Europe. Although the emphasis differed depending on the individual university and graduate program, American philosophy students at that time were reading Wittgenstein, Ryle, Ayer, Austin, the above-mentioned thinkers from the Vienna circle, Kierkegaard, Nietzsche, Camus, Sartre, Husserl, Heidegger, Marcel, or Merleau-Ponty. The professionally oriented graduate schools were often characterized more by the technical accompaniment of logic than by that of languages. Increasingly, argumentation superseded interpretation as the proper mode of philosophical discourse, whether found verbally or as written in the learned journals. Whatever else one wants to say about this development of philosophy in America after the war, it remains incontrovertible that interest in classical American philosophy had all but disappeared from the academic philosophical scene.

From one point of view, the comparative neglect of classical American philosophy after the Second World War is baffling. Surely, no other major Western culture would so completely abandon its own philosophical tradition. Can one think of French philosophy without constant, even if critical, recourse to Descartes? Can one similarly think of German philosophy without relation to Kant or British philosophy without relation to Hume? (As a general response, the answer would be no!) Yet from another point of view, the neglect is understandable, even if lamentable. America, again by tradition, has prided itself on being ever open to novelty, be it ideas or things. Less praiseworthy, but also endemic to American culture, has been its susceptibility to the belief that native culture is inferior to that spawned elsewhere. This proceeds from a complex historical dialectic between a peculiar American version of the oriental doctrine of "face" and a long-standing sense of cultural inferiority, the latter healed apparently only by periodically imported European wisdom. As with other remarks made above, these contentions also deserve extensive commentary, but they too would take us beyond the mandate of the present essay.

Lest the reader doubt the neglected status of classical American philosophy in the 1960s, I offer some autobiographical comments. When I set out in 1965 to prepare a comprehensive edition of the works of William James, the publication scene was revealing. I found multiple paperback editions of the popular writings of James in print: *The Varieties of Religious Experience, Pragmatism,* and *The Will to Believe and Other Essays in Popular Philosophy.* They were casually "introduced," if introduced at all, and poorly printed. James's major philosophical writings, such as *Essays in Radical Empiricism* and *A Pluralistic Universe,* were out of print and difficult to obtain. In response to this situation, I published *The Writings of William James* (New York: Random House, 1967; Chicago: University of Chicago Press, 1977), which included a complete text of *Pragmatism* and a complete text of Ralph Barton Perry's 1943 edition of *Essays in Radical Empiricism* and *A Pluralistic Universe.* Appended to this volume was an updated and corrected version of Ralph Barton Perry's "Annotated Bibliography of the Writings of William James."

The response to this volume was revealing. A consensus revealed surprise at the range of James's interests, fascination with the comparative contemporaneity of his thought, and, significantly, an acknowledgment of his technical philosophical virtuosity. Soon after this publication of the *Writings of William James,* other editions appeared: some claimed James for phenomenology (Bruce Wilshire, *William James: The Essential Writings* [New York: Harper and Row, 1971]) and others pointed to his catholicity of interests, philosophical as well as literary (Andrew J. Reck, ed., *Introduction to William James* [Bloomington: Indiana University Press, 1967]; John K. Roth, ed., *The Moral Equivalent of War and Other Essays* [New York: Harper and Row, 1971]; Gay Wilson Allen, ed., *A William James Reader* [Boston: Houghton Mifflin, 1972]).

A similar situation existed when I began to prepare a comprehensive edition of the writings of Josiah Royce. Virtually all of his works were out of print, and the few to escape that fate were published without introduction and without scholarly apparatus. Royce was still regarded by many as a throwback to the German idealists. He was thought to be a derivative thinker, and there was little acknowledgment of the extensive development in his thought or of the range of his interests. In 1968, prodded by the editorial wisdom of Morris Philipson, the University of Chicago Press set out to present the works of Royce in a comprehensive format. The first volume was an edition of Royce's book *The Problem of Christianity,* published originally in 1913. The Chicago edition of this work has a perceptive and detailed introduction by John E. Smith. In 1969, the Chicago series was continued by the publication of *The Basic Writings of Josiah Royce,* in two volumes, which I edited. Included in these volumes was "An Annotated Bibliography of the Published Works of Josiah Royce" by Ignas Skrupskelis. As with the earlier mentioned response to the James volume, so too here did the reviewers stress their surprise at the variety of Royce's writings, especially with regard to his work in social philosophy and American history and religion. The fourth volume of this series was published in 1974, entitled *The Letters of Josiah Royce,* edited by John Clendenning. The fifth and final volume, a biography of Royce by Clendenning, is now in preparation at the University of Wisconsin Press. At this writing, the Chicago series is the most substantial version of Royce now in print. There are no present plans, unfortunately, for a collected and critical edition of his writings. This is especially to be regretted because the Royce archives at Harvard University contain a considerable amount of unpublished papers, notably on logic, which merit wider public attention.

In the late 1960s, John Dewey's writings were better represented than those of James or Royce. The standard comprehensive edition was that of

Joseph Ratner, *Intelligence in the Modern World* (New York: Modern Library, 1939), but it had the defect of presenting many excerpted materials and following themes designated as significant by the editor rather than by Dewey himself. In 1960, Richard Bernstein edited a helpful collection of Dewey's essays, *On Experience, Nature and Freedom* (Indianapolis: Bobbs [Liberal Arts], 1960). All but one of these essays, however, were confined to Dewey's work after 1930. Another coherent collection of Dewey's writings was to be found in *John Dewey on Education*, edited by Reginald Archambault (New York: Modern Library, 1964). At this time, most of Dewey's original books were still in print, even if only in paperback editions. An attempt to provide a minimally comprehensive edition of Dewey's writings can be found in my two-volume edition, *The Philosophy of John Dewey* (Chicago: University of Chicago Press, 1981).

The upshot of these developments with regard to the works of James, Royce, and Dewey is that an effort was made to provide competent and comprehensive editions of their works and to overcome the haphazard and casual presentations of their major writings. These efforts, at least in the case of Dewey and James, acted as a creative backdrop to a major breakthrough on the American philosophical scene. For the first time, national funding was provided for a collected critical edition of the writings of philosophers. The first venture, largely supported by the National Endowment for the Humanities, was that devoted to the works of John Dewey. Originated by the Center for Dewey Studies of Southern Illinois University at Carbondale, and partially supported by a grant from the John Dewey Foundation and from Mr. Corliss Lamont, the entire project is edited by Jo Ann Boydston. The first five volumes are published as "The Early Works, 1882–1898." They include Dewey's early essays, his writings on Leibniz, psychology, and ethics, and his periodic and episodic pieces during that period. The next group of volumes are referred to as "The Middle Works, 1899–1924." All fifteen volumes projected for this period have been published, containing Dewey's classic writings on education, his many journal articles and book reviews of that time, and his important work of 1903, *Studies in Logical Theory*. "The Later Period, 1925–1953," is projected as having sixteen volumes. As of this writing, seven volumes have been published, including the very important text of *Experience and Nature*. To this will be added an index and other important editorial information. Some ten volumes of correspondence await confirmation as to actual publication. Of the volumes published thus far, it can be said that they are characterized by helpful introductions, accurately emended texts, and impeccable editorial supervision by Ms. Boydston. When this massive project is completed, even serious students of Dewey will be awed anew at his prodigious output, his learning, and above all his extraordinary ability to sustain intellectual quality over such an extensive span of time and work.

Between the publication of "The Early Works" and the initial volumes of "The Middle Works," the National Endowment for the Humanities funded a second proposal for a collected, critical edition of the writings of a major classical American philosopher, William James. Founded by Frederick Burkhardt and John J. McDermott, and sponsored by the American Council of Learned Societies, this edition, inclusive of unpublished writings, is projected to be sixteen volumes. The general editor is Frederick Burkhardt and the textual editor is Fredson Bowers. The publisher is Harvard University Press. The introductions to these James volumes are much more extensive than those found in the Dewey edition, and take as their task to provide the genesis of the text, its major contentions, and an analysis of the critical response to the text over the years of its existence. The James edition has not been published in chronological order, although when finished it can be read that way. Thus far thirteen volumes have been published, comprising a three-volume edition of *The Principles of Psychology* and ten other titles. As with the Dewey volumes, this edition of James establishes an exact text, inclusive of James's emendations, subsequent to the first printing. In the James volumes, an added feature is the work of Ignas Skrupskelis, who has traced every reference or allusion made by James to its original source. The result is a veritable map to the panoply of persons and issues which laced the European and American intellectual scenes of the late nineteenth and early twentieth centuries.

The collected critical editions of James and Dewey, when completed, will provide the student of American philosophy with a vast amount of philosophical and cultural material from which to assess their significance as thinkers. Provided also will be a rich context for the understanding of almost a century of vibrant philosophical activity. Although not as technically proficient or nearly as complete, the Chicago series of Royce volumes adds a still further enriching context for understanding that period in American and European cultural history.

I turn now to the last three thinkers of the classical period, C. S. Peirce, George Santayana, and George H. Mead. The story of Peirce's inability to publish most of his writings during his lifetime is now a depressing biographical chapter in any history of American philosophy. After his death in 1914, many boxes of his papers were sold to Harvard University, where they languished for years, uncatalogued and unsung. Due to the efforts of two young philosophers then at Harvard University, Charles Hartshorne and Paul Weiss, six volumes of these papers were published between 1931 and 1935.[5] In 1958, this series was brought to a completion by the publication of the seventh and eighth volumes under the editorial supervision of Arthur W. Burks. Before and during this time, several smaller anthologies of Peirce's writings were published: *Chance, Love and Logic,* ed. Morris R. Cohen (New York: Harcourt, Brace and Co., 1923); *The Philosophy of Peirce,* ed. Justus Buchler (London: Routledge and Kegan Paul, 1940); *Charles S. Peirce, Essays in the Philosophy of Science,* ed. Vincent Tomas (New York: Liberal Arts Press, 1957); *Charles S. Peirce, Values in a Universe of Chance,* ed. Philip P. Wiener (New York: Doubleday, 1958). A much later collection of *The Essential Writings* of Peirce was edited by Edward C. Moore (New York: Harper and Row, 1972).

The collected papers of Peirce, however, did not exhaust the treasure trove of his writings. This was made clear with the publication of Richard Robin's *Annotated Catalogue of the Papers of C. S. Peirce* (Amherst: University of Massachusetts Press, 1967). Robin's catalogue made clear that the *Collected Papers,* although a magnificent endeavor in its time, fell short in scope and in editorial organization. It came, then, as very welcome news when the National Endowment for the Humanities announced its funding support of the publication of a collected and critical edition of Peirce's works. This edition, to be prepared chronologically, will be under the supervision of the distinguished Peirce scholar Max H. Fisch. When completed and joined with the edition of Peirce's mathematical writings edited by Carolyn Eisele, we shall have extant virtually all of Peirce's work, arranged and edited in the best tradition of scholarship. At present, two volumes have been published by Indiana University Press, taking Peirce's writings from 1857 until 1871, inclusive of biographical material by Max Fisch.

With regard to the work of George Santayana, a similar program is underway. Santayana's writings have been periodically reprinted in paperback editions, and two volumes have been devoted to his unpublished writings; these are *Santayana: Animal Faith and Spiritual Life,* ed. John Lachs (New York: Appleton-Century-Crofts, 1967), and *Physical Order and Moral Liberty,* ed. John Lachs and Shirley Lachs (Nashville: Vanderbilt University Press, 1969). Other collections of Santayana's essays have appeared, and it can be said that a high proportion of his works are available in one form or another. Yet, as with the other classical American philosophers, his reputation has suffered from the unavailability of a comprehensive edition of his writings. This situation has been rectified by a grant from the National Endowment for the Humanities on behalf of the editor, Herman Saatkamp, Jr., to publish a critical edition of the writings of George Santayana, to be published by the M.I.T. Press.

The last thinker under direct consideration is George H. Mead. A colleague of John Dewey for ten years at the University of Chicago, Mead remained there after Dewey's departure. A profound teacher, he published comparatively little in his lifetime. After his death, many of Mead's manuscripts and lectures were published, including *The Philosophy of the Present* (Chicago: Open Court, 1932); *Mind, Self and Society* (Chicago: University of Chicago Press, 1934); *Movements of Thought in the Nineteenth Century* (Chicago: University of Chicago Press, 1936); and *The Philosophy of the Act* (Chicago: University of Chicago Press, 1938). These volumes are still in print and have been supplemented by the publication of Andrew J. Reck's edition of most of Mead's previously published essays under the title of *Selected Writings* (Indianapolis: Bobbs-Merrill, 1964). A bibliography of Mead's writings, including details about his unpublished work, can be found in David Miller's authoritative study, *George Herbert Mead—Self, Language and the World* (Austin: University of Texas Press, 1973). Miller has also published *The Individual and the Social Self: Unpublished Work of George Herbert Mead* (Chicago: University of Chicago Press, 1982).

In addition to the extraordinary developments in the area of scholarly editions of the writings of the classical American philosophers, the last ten years has also witnessed the publication of important works in the area of secondary literature. The two standard works in the history of American philosophy have been by Herbert Schneider, 1946, and by Joseph Blau, 1952. In 1977, there appeared an impressive two-volume study entitled *A History of Philosophy in America* (New York: G. P. Putnam's Sons, 1977). Written by Elizabeth Flower and Murray Murphey, it is thorough and philosophically sophisticated. Its range is from the Puritans to C. I. Lewis, and it has taken its place as the standard history of American philosophy despite its title, which announces "Philosophy in America."

In the last decade, two important biographies have been published: Gay Wilson Allen's *William James* (New York: Viking Press, 1967), and *The Life and Mind of John Dewey* (Carbondale: Southern Illinois University Press, 1973), by George Dykhuizen. As mentioned earlier, a biography of Royce by John Clendenning is in progress, and so too is one of Whitehead by Victor Lowe, *Alfred North Whitehead: The Man and His Work,* vol. 1 (Baltimore: The Johns Hopkins University Press, 1985). Of note also in this regard is the recent publication of *The Poems of John Dewey,* edited by Jo Ann Boydston (Carbondale: Southern Illinois University Press, 1977). As with all of Ms. Boydston's editing, this volume is a model of scholarship, and her introduction provides a lucid account of the circumstances surrounding Dewey's writing of poetry and an accompanying perspective on a heretofore little known aspect of Dewey's life.

Commentaries on the American philosophers have also increased both in quantity and quality. As a further testament to the renascence of American philosophy, in 1974 the Society for the Advancement of American Philosophy was founded. Now in its twelfth year, the Society has over 600 active members and meets four times a year. The quarterly journal *Transactions of the Charles S. Peirce Society* has widened its focus to become "A Quarterly Journal in American Philosophy." This renewal of interest, coupled with the publication of collected critical editions of the classic American philosophers, should considerably enhance the quality of work in American philosophy. Assuming that the editions are published as planned, the year 1990 should bring us over 100 volumes of superbly edited works in American philosophy.

Aside from the sheer aesthetic and editorial importance of these events, what significance accrues for the study of philosophy in the widest sense of that term? First, it gives to those who are teaching and writing philosophy in America a local touchstone from which to understand essential dimensions of contemporary philosophy. The work of contemporary philosophers as diverse as W. V. O. Quine, Nelson Goodman, Wilfred Sellars, Richard Rorty, and Hilary Putnam is inseparable from the influences of the earlier classical American period.

Second, European philosophers are used to working from a tradition which is characterized not only by brilliance but by girth. In the past, American philosophy was represented by isolated works, leaving the enormous scope of each major thinker hidden from view. The publication of the respective collected works will present an imposing and coherent body of materials from which to proceed. In short, the tradition of classical American philosophy will take its public place among the other great and warranted philosophical traditions of the past. This will give a new generation, whatever its geographical location, an opportunity to evaluate the continuing worth of American philosophy.

Finally, quite aside from the importance of the renewed availability of the works of the American philosophers, we stress here the intrinsic importance of the works themselves. The American philosophers address themselves, at one time or another, to virtually every significant philosophical theme, most often in a language which is accessible and rich. Their disputes, insights, and failings constitute one of the truly creative philosophical clusterings in the history of philosophy. Their work is seminal for our work, and the general admonition of Santayana is still to the point: those of us who forget the past will be condemned to relive it. Such a reliving would be done in ignorance, which is certainly an unforgivable condition for philosophers.

SELECTED SECONDARY SOURCES

This bibliographical appendix will provide the reader with some knowledge of recent activity in the field of American philosophy. The books listed here are in addition to those mentioned in the text.

Allen, Gay Wilson, *William James* (New York: Viking Press, 1967). Based on the Harvard collection of James's family papers, this is now the standard biography.

Ames, Van Meter, *Zen and American Thought* (Honolulu: University of Hawaii Press, 1962). Ames writes provocative chapters on the important American literary and philosophical thinkers, each from a Zen perspective.

Apel, Karl-Otto, *Charles S. Peirce: From Pragmatism to Pragmaticism* (Amherst: University of Massachusetts Press, 1981). A detailed analysis of the genesis of Peirce's philosophy from the perspective of a sympathetic but critical German philosopher.

Ayer, A. J., *The Origins of Pragmatism* (San Francisco: Freeman, Cooper and Company, 1968). The concentration here is on the central themes of the philosophy of Peirce and James.

Barzun, Jacques, *A Stroll with William James* (New York: Harper and Row, 1983). A brilliant "conversation" with the thought of William James by one of America's most elegant and incisive men of letters.

Bernstein, Richard, *John Dewey* (New York: Washington Square Press, 1967). An excellent introduction to Dewey's philosophy.

Blewett, John, ed., *John Dewey: His Thought and Influence* (New York: Fordham University Press, 1960). A centennial celebration of Dewey's birthday in 1959, this book features an extraordinary essay by Robert C. Pollock on "Process and Experience."

Boler, John F., *Charles Peirce and Scholastic Realism* (Seattle: University of Washington Press, 1963). A careful analysis of the influence of Duns Scotus on the philosophy of Peirce.

Cahn, Steven M., ed., *New Studies in the Philosophy of John Dewey* (Hanover, N.H.: University Press of New England, 1977). A collection of essays which focus alternately on Dewey's social philosophy, metaphysics, aesthetics, episte-mology, ethics, and philosophy of education.

Clebsch, William, *American Religious Thought* (Chicago: University of Chicago Press, 1973). A provocative and insightful treatment of the thought of Jonathan Edwards, Emerson, and especially James.

Conkin, Paul K., *Puritans and Pragmatists* (New York: Dodd, Mead and Company, 1968). This book is extremely informative as to the lives and times of the major figures in American intellectual history.

Corti, Walter Robert, *The Philosophy of George Herbert Mead* (Hamburg: Felix Meiner Verlag, 1973). A collection of essays by European and American scholars on the range of Mead's thought. It includes a bibliography of Mead's writings.

———, *The Philosophy of William James* (Hamburg: Felix Meiner Verlag, 1976). A collection of essays devoted to the life and thought of William James. A helpful bibliography of secondary sources is included.

Cotton, J. Harry, *Royce on the Human Self* (Cambridge: Harvard University Press, 1954). Regarded as a classic in Royce scholarship, this book is a systematic study of the importance of self in relation to Royce's total philosophical work.

Coughlan, Neil, *Young John Dewey: An Essay in American Intellectual History* (Chicago: University of Chicago Press, 1973). An interpretation of Dewey's personal values during his formative years.

Curti, Merle, *Human Nature in American Thought* (Madison: University of Wisconsin Press, 1980). An overview of American intellectual history by its leading historian of ideas.

Damico, Alfonso J., *Individuality and Community: The Social and Political Thought of John Dewey* (Gainesville: University Presses of Florida, 1978). This book seeks to show the importance of Dewey's philosophical thought for his social and political judgments.

Deledalle, Gérard, *Histoire de la Philosophie Américaine* (Paris: Presses Universi-taires de France, 1954). An overview from Europe's leading interpreter of Amer-ican philosophy.

———, *L'Idée d'Expérience dans la Philosophie de John Dewey* (Paris: Presses Universitaires de France, 1967). A chronological history of Dewey's notion of experience from 1904 until 1952.

———, *La Philosophie Américaine* (Lausanne: L'Age D'Homme, 1983). An imaginative and interpretive history of American philosophy.

———, *Théorie et Pratique du Signe* (Paris: Payot, 1979). Beginning with a discus-sion of Saussure, this work is an analysis of Peirce's semiotics.

Dykhuizen, George, *The Life and Mind of John Dewey* (Carbondale: Southern Illinois University Press, 1973). The first detailed biography of John Dewey. It provides the personal and professional context necessary to understand Dewey's writings.

Eames, S. Morris, *Pragmatic Naturalism* (Carbondale: Southern Illinois University Press, 1977). A pragmatic philosophical approach to the problems of nature, knowledge, values, and education.

Easton, Loyd D., *Hegel's First American Followers* (Athens: Ohio University Press, 1966). A presentation of the thought of four early German-American Hegelians, accompanied by a translation of several of their essential writings.

Feinstein, Howard M., *Becoming William James* (Ithaca: Cornell University Press, 1984). A psychological biography of the young William James and his family.

Fiering, Norman, *Jonathan Edwards' Moral Thought and Its British Context* (Chapel Hill: University of North Carolina Press, 1981). A perceptive and historically informed widening of the sources necessary to understand the thought of Jonathan Edwards.

Fontinell, Eugene, *Toward a Reconstruction of Religion* (New York: Doubleday and Co., 1970). A thoughtful application of American pragmatism to traditional religious questions.

Ford, Marcus Peter, *William James's Philosophy: A New Perspective* (Amherst: University of Massachusetts Press, 1982). A cogent defense of the controversial claim that William James was a pan-psychist.

Fuss, Peter, *The Moral Philosophy of Josiah Royce* (Cambridge: Harvard University Press, 1965). A monograph devoted to the development of Royce's ethical theory in relation to his epistemology and theory of community.

Goetzmann, William H., *The American Hegelians* (New York: Alfred A. Knopf, 1973). A valuable anthology of the writings of the American Hegelians with an appended annotated bibliography.

Goudge, Thomas A., *The Thought of C. S. Peirce* (New York: Dover Publications, Inc., 1969). Originally published in 1950, this is still a well-regarded general treatment of Peirce's work.

Gouinlock, James, *The Moral Writings of John Dewey* (New York: Hafner Press, 1976). A helpful and well-selected compilation of Dewey's writings on moral philosophy and social ethics.

Gunn, Giles, ed., *New World Metaphysics* (New York: Oxford University Press, 1981). An imaginative presentation of classical material on the American point of view.

Harris, Leonard, *Philosophy Born of Struggle: Anthology of Afro-American Philosophy from 1917* (Dubuque: Kendall-Hunt Publishing Company, 1983). The only detailed collection of writings from Afro-American philosophers, this book is of considerable philosophical and cultural interest.

Howie, John, and Thomas O. Buford, eds., *Contemporary Studies in Philosophical Idealism* (West Dennis, Mass.: Claude Stark & Co., 1975). Vigorous restatements of the American idealist tradition.

Kuklick, Bruce, *Josiah Royce* (Indianapolis and New York: Bobbs-Merrill Company, Inc., 1972). This is an intellectual biography of Royce with a unique focus on his work in logic and methodology.

Levinson, Henry Samuel, *The Religious Investigations of William James* (Chapel Hill: University of North Carolina Press, 1981). The best and most detailed analysis of James's philosophy of religion and his classic work, *The Varieties of Religious Experience*.

Madden, Edward H., *Chauncey Wright and the Foundations of Pragmatism*

(Seattle: University of Washington Press, 1963). A brilliant intellectual biography of Wright, the informal teacher of the young Peirce and James.

McDermott, John J., *The Culture of Experience: Philosophical Essays in the American Grain* (New York: New York University Press, 1976). This book is concerned with the significance of the writings of James and Dewey for an analysis and critique of contemporary culture.

————, *Streams of Experience: Reflections on the History and Philosophy of American Culture* (Amherst: University of Massachusetts Press, 1986). A second series of essays on the American culture of experience.

Merrill, Kenneth R., and Robert W. Shahan, eds., *American Philosophy: From Edwards to Quine* (Norman: University of Oklahoma Press, 1977). An overview of American philosophy, including essays on the transcendentalists, Royce, and Santayana.

Miller, David L., *George Herbert Mead* (Austin: University of Texas Press, 1973). An excellent, comprehensive study of the thought of Mead.

Mills, C. Wright, *Sociology and Pragmatism* (New York: Paine-Whitman Publishers, 1964). An attempt to provide an analysis of the social and political context which gave rise to pragmatism.

Moore, Edward C., *American Pragmatism: Peirce, James and Dewey* (New York: Columbia University Press, 1961). Interpretive essays which are concerned with ethics, religion, epistemology, and metaphysics.

Morganbesser, Sidney, ed., *Dewey and His Critics* (New York: Journal of Philosophy, Inc., 1977). A collection of essays by John Dewey and polemical rejoinders by his peers. All of them are reprinted from the *Journal of Philosophy*.

Morris, Charles, *The Pragmatic Movement in American Philosophy* (New York: George Braziller, 1970). The focus here is on semiotics, axiology, methodology, and cosmology in the thought of James, Peirce, Dewey, and Mead.

Mulvaney, Robert, and Philip Zeltner, *Pragmatism: Its Sources and Prospects* (Columbia: University of South Carolina Press, 1981). Contains expansive essays by Thayer, Gellner, Quine, McDermott, and Gouinlock on the controverted position of pragmatism in contemporary philosophy.

Munson, Thomas N., *The Essential Wisdom of George Santayana* (New York: Columbia University Press, 1962). A synoptic view of Santayana's thought gathered around the theme of his notion of essence.

Murphey, Murray, *The Development of Peirce's Philosophy* (Cambridge: Harvard University Press, 1961). A controversial and learned interpretation of Peirce which holds that Peirce never attained any systematic version of his own thought.

Novak, Michael, *American Philosophy and the Future* (New York: Charles Scribner's Sons, 1968). Original interpretations of the American philosophers, often with contemporary cultural themes in mind.

Oppenheim, Frank M., *Royce's Voyage Down Under* (Lexington: University of Kentucky Press, 1980). A sensitive reporting of Royce's mental breakdown in 1888 and his recuperative voyage to Australia.

Petras, John W., *George Herbert Mead: Essays on His Social Philosophy* (New York: Teachers College Press, 1968). A collection of Mead's essays on social and educational problems.

Potter, Vincent G., S.J., *Charles S. Peirce on Norms and Ideals* (Amherst: University of Massachusetts Press, 1967). This book is devoted to the importance of the categories in Peirce's doctrine of the normative sciences.

"Psychological Studies of the James Family," *Psychohistory Review* 7, nos. 1–2 (Summer-Fall 1979). Essays on Henry James, Sr., Mary Robertson James, William James, and Henry James, Jr.

Robinson, Daniel, *Royce and Hocking: American Idealists* (Boston: The Christopher Publishing House, 1968). A comparative study which contains some interesting correspondence of both Royce and Hocking to their contemporaries.

Rorty, Richard, *Consequences of Pragmatism* (Minneapolis: University of Minnesota Press, 1982). A series of controversial and iconoclastic philosophical essays, including the well-known ironic piece "Philosophy in America Today."

———, *Philosophy and the Mirror of Nature* (Princeton: Princeton University Press, 1979). A refreshing and learned work which calls for the thought of William James and John Dewey to be returned to the center of contemporary philosophical conversation.

Rosenthal, Sandra B., *The Pragmatic A Priori* (St. Louis: Warren H. Green, Inc., 1976). An examination of the epistemology of C. I. Lewis.

Roth, John K., *The Philosophy of Josiah Royce* (Indianapolis: Hackett Publishing Company, 1982). A well-chosen volume of selections from the writings of Josiah Royce.

Rucker, Darnell, *The Chicago Pragmatists* (Minneapolis: University of Minnesota Press, 1969). The story of the imaginative work in philosophy and the social sciences as found at the University of Chicago from 1895 until 1930.

Saatkamp, Herman J., Jr., and John Jones, *George Santayana: A Bibliographical Checklist, 1880–1980* (Bowling Green, Ohio: Philosophy Documentation Center, 1982). Contains primary and secondary sources as well as dissertations and manuscripts.

Scheffler, Israel, *Four Pragmatists* (New York: Humanities Press, 1974). Although other topics are considered, this is fundamentally an epistemological critique of the philosophy of James, Peirce, Mead, and Dewey.

Seigfried, Charlene, *Chaos and Context* (Athens: Ohio University Press, 1978). A trenchant and detailed study of James's notion of pure experience.

Singer, Beth J., *The Rational Society* (Cleveland: Press of Case Western Reserve University, 1970). An examination of Santayana's social and political philosophy.

Smith, John E., *Purpose and Thought: The Meaning of Pragmatism* (New Haven: Yale University Press, 1978). An original and thorough analysis of pragmatist epistemology.

———, *The Spirit of American Philosophy* (New York: Oxford University Press, 1963). A perceptive treatment of the originality of American philosophy.

———, *Themes in American Philosophy* (New York: Harper and Row, 1970). A rich examination of the themes of purpose, experience, and community.

Suckiel, Ellen Kappy, *The Pragmatic Philosophy of William James* (South Bend: University of Notre Dame Press, 1982). A careful study of James's thought with a concentration on his epistemology.

Taylor, Eugene, *William James on Exceptional Mental States* (New York: Charles Scribner's Sons, 1983). A remarkable reconstruction of James's manuscripts for the Lowell Lectures of 1896.

Thayer, H. S., *Meaning and Action* (Indianapolis and New York: Bobbs-Merrill Company, Inc., 1968). A thorough and critical history of pragmatism, including an analysis of the European influences.

White, Morton, *The Philosophy of the American Revolution* (New York: Oxford University Press, 1978). A penetrating analysis of the complex strands which lace the philosophical foundations of the American Revolution.

——, *Pragmatism and the American Mind* (New York: Oxford University Press, 1973). A collection of White's essays on the American philosophers and on the philosophical dimensions in American intellectual history.

——, *Science and Sentiment in America* (New York: Oxford University Press, 1972). An interpretive and often critical history of American philosophy from the seventeenth century forward.

Wiener, Philip P., *Evolution and the Founders of Pragmatism* (Cambridge: Harvard University Press, 1949). The classic statement of the influence of Darwinism on American philosophy.

Wild, John, *The Radical Empiricism of William James* (Garden City, N.Y.: Doubleday and Company, Inc., 1969). A view of James's thought which finds it anticipatory and continuous with European phenomenology and existentialism.

Wilshire, Bruce, *William James and Phenomenology: A Study of "The Principles of Psychology"* (Bloomington: Indiana University Press, 1968). A study of James's *Principles of Psychology* from the perspective of Husserlian phenomenology.

Zeltner, Philip, *John Dewey's Aesthetic Philosophy* (Amsterdam: B. R. Gruner, 1975). The focus here is on Dewey's notion of experience as aesthetic.

Of special importance are the forthcoming studies of William James by Gerald Myers and of John Dewey by Ralph W. Sleeper.

NOTES

PREFACE

1 William James, *Essays in Radical Empiricism* (Cambridge: Harvard University Press, 1976), p. 121.
2 William James, *Essays in Philosophy* (Cambridge: Harvard University Press, 1978), p. 190.

I THE CULTURAL IMMORTALITY OF PHILOSOPHY AS HUMAN DRAMA

1 Plato, "Republic," *Plato: The Collected Dialogues* (New York: Pantheon Books, 1961), pp. 747–53.
2 Plato, "Meno," ibid., pp. 354–84.
3 Ibid., p. 363.
4 Cf. Herbert Marcuse, "Love Mystified: A Critique," in *Negations* (Boston: Beacon Press, 1969), p. 243: "Waking up from sleep, finding the way out of the cave is work within the cave; slow painful work with and *against* the prisoners in the cave. Everywhere, even in your own land which is not yet found, not yet free, there are those who do this work, who risk their lives for it—they fight the real fight, the political fight. You have revealed the latent, the true content of politics—you know that the political fight is the fight for the whole; not the mystical whole, but the very unmystical, antagonistic whole of our life and that of our children—the only life that is."
5 Cf. Norman O. Brown, "Love Mystified: A Reply," in *Negations,* p. 246: "The next generation needs to be told that the real fight is not the political fight, but to put an end to politics. From politics to metapolitics." For a commentary on this dispute between Brown and Marcuse about the meaning of the "cave," see John J. McDermott, *The Culture of Experience: Philosophical Essays in the American Grain* (New York: New York University Press, 1976), pp. 126–32.
6 William Shakespeare, *Hamlet,* in *The Complete Works of William Shakespeare* (London: Oxford University Press, 1905), p. 878.
7 Augustine, "On the Trinity," in *Basic Writings of Saint Augustine,* vol. 2 (New York: Random House, 1948), p. 673.
8 John 1:14.

9 John 1:1.

10 Marcus Aurelius, *Meditations* (Chicago: Henry Regnery Co., 1956), pp. 18–19.

11 John 1:9.

12 Baruch Spinoza, "On the Improvement of the Understanding," in *The Chief Works of Benedict De Spinoza*, vol. 2 (New York: Dover Publications, 1951), pp. 1–41.

13 Cf. William James, "Quelques considérations sur la méthode subjective," in *Essays in Philosophy* (Cambridge: Harvard University Press, 1978), p. 24: "Il y a donc des cas où *une* croyance crée sa propre vérification."

14 John Donne, *The Complete Poetry and Selected Prose of John Donne* (New York: Modern Library, 1952), p. 191.

15 Blaise Pascal, *Pensées* (New York: Modern Library, 1941), p. 75.

16 René Descartes, "Discourse on Method," in *The Essential Writings* (New York: Harper and Row, 1977), p. 134.

17 Immanuel Kant, *Kant's Inaugural Dissertation and Early Writings on Space* (Chicago: Open Court Publishing Co., 1929), pp. 53, 56, 59, 61.

18 G. W. F. Hegel, *Reason in History* (New York: Liberal Arts Press, 1953), p. 27.

19 *The Marx-Engels Reader*, ed. Robert C. Tucker (New York: W. W. Norton and Co., 1978), p. 4.

20 Ibid., pp. 70–79.

21 *Marx and Engels: Basic Writings on Politics and Philosophy*, ed. Lewis S. Feuer (New York: Anchor Books, 1959), p. 245.

22 Friedrich Nietzsche, *The Will to Power* (New York: Vintage Books, 1968), p. 8.

23 Cf. Friedrich Nietzsche, "The Birth of Tragedy," in *Basic Writings of Nietzsche*, ed. Walter Kaufman (New York: Modern Library, 1968), pp. 56–121.

24 Friedrich Nietzsche, "The Gay Science," in *The Portable Nietzsche*, ed. Walter Kaufman (New York: Viking Press, 1943), pp. 95–96.

25 Nietzsche, "The Dawn," in ibid., p. 92.

26 Nietzsche, "The Gay Science," in ibid., p. 297.

27 William James, "The Teaching of Philosophy in Our Colleges," in *Essays in Philosophy*, p. 4.

28 William James, *The Varieties of Religious Experience* (New York: Longmans, Green and Co., 1902), p. 160. Masked as coming from a "French correspondent," this text is actually autobiographical. The term "vastation" is taken from the eighteenth-century mystic-philosopher Emmanuel Swedenborg and refers to the projecting of our inner self outward, such that we behold ourself anew, usually in a grotesque form. The attempt is to purify inner evil, although the frightening character of the experience holds the center of the attention.

29 William James, "Diary," in *The Writings of William James*, ed. John J. McDermott (Chicago: University of Chicago Press, 1977), p. 8.

30 *The Letters of Josiah Royce*, ed. John Clendenning (Chicago: University of Chicago Press, 1970), p. 586.

31 William James, "Introduction to the Literary Remains of the Late Henry James," in *Essays in Religion and Morality* (Cambridge: Harvard University Press, 1982), p. 62.

32 William James, *Pragmatism* (Cambridge: Harvard University Press, 1975), p. 123.

33 Cf. Ralph Barton Perry, *The Thought and Character of William James*, vol. 2 (Boston: Little, Brown and Co., 1935), p. 700.

34 William James, *A Pluralistic Universe* (Cambridge: Harvard University Press, 1977), p. 39.

35 Ibid., pp. 130–31.

36 Voltaire, "La Henriade," in *Les Oeuvres Complètes de Voltaire*, vol. 2 (Geneva: Institut et Musée Voltaire, 1970), p. 575.

2 SPIRES OF INFLUENCE

1 *American Philosophic Addresses, 1700–1900*, ed. Joseph L. Blau (New York: Columbia University Press, 1946); *Men and Movements in American Philosophy* (Englewood Cliffs, N.J.: Prentice-Hall, 1952); "Emerson's Transcendentalist Individualism as a Social Philosophy," *Review of Metaphysics* 31, no. 1 (September 1977): 80–92.

2 Robert C. Pollock, "Ralph Waldo Emerson—The Single Vision," in *American Classics Reconsidered*, ed. Harold Gardiner (New York: Scribner's, 1958), pp. 15–58.

3 George Herbert Mead tends to speak of Emerson only in the context of Concord transcendentalism. Ironically, in lamenting the failure of the transcendentalists to develop a distinctive doctrine of American self-consciousness, Mead overlooks the powerful voice of Emerson in precisely that regard. Mead, "The Philosophies of Royce, James and Dewey in Their American Setting," in *Selected Writings*, ed. Andrew J. Reck (Indianapolis: Bobbs-Merrill, 1964), pp. 377–78.

4 Charles Sanders Peirce, *Collected Papers*, ed. Charles Hartshorne and Paul Weiss, vol. 6 (sec. 102) (Cambridge: Harvard University Press, 1934), pp. 86–87. Peirce also was fond of quoting and mocking Emerson's poem on the Sphinx, especially the line, "Of thine eye, I am eyebeam," ibid., vol. 1 (sec. 310), pp. 153–54, and vol. 3 (sec. 404), p. 252. Some unpublished material on Peirce's "boyhood impressions" of Emerson can be found in "Manuscript—296" as recorded in the *Annotated Catalogue of the Papers of Charles S. Peirce*, ed. Richard Robin (Amherst: University of Massachusetts Press, 1967), p. 31.

5 Ralph Waldo Emerson, "The American Scholar," in *The Complete Works of Ralph Waldo Emerson*, vol. 1 (Boston: Houghton Mifflin, 1903–1904), p. 86.

6 Emerson, "Nature," in ibid., p. 3.

7 Emerson, "The Divinity School Address," in ibid., p. 135.

8 Ibid., p. 151.

9 Emerson, "American Scholar," p. 95. The use of "he" and "man" in this text and in subsequent texts is to be read in the present essay as referring also to "she" and "woman."

10 Ibid., p. 99.

11 Emerson, "Fate," in ibid., vol. 6, p. 3. For a similar attitude, see William James, *The Varieties of Religious Experience* (New York: Longmans, Green and Co., 1902), p. 489. "Knowledge about life is one thing; effective occupation of a place in life, with its dynamic currents passing through your being, is another."

12 Texts in support of this position abound in the writings of John Dewey. Among others are Dewey, *Reconstruction in Philosophy*, vol. 12 (1982) of *The Middle Works* (Carbondale: Southern Illinois University Press, 1976–83), p. 132. "Experience carries principles of connection and organization within itself." And again, p. 134, "What Shakespeare so pregnantly said of nature, it is 'made better by no mean, but nature makes that mean,' becomes true of experience."

13 For a historical and philosophical treatment of the genesis of James's doctrine of radical empiricism, see John J. McDermott, "Introduction" to William James, *Essays in Radical Empiricism* (Cambridge: Harvard University Press, 1976), pp. xi–xlviii. Dewey's doctrine of radical empiricism is best found in *The Influence of Darwinism on Philosophy and Other Essays in Contemporary Philosophy* (New York: Holt, 1910).

14 Emerson, "American Scholar," p. 111. For a richer description of the extreme variety of audience responses to Emerson's oration of 1837, see Bliss Perry, "Emerson's Most

Famous Speech," in *Ralph Waldo Emerson—A Profile*, ed. Carl Bode (New York: Hill and Wang, 1969), pp. 52–65. Oliver Wendell Holmes heard the oration as an "intellectual Declaration of Independence" and James Russell Lowell viewed it as "our Yankee version of a lecture by Abelard, our Harvard parallel to the last public appearances of Schelling."

15 Emerson, "American Scholar," p. 111.
16 Emerson, "Experience," in *Works*, vol. 6, p. 308 n. 1. "Everything in the Universe goes by indirection. There are no straight lines."
17 Ibid., p. 68. William James holds a similar position. "Notebook" entry of 1903 as found in Ralph Barton Perry, *The Thought and Character of William James*, vol. 2 (Boston: Little, Brown and Co., 1935), p. 700 (cited above, pp. 25–26).
18 *The Journals of Ralph Waldo Emerson*, vol. 9 (Boston: Houghton Mifflin, 1909–14), pp. 277–78.
19 Emerson, "Nature," p. 34.
20 Emerson, "Education," in *Works*, vol. 10, p. 132.
21 Emerson, "The Poet," in *Works*, vol. 3, p. 18.
22 Emerson, "Nature," p. 32.
23 Peirce, *Collected Papers*, vol. 5, p. 37.
24 John Dewey, *Experience and Nature*, vol. 1 (1981) of *The Later Works* (Carbondale: Southern Illinois University Press, 1981–), p. 43.
25 Emerson, "Nature," p. 31.
26 *The Letters of Josiah Royce*, ed. John Clendenning (Chicago: University of Chicago Press, 1970), p. 586 (cited above, p. 24).
27 Josiah Royce, *The Problem of Christianity* (Chicago: University of Chicago Press, 1968 [1913]), p. 294.
28 William James, *Pragmatism* (Cambridge: Harvard University Press, 1975), p. 9.
29 Ibid., p. 99.
30 Ibid., p. 123.
31 James Papers, Houghton Library, Harvard University (bMs AM 1092, box L, notebook N²).
32 James, *Essays in Radical Empiricism*, p. 42.
33 Cited in Gay Wilson Allen, *William James—A Biography* (New York: Viking, 1967), pp. 186–87.
34 Emerson, "American Scholar," pp. 89–90.
35 William James, "Address at the Emerson Centenary in Concord," in *Essays in Religion and Morality* (Cambridge: Harvard University Press, 1982), p. 109–15. For a contrast of James's hagiographic approach to others more critical and substantive, the reader should consult two collections of essays: *Emerson*, ed. Milton Konvitz and Stephen Whicher (Englewood Cliffs, N.J.: Prentice-Hall, 1962) and *The Recognition of Ralph Waldo Emerson—Selected Criticism since 1837*, ed. Milton Konvitz (Ann Arbor: University of Michigan Press, 1972). It is striking that in the vast secondary literature on Emerson, distinctively philosophical considerations are virtually absent.
36 James was not always complimentary to Emerson. In *The Varieties of Religious Experience*, for example, he criticized Emerson for tending toward "abstraction" on the religious question (pp. 32, 56). For a discussion of James's ambivalence on Emerson, see F. O. Mathiessen, *The American Renaissance* (New York: Oxford University Press, 1941), pp. 53–54 n.
37 James, *Essays in Religion and Morality*, p. 114.
38 Emerson, "American Scholar," pp. 96–97.

39 James, *Essays in Religion and Morality,* p. 114. The potential capacity for "transfiguration" of fact as subject to human will is not a strange contention for William James, as can
be seen in his own doctrine of "The Will to Believe." Could it have some expressive origin
in Emerson's "Nature"? "Build therefore your own world. As fast as you conform your
life to the pure idea in your mind, that will unfold its great proportions. A correspondent
revolution in things will attend the influx of the spirit" (*Works,* vol. 1, p. 76).

40 What could be more Emersonian than James's remark in his "Sentiment of Rationality"
that "the inmost nature of the reality is congenial to powers which you possess"? (*The
Will to Believe* [Cambridge: Harvard University Press, 1979], p. 73). See also *The
Writings of William James,* ed. John J. McDermott (Chicago: University of Chicago Press,
1977), p. 331. In preparation for his "Address," James did read Emerson, "volume
after volume," but came away with "a moral lesson" rather than distinctive philosophical
insight. Cf. *The Letters of William James,* ed. Henry James III, 2 vols. (Boston: Atlantic
Monthly Press, 1920), p. 190.

41 James, *Letters of William James,* pp. 234–35. For another contrast of Emerson and
Santayana, see John Crowe Ransom, "Art and Mr. Santayana," *Santayana: Animal
Faith and Spiritual Life,* ed. John Lachs (New York: Appleton-Century-Crofts, 1967),
pp. 403–4.

42 George Santayana, *The Letters of George Santayana,* ed. Daniel Cory (New York:
Scribner's, 1955), pp. 81–82.

43 George Santayana, "The Optimism of Ralph Waldo Emerson," in *George Santayana's
America,* ed. James Ballowe (Urbana: University of Illinois Press, 1967), p. 84. Another
little-known piece of Santayana on Emerson is "Emerson the Poet," a centennial contribution of 1903. Although in this essay Santayana speaks of Emerson as often bland, he
praises him for self-direction and a deep and unyielding sense of personal liberty. See
Santayana on America, ed. Richard C. Lyon (New York: Harcourt, 1968), pp. 268–83.

44 George Santayana, "The Genteel Tradition in American Philosophy," in *Winds of
Doctrine* (London: J. M. Dent, 1913), pp. 192–93.

45 George Santayana, "Emerson," in *Interpretations of Poetry and Religion* (New York:
Scribner's, 1900), p. 218.

46 Ibid., p. 233.

47 Santayana, *Letters,* pp. 225–26.

48 Ignas K. Skrupskelis, "Annotated Bibliography of the Publications of Josiah Royce," in
The Basic Writings of Josiah Royce, ed. John J. McDermott, vol. 2 (Chicago: University
of Chicago Press, 1969), pp. 1167–226.

49 Josiah Royce, *William James and Other Essays* (New York: Macmillan, 1911), pp. 3–4,
5–6.

50 John Dewey, "Ralph Waldo Emerson," in *Characters and Events,* vol. 1 (New York:
Holt, 1929), p. 71.

51 Ibid., p. 74.

52 Ibid., p. 70.

53 Ibid., p. 75.

54 Dewey takes a similar position in *Art as Experience* (New York: Capricorn, 1958
[1934]), p. 11: "Theory can start with and from acknowledged works of art only when
the esthetic is already compartmentalized, or only when works of art are set in a niche
apart instead of being celebrations, recognized as such, of the things of ordinary experience. Even a crude experience, if authentically an experience, is more fit to give a clue to
the intrinsic nature of esthetic experience than is an object already set apart from any
other mode of experience."

55 Dewey, "Ralph Waldo Emerson," p. 75.
56 Ibid., p. 77.

3   THE PROMETHEAN SELF AND COMMUNITY IN THE
PHILOSOPHY OF WILLIAM JAMES

1   *The Letters of William James,* ed. Henry James III, vol. 2 (Boston: Atlantic Monthly Press, 1920), p. 90. The "Headnote" is from *Memories and Studies* (New York: Longmans, Green and Co., 1911), p. 102.
2   John Dewey, "The Vanishing Subject in the Psychology of James," *Problems of Men* (New York: Philosophical Library, 1946), p. 396.
3   William James, *Essays in Radical Empiricism* (Cambridge: Harvard University Press, 1976).
4   For a discussion of the occasion of these crisis texts, see Gay Wilson Allen, *William James—A Biography* (New York: Viking Press, 1967), pp. 162–70. The three texts are cited in full in *The Writings of William James,* ed. John J. McDermott (Chicago: University of Chicago Press, 1977 [1967]), pp. 6–8.
5   See, e.g., "Psychological Studies of the James Family," *Psychohistory Review* 7 (Summer-Fall 1979): 5–70.
6   William A. Clebsch, *American Religious Thought* (Chicago: University of Chicago Press, 1973), p. 142.
7   James, *Writings of William James,* p. 7.
8   Ibid., p. 6.
9   Ibid., pp. 7–8.
10 See William James, *Pragmatism* (Cambridge: Harvard University Press, 1975), p. 99: "Woe to him whose beliefs play fast and loose with the order which realities follow in his experience: they will lead him nowhere or else make false connexions."
11 Ibid., p. 123; as cited earlier (see chap. 1, p. 25). James stresses the Promethean character of the human self.
12 See David Hume, *A Treatise of Human Nature* (Oxford: Clarendon Press, 1958), pp. 251–63.
13 William James, *The Principles of Psychology,* vol. 1 (Cambridge: Harvard University Press, 1981), p. 336.
14 William James, *Psychology: Briefer Course* (Cambridge: Harvard University Press, 1984), pp. 190–91.
15 For an explicitly physical account of self-consciousness by James, see *Principles,* vol. 1, p. 288: "In a sense, then, it may be truly said that, in one person at least, *the 'Self of selves,' when carefully examined, is found to consist mainly of the collection of these particular motions in the head or between the head and throat.* I do not for a moment say that this is *all* it consists of, for I fully realize how desperately hard is introspection in this field. But I feel quite sure that these cephalic motions are the portions of my innermost activity of which I am *most distinctly aware.* If the dim portions which I cannot yet define should prove to be like unto these distinct portions in me, and I like other men, *it would follow that our entire feeling of spiritual activity, or what commonly passes by that name, is really a feeling of bodily activities whose exact nature is by most men overlooked.*"
16 William James, *The Meaning of Truth* (Cambridge: Harvard University Press, 1975), pp. 6–7.
17 James, *Pragmatism,* p. 9.

18 James, *Essays in Radical Empiricism*, p. 86 n.

19 James, *Psychology: Briefer Course*, p. 158.

20 William James, *The Varieties of Religious Experience* (New York: Longmans, Green and Co., 1902), p. 498.

21 William James, *A Pluralistic Universe* (Cambridge: Harvard University Press, 1977), p. 139.

22 James, *Varieties of Religious Experience*, p. 499.

23 Ibid.

24 James, *Principles*, vol. 1, pp. 281–82.

25 I have made some earlier efforts in this direction. See John J. McDermott, *The Culture of Experience: Philosophical Essays in the American Grain* (New York: New York University Press, 1976).

26 A phenomenology of these relational pairs can be found in "Life Is in the Transitions," in ibid., pp. 104–10.

27 James, *Essays in Radical Empiricism*, p. 35.

28 James, *Pragmatism*, p. 30. For the full text, see below, chap. 7, p. 110.

29 Blaise Pascal, *Pensées* (New York: Modern Library, 1941), p. 75. For other discussions of homelessness, see above, chap. 1, p. 13, and below, chap. 4, p. 68, and chap. 8, p. 135.

30 The works of Edward Hall, Robert Sommer, Kevin Lynch, and Erving Goffman are exceptions to this judgment. See also Raymond P. McDermott, "Social Relations as Contexts for Learning," *Harvard Educational Review* 47 (May 1977): 198–213.

31 See James, "On Some Omissions of Introspective Psychology," as cited in *Essays in Radical Empiricism*, p. xix, where he writes that we should avoid "the error, namely, of supposing that where there is *no* name no entity can exist. All *dumb* psychic states have, owing to this error, been coolly suppressed; or, if recognised at all, have been named after the substantive perception they led to, as thoughts 'about' this object or 'about' that, the stolid word *about* engulfing all their delicate idiosyncracies in its monotonous sound. Thus the greater and greater accentuation and isolation of the substantive parts have continually gone on."

32 James, *A Pluralistic Universe*, p. 145.

33 James, *Varieties of Religious Experience*, pp. 501–2.

4   TRANSIENCY AND AMELIORATION

1 The most dramatic recent defense of the cycle as a principle of historical explanation is to be found in N. O. Brown, *Closing Time* (New York: Random House, 1973).

2 For support of this judgment see Clifford Geertz, *The Interpretation of Culture* (New York: Basic Books, 1973), p. 43. "However, even if I am wrong (as, admittedly, many anthropologists would hold) in claiming that the *consensus gentium* approach can produce neither substantial universals nor specific connections between cultural and non-cultural phenomena to explain them, the question still remains whether such universals should be taken as the central elements in the definition of man, whether a lowest-common-denominator view of humanity is what we want anyway. This is, of course, now a philosophical question, not as such a scientific one; but the notion that the essence of what it means to be human is most clearly revealed in those features of human culture that are universal rather than in those that are distinctive to this people or that is a prejudice we are not necessarily obliged to share. Is it in grasping such general facts—that man has

everywhere some sort of 'religion'—or in grasping the richness of this religious phenomenon or that—Balinese trance or Indian ritualism, Aztec human sacrifice or Zuni raindancing—that we grasp him? Is the fact that 'marriage' is universal (if it is) as penetrating a comment on what we are as the facts concerning Himalayan polyandry, or those fantastic Australian marriage rules, or the elaborate bride-price systems of Bantu Africa? The comment that Cromwell was the most typical Englishman of his time precisely in that he was the oddest may be relevant in this connection, too: it may be in the cultural particularities of people—in their oddities—that some of the most instructive revelations of what it is to be generically human are to be found; and the main contribution of the science of anthropology to the construction—or reconstruction—of a concept of man may then lie in showing us how to find them."

3 The emergence of narcissism in America has already been catalogued by Christopher Lasch, *The Culture of Narcissism—American Life in an Age of Diminishing Expectations* (New York: W. W. Norton and Co., 1978). Lasch writes, "Liberalism, the political theory of the ascendant bourgeoisie, long ago lost the capacity to explain events in the world of the welfare state and the multinational corporation; nothing has taken its place. Politically bankrupt, liberalism is intellectually bankrupt as well. The sciences it has fostered, once confident of their ability to dispel the darkness of the ages, no longer provide satisfactory explanations of the phenomena they profess to elucidate. Neoclassical economic theory cannot explain the coexistence of unemployment and inflation; sociology retreats from the attempt to outline a general theory of modern society; academic psychology retreats from the challenge of Freud into the measurement of trivia. The natural sciences, having made exaggerated claims for themselves, now hasten to announce that science offers no miracle cures for social problems.

"In the humanities, demoralization has reached the point of a general admission that humanistic study has nothing to contribute to an understanding of the modern world. Philosophers no longer explain the nature of things or pretend to tell us how to live. Students of literature treat the text not as a representation of the real world but as a reflection of the artist's inner state or mind. Historians admit to a 'sense of the irrelevance of history,' in David Donald's words, 'and of the bleakness of the new era we are entering' " (pp. xiii–xiv).

4 On behalf of an extensive literature, see David W. Marcell, *Progress and Pragmatism—James, Dewey, Beard and the American Idea of Progress* (Westport: Greenwood Press, 1974).

5 "The Practical Significance of Pessimism," in *Fugitive Essays of Josiah Royce*, ed. Jacob Loewenberg (Freeport: Books for Libraries Press, 1968 [1920]), p. 152.

6 Perry Miller, *Errand Into the Wilderness* (Cambridge: Harvard University Press, 1956), p. 7.

7 Sacvan Bercovitch holds that this second form of the jeremiad possesses the pervasive theme of affirmation and exultation. See *The American Jeremiad* (Madison: University of Wisconsin Press, 1978), p. 6.

8 Ralph Waldo Emerson, "Nature," in *The Complete Works of Ralph Waldo Emerson,* vol. 1 (Boston: Houghton Mifflin, 1903–1904), p. 3.

9 Ralph Waldo Emerson, "The American Scholar," in ibid., vol. 1, p. 81.

10 Alfred Kazin, *On Native Grounds* (New York: Anchor Books, 1956), pp. ix–x.

11 Walt Whitman, *Democratic Vistas* (New York: Liberal Arts Press, 1949), p. 9.

12 Ibid., p. 59.

13 See *The Shock of Recognition,* ed. Edmund Wilson (New York: Farrar, Straus and Cudahy, 1955), p. 259.

14 Ibid., p. 262.

15 Gabriel Marcel, *Homo Viator* (Chicago: Henry Regnery Co., 1951), p. 153.

16 Karl Jaspers, *Man in the Modern Age* (New York: Anchor Books, 1957 [1931]), pp. 2–3.

17 Alexis de Tocqueville, *Democracy in America,* vol. 1 (New York: Vintage Books, 1959 [1835]), p. 303.

18 George Santayana, *Character and Opinion in the United States* (New York: Doubleday Anchor Books, 1956 [1920]), pp. 106–7.

19 As symbolic sustenance of this judgment, witness the attitude of John Cotton before and after his journey to New England. In his farewell sermon to John Winthrop's company, then leaving for the new world, John Cotton took as his text 2 Samuel 7:10: "Moreover I will appoint a place for my people Israel, and I will plant them, that they may dwell in a place of their owne, and move no more." See John Cotton, "God's Promise to His Plantation," *Old South Leaflets* (London, 1630), no. 3. Once in the New World, Cotton could write in "A Reply" to Roger Williams, "The Jurisdiction (whence a man is banished) is but small, and the Countrey round about it, large and fruitful: where a man may make his choice of variety of more pleasant, and profitable seats, than he leaveth behind him. In which respect, Banishment in this countrye, is not counted so much a confinement, as an enlargement." Cited in Sidney Mead, "The American People: Their Space, Time and Religion," in *The Lively Experiment* (New York: Harper and Row, 1964), p. 13.

20 Even Josiah Royce came to this position. In 1885, he wrote that "we go to seek the Eternal, not in experience, but in the thought that thinks experience." *The Religious Aspect of Philosophy* (Boston: Houghton Mifflin, 1885), p. 289. By 1913, Royce had fully absorbed the thrust of America in his own life and thought to such an extent that he wrote, "In brief, then, the real world is the Community of Interpretation which is constituted by the two antithetic ideas, and their mediator or interpreter, whatever or whoever that interpreter may be. If the interpretation is a reality, and if it truly interprets the whole of reality, then the community reaches its goal, and the real world includes its own interpreter. Unless both the interpreter and the community are real, there is no real world." *The Problem of Christianity* (Chicago: University of Chicago Press, 1968), p. 339.

21 See Louis Simpson, "In California," *At the End of the Open Road* (Middletown: Wesleyan University Press, 1963), p. 11:

> Lie back, Walt Whitman.
> There, on the fabulous raft with the King and the Duke!
> For the white row of the Marina
> Faces the Rock. Turn round the wagons here.

22 *The Collected Poems of Henry David Thoreau,* ed. Carl Bode (Baltimore: Johns Hopkins University Press, 1964), p. 135.

23 T. S. Eliot, "East Coker," *Four Quartets* (London: Faber and Faber, 1949), p. 31.

5 AMERICA

1 J. Hector St. John de Crèvecoeur, *Letters from an American Farmer* (New York: E. P. Dutton, 1957 [1782]), p. 39. "What then is the American, this new man? He is either an European, or the descendant of an European, hence that strange mixture of blood, which you will find in no other country. I could point out to you a family whose grandfather was an Englishman, whose wife was Dutch, whose son married a French woman, and whose

present four sons have now four wives of different nations. *He* is an American, who leaving behind him all his ancient prejudices and manners, receives new ones from the new mode of life he has embraced, the new government he obeys, and the new rank he holds. He becomes an American by being received in the broad lap of our great *Alma Mater*. Here individuals of all nations are melted into a new race of men, whose labours and posterity will one day cause great changes in the world. Americans are the western pilgrims, who are carrying along with them that great mass of arts, sciences, vigour, and industry which began long since in the east; they will finish the great circle."

2 Cf. Pico della Mirandola, *Oration on the Dignity of Man* (Chicago: Henry Regnery Co., 1956).

3 Cf. Ralph Waldo Emerson, *The Complete Works of Ralph Waldo Emerson* (Boston: Houghton Mifflin, 1903–1904): "Nature," vol. 1, p. 3; "Civilization," vol. 7, p. 28; "Self-Reliance," vol. 2, pp. 49–50. Emerson's statement, "Do your own work" was a change from his earlier line, "Do your own thing," which can be found in an 1839 edition of "Self-Reliance."

4 Emerson, "Education," in ibid., vol. 10, p. 132.

5 *The Journals of Ralph Waldo Emerson*, vol. 9 (Boston: Houghton Mifflin, 1909–14), p. 277. For the full text, see above, chap. 2, pp. 33–34.

6 Cf. Edmund Wilson, *The Shock of Recognition* (New York: Farrar, Straus and Cudahy, 1943), p. 259.

7 Walt Whitman, *Democratic Vistas* (New York: Liberal Arts Press, 1949), p. 52.

8 Ibid., p. 18.

9 William James, "Thomas Davidson: A Knight-Errant of the Intellectual Life," in *Memories and Studies* (New York: Longmans, Green and Co., 1911), p. 102.

10 *The Letters of William James,* ed. Henry James III, vol. 2 (Boston: Atlantic Monthly Press, 1920), p. 90. A longer excerpt from this letter is found above, at the beginning of chap. 3, p. 44.

11 Cf. Ralph Barton Perry, *The Thought and Character of William James,* vol. 2 (Boston: Little, Brown and Co., 1935), p. 700, as cited earlier, chap. 1, pp. 25–26.

12 Josiah Royce, "An Autobiographical Sketch," in *The Basic Writings of Josiah Royce,* ed. John J. McDermott, vol. 1 (Chicago: University of Chicago Press, 1969), p. 34.

13 Josiah Royce, *California: A Study of American Character* (Boston: Houghton Mifflin Co., 1886), p. 501.

14 Josiah Royce, *The Problem of Christianity* (Chicago: University of Chicago Press, 1968 [1918]), p. 325.

15 John Dewey, *Individualism, Old and New,* vol. 5 (1984) of *The Later Works* (Carbondale: Southern Illinois University Press, 1981–), p. 80.

16 Ibid., pp. 66–67.

17 John Dewey, *The Public and Its Problems,* vol. 2 (1984) of *The Later Works,* pp. 329–30.

18 Ibid., p. 328.

19 We are in obvious debt here to Immanuel Kant, *The Critique of Pure Reason* (London: Macmillan and Co., Ltd., 1953), p. 635. "All the interests of my reason, speculative as well as practical, combine in the three following questions:

    1. What can I know?
    2. What ought I to do?
    3. What may I hope?"

To which is added a fourth question ("What is man?") found in Kant's "Introduction" to his *Logic* (New York: Library of Liberal Arts, 1974), p. 29.

20 William Manchester, *The Glory and the Dream: A Narrative History of America, 1932–1972* (Boston: Little, Brown and Co., 1974), p. 3.

21 John Dewey, *Human Nature and Conduct*, vol. 14 (1983) of *The Middle Works* (Carbondale: Southern Illinois University Press, 1976–83), p. 227.

6 CLASSICAL AMERICAN PHILOSOPHY

1 Cf. Robert McNamara, "Time Bomb or Myth: The Population Problem," *Foreign Affairs* 62, no. 5 (Summer 1984): 1107–32.

2 Robert Jay Lifton and Kai Erikson, "Nuclear War's Effect on the Mind," *Indefensible Weapons*, ed. Robert Jay Lifton and Richard Falk (New York: Basic Books, 1982), pp. 274–75.

3 William James, *Pragmatism* (Cambridge: Harvard University Press, 1975), p. 91.

4 The doctrines of fallibilism and tychism in the thought of Charles Sanders Peirce, the social criticism of George Santayana, and the social philosophy of George Herbert Mead are also relevant here. Another way of putting the position of Santayana and Mead, with regard to the potential transcendence of "local" thought, is found in T. S. Eliot, "American Literature and American Language," in *To Criticize the Critic* (New York: Farrar, Straus and Giroux, 1965), p. 54. In singling out a "landmark of a national literature," Eliot writes that it has "the strong local flavour combined with unconscious universality."

5 George Santayana, *Character and Opinion in the United States* (New York: Doubleday Anchor Books, 1956 [1920]), p. 20. A further gloss on the philosophical articulation of the American native soil is found in George Herbert Mead, "The Philosophies of Royce, James and Dewey in Their American Setting," *International Journal of Ethics* 40 (1929–30): 211–31.

6 John Dewey, *The Need for a Recovery of Philosophy*, vol. 10 (1980) of *The Middle Works* (Carbondale: Southern Illiinois University Press, 1976–83), p. 6.

7 In the phrase "takes the finite at dead-reckoning," the philosophical pun is intended, for it is our unrequited death that is the ontological bane of our existence and yet it must be reckoned.

8 It is of note here that aside from other afflictions, James lost an infant son; Dewey lost an older brother, two young children, and an adolescent grandson; and one of Royce's children was a victim of severe mental illness. Offenses to the innocent tend to drive one into the bosom of an alleged Infinite or into the potential healing of the shadows of time. They took the latter route.

9 James, *Pragmatism*, p. 30.

10 For a clarifying and perceptive discussion of the originality of pragmatic truth as developed by William James, see H. S. Thayer, "Introduction," *The Meaning of Truth* (Cambridge: Harvard University Press, 1975), pp. xxv–xliii.

11 James, *Pragmatism*, pp. 78–79. In a response to this paper, both Alan Rosenberg and Gary Brodsky point to the snare facing the pluralist position, namely, the existence of the fanatic. A genuine pluralist position allows all persuasions to have their say, yet that of the fanatic will close discussion forever. In response, I invoke Dewey's maxim of "warranted assertions," which holds that the accrued history of human experience has rendered certain positions and activities, such as slavery and genocide, as permanently dehumanizing and therefore unacceptable to the human community. The open question is whether

fanaticism and terrorism come under that stricture and whether opposing them violates a genuine pluralism. I do think that they are liable to such a critique and I do not think that this obviates pluralism, on the grounds that if they prevail nothing human can grow.

12 Charles Sanders Peirce, "The Fixation of Belief," in *Collected Papers of Charles Sanders Peirce*, ed. Charles Hartshorne and Paul Weiss, vol. 5 (Cambridge: Harvard University Press, 1934), pp. 233–47.

13 Josiah Royce, "Provincialism," in *The Basic Writings of Josiah Royce*, ed. John J. McDermott, vol. 2 (Chicago: University of Chicago Press, 1969), p. 1069.

14 Josiah Royce, *The Problem of Christianity* (Chicago: University of Chicago Press, 1968), p. 337.

15 Ibid., p. 339.

16 James, *Pragmatism*, p. 94.

17 William James, "Faith and the Right to Believe," in *The Writings of William James*, ed. John J. McDermott (Chicago: University of Chicago Press, 1977), p. 739.

18 John Dewey, "Renascent Liberalism," in *The Philosophy of John Dewey*, ed. John J. McDermott, vol. 2 (Chicago: University of Chicago Press, 1981), pp. 646–47.

19 William James, "The Sentiment of Rationality," in *The Will to Believe* (Cambridge: Harvard University Press, 1979), p. 73.

7   A RELATIONAL WORLD

1 William James, *The Will to Believe* (Cambridge: Harvard University Press, 1979), p. 144. See also *The Writings of William James*, ed. John J. McDermott (Chicago: University of Chicago Press, 1977), p. 613. James was not unaware of the danger involved in revolutionary ideas, for in 1878 he writes that "we have never had an example in history of a highly intellectual race, in which prudence was the ruling passion." Cf. Ralph Barton Perry, *The Thought and Character of William James*, vol. 2 (Boston: Little, Brown and Co., 1935), p. 35.

2 William James, *The Meaning of Truth* (Cambridge: Harvard University Press, 1975), pp. 6–7. See also James, *Writings of William James*, p. 136 (cited above, pp. 49–50).

3 William James, *The Principles of Psychology*, vol. 2 (Cambridge: Harvard University Press, 1981), p. 961 (italics in the original).

4 For a more detailed analysis of radical empiricism, see John J. McDermott, "Introduction," to William James, *Essays in Radical Empiricism* (Cambridge: Harvard University Press, 1976), pp. xi–xlviii; and John J. McDermott, "Life Is in the Transitions," in *The Culture of Experience: Philosophical Essays in the American Grain* (New York: New York University Press, 1976), pp. 99–117.

5 William James, *Pragmatism* (Cambridge: Harvard University Press, 1975), p. 30 (italics in the original). See also James, *Writings of William James*, p. 379.

6 Cf. John J. McDermott, "To Be Human Is to Humanize: A Radically Empirical Aesthetic," in *Culture of Experience*, pp. 21–62.

7 William James, *A Pluralistic Universe* (Cambridge: Harvard University Press, 1977), p. 145 (italics in the original). See also James, *Writings of William James*, pp. 806–7.

8 Perry, *Thought and Character of William James*, vol. 2, p. 700 (cited above, chap. 1, pp. 25–26).

9 James, *Will to Believe*, pp. 6–7. See also James, *Writings of William James*, p. 135.

10 William James, *Essays in Religion and Morality* (Cambridge: Harvard University Press,

1982), pp. 162–73. See also James, *Writings of William James,* pp. 660–71.

11 John Dewey, "The Development of American Pragmatism," in *The Philosophy of John Dewey,* ed. John J. McDermott, vol. 1 (Chicago: University of Chicago Press, 1981), pp. 50–51.

12 Cf. John Dewey, *Lectures in China, 1919–1920,* ed. Robert W. Clopton and Tsuin-Chen Ou (Honolulu: University Press of Hawaii, 1973).

13 A balanced view of Dewey's contributions and limitations during his China sojourn is found in Thomas Berry, "Dewey's Influence in China," in *John Dewey: His Thought and Influence,* ed. John Blewett (New York: Fordham University Press, 1960), pp. 199–232.

14 John Dewey, *Democracy and Education,* vol. 9 (1980) of *The Middle Works* (Carbondale: Southern Illinois University Press, 1976–83), p. 153 (italics in the original).

15 John Dewey, *Experience and Nature,* vol. 1 (1981) of *The Later Works* (Carbondale: Southern Illinois University Press, 1981–), p. 172.

16 John Dewey, *The Quest for Certainty,* vol. 4 (1984) of *The Later Works,* p. 224. See also Dewey, "The Construction of Good," in *Philosophy of John Dewey,* vol. 2, p. 595.

17 Dewey, *Experience and Nature,* pp. 12–13.

18 Clifford Geertz, *The Interpretation of Cultures* (New York: Basic Books, 1973), pp. 24–25. Cf. Geertz, *Local Knowledge* (New York: Basic Books, 1983).

19 Dewey, *Experience and Nature,* p. 392.

20 Dewey, *Philosophy of John Dewey,* vol. 2, p. 539.

21 Dewey, *Experience and Nature,* pp. 40–41.

22 Dewey, *Democracy and Education,* p. 200.

23 John Dewey, *Education Today* (New York: G. P. Putnam's Sons, 1940), p. 298.

24 Cited in Jacques le Goff, *The Birth of Purgatory* (Chicago: University of Chicago Press, 1984), pp. 49–50.

8 THE AESTHETIC DRAMA OF THE ORDINARY

1 Cited in Serge Chermayeff and Christopher Alexander, *Community and Privacy* (New York: Anchor Books, 1965), p. 29.

2 Larry L. King, "The Last Frontier," *The Old Man and Lesser Mortals* (New York: Viking Press, 1975), p. 207.

3 Cf. the moving and poignant scene of "eviction" in Ralph Ellison, *Invisible Man* (New York: Vintage Books, 1972 [1952]), pp. 261–77.

4 The master of "things" and "boxes" is, of course, Joseph Cornell. Indeed, he is the master of things in boxes, known forever as Cornell boxes. Only those who have experienced these "boxes" can appreciate Cornell's extraordinary ability to merge the surrealism of the imagination and the obviousness of things as a "memorial to experience." Cf. Diane Waldman, *Joseph Cornell* (New York: George Braziller, Inc., 1977), and Kynaston McShine, *Joseph Cornell* (New York: The Museum of Modern Art, 1981). As with Cornell, by "things" we mean, as does William James, bundles of relations. Things are not construed here as Aristotelian essences, much less as conceptually rendered boxes.

5 Rainer Maria Rilke, "The Ninth Elegy," *Duino Elegies* (New York: W. W. Norton, 1939), p. 73.

6 Ralph Waldo Emerson, "The American Scholar," in *Works,* vol. 1 (Boston: Houghton Mifflin, 1903–1904), pp. 96–97.

7 Cf. William Blake, "Auguries of Innocence," *The Poetry and Prose of William Blake,* ed. David V. Erdman (New York: Anchor Books, 1965), p. 481.

> To see a World in a Grain of Sand
> And a Heaven in a Wild Flower,
> Hold Infinity in the palm of your hand
> And Eternity in an hour.

9 EXPERIENCE GROWS BY ITS EDGES

1 The full passage from which the title of this chapter is taken was cited in chap. 2, p. 37, and can be found in William James, *Essays in Radical Empiricism* (Cambridge: Harvard University Press, 1976), p. 42.

2 Maurice Merleau-Ponty, *Phenomenology of Perception,* trans. Colin Smith (New York: Humanities Press, 1962), p. viii (emphasis is in the original).

3 Cf. Sandra B. Rosenthal and Patrick L. Burgeois, *Pragmatism and Phenomenology: A Philosophic Encounter* (Amsterdam: B. R. Grüner Publishing Co., 1980). Pioneer efforts in this direction were provided by the work of James M. Edie. See his "Introduction" to Pierre Thévenaz, *What is Phenomenology? and Other Essays* (Chicago: Quadrangle Books, 1962), pp. 13–36; James M. Edie, "Notes on the Philosophical Anthropology of William James," in *An Invitation to Phenomenology,* ed. James M. Edie (Chicago: Quadrangle Books, 1965), pp. 110–32; and Bruce Wilshire, *William James and Phenomenology* (Bloomington: Indiana University Press, 1968).

4 Cf. John Dewey, "Having an Experience," in *The Philosophy of John Dewey,* ed. John J. McDermott, vol. 2 (Chicago: University of Chicago Press, 1981), p. 555. Dewey writes here of the inchoate, of the "distractions," "dispersions," "extraneous interruption" and "inner lethargy" which dog all of our attendings.

5 Merleau-Ponty, *Phenomenology of Perception,* p. 203.

6 John E. Smith, "The Course of American Philosophy," in *Themes in American Philosophy: Purpose, Experience and Community* (New York: Harper Torchbooks, 1970), p. 135.

7 Cf. Arthur Bentley, "The Human Skin: Philosophy's Last Line of Defense," in *Inquiry into Inquiries* (Boston: Beacon Press, 1954), pp. 195–211.

8 Cf. Rollo May et al., *Existence* (New York: Basic Books, 1958), especially "The Case of Ellen West," pp. 237–364. Subsequent steps in a phenomenology of the body have been taken in *The Philosophy of the Body,* ed. Stuart Spicker (Chicago: Quadrangle Books, 1970), and in Richard M. Zaner, *The Context of Self: A Phenomenological Inquiry Using Medicine as a Clue* (Athens: Ohio University Press, 1981).

9 Oliver Sacks, *Awakenings* (New York: E. P. Dutton, 1983).

10 Ibid., p. 316.

11 Ibid., p. 328.

12 Cf. A. R. Luria, *The Man with a Shattered World* (New York: Basic Books, 1972).

13 Ibid., pp. 46–49.

14 William James, *The Varieties of Religious Experience* (New York: Longmans, Green and Co., 1902), pp. 298–99.

15 John Dewey, *Human Nature and Conduct,* vol. 14 (1983) of *The Middle Works* (Carbondale: Southern Illinois University Press, 1976–83), p. 195.

16 Merleau-Ponty, *Phenomenology of Perception,* p. xix (italics in the original).

17 For a discussion of James's radical empiricism, see Smith, *Themes,* pp. 26–41; and John J. McDermott, "Introduction," to James, *Essays in Radical Empiricism,* pp. xi–xlviii.

18 Cf. Nelson Goodman, *Ways of Worldmaking* (Indianapolis: Hackett Publishing Co., 1978). Acknowledging the influence of James, Goodman writes, "Our universe, so to

speak, consists of these ways rather than of a world or of worlds" (p. 3); "universes of worlds as well as worlds themselves may be built in many ways" (p. 5).

19 William James, *The Principles of Psychology,* vol. 2 (Cambridge: Harvard University Press, 1981), p. 961 (italics in the original).

20 Ibid., p. 959 (italics and emphasis in the original).

21 Michel Foucault, *The Order of Things* (New York: Pantheon Books, 1970), p. 9. Cf. the ironically perceptive critique of the deception of words in Michel Foucault, *This Is Not a Pipe* (Berkeley: University of California Press, 1982).

22 James, *Principles,* vol. 1, p. 273. See also William James, "The Stream of Thought," in *The Writings of William James,* ed. John J. McDermott (Chicago: University of Chicago Press, 1977), p. 70.

23 James, *Principles,* vol. 1, p. 274. See also James, *Writings of William James,* p. 70.

24 William James, *Talks to Teachers on Psychology* (Cambridge: Harvard University Press, 1983), p. 138. See also James, "On a Certain Blindness in Human Beings," in James, *Writings of William James,* p. 634.

25 Maurice Merleau-Ponty, *The Primacy of Perception,* ed. James M. Edie (Evanston: Northwestern University Press, 1964), pp. 100–108.

26 David Riesman et al., *The Lonely Crowd* (New Haven: Yale University Press, 1950).

27 For an exquisite instance of a symbiotic relationship, witness that of the jellyfish and the nudibranch in the Bay of Naples, as described by Lewis Thomas, *The Medusa and the Snail* (New York: Bantam Books, 1980), pp. 3–4:

> Sometimes there is such a mix-up about selfness that two creatures, each attracted by the molecular configuration of the other, incorporate the two selves to make a single organism. The best story I've ever heard about this is the tale told of the nudibranch and medusa living in the Bay of Naples. When first observed the nudibranch, a common sea slug, was found to have a tiny vestigial parasite, in the form of a jellyfish, permanently affixed to the ventral surface near the mouth. In curiosity to learn how the medusa got there, some marine biologists began searching the local waters for earlier developmental forms, and discovered something amazing. The attached parasite, although apparently so specialized as to have given up living for itself, can still produce offspring, for they are found in abundance at certain seasons of the year. They drift through the upper waters, grow up nicely and astonishingly, and finally become full-grown, handsome, normal jellyfish. Meanwhile, the snail produces snail larvae, and these too begin to grow normally, but not for long. While still extremely small, they become entrapped in the tentacles of the medusa and then engulfed within the umbrella-shaped body. At first glance, you'd believe the medusae are now the predators, paying back for earlier humiliations, and the snails the prey. But no. Soon the snails, undigested and insatiable, begin to eat, browsing away first at the radial canals, then the borders of the rim, finally the tentacles, until the jellyfish becomes reduced in substance by being eaten while the snail grows correspondingly in size. At the end, the arrangement is back to the first scene, with a full-grown nudibranch basking, and nothing left of the jellyfish except the round, successfully edited parasite, safely affixed to the skin near the mouth.

28 John Dewey, "The Need of a Theory of Experience," in *The Philosophy of John Dewey,* vol. 2, p. 508 (italics in the original).

29 Cf. R. E. L. Masters and Jean Houston, *The Varieties of Psychedelic Experience* (New York: Dell Publishing Co., 1966).

30 Franz Kafka, *Letter to His Father* (New York: Schocken Books, 1953), p. 17.
31 Cf. Martin Heidegger, *What Is a Thing?* (South Bend: Gateway Editions, 1967), pp. 82–85.

10 THE INEVITABILITY OF OUR OWN DEATH

1 Cf. David Cole Gordon, *Overcoming the Fear of Death* (Baltimore: Penguin Books, 1972), p. 13.
2 Susan Sontag, *Illness as Metaphor* (New York: Vintage Books, 1979), p. 3.
3 For a profound analysis of capital punishment, see Albert Camus, "Reflections on the Guillotine," in *Resistance, Rebellion and Death* (New York: Alfred Knopf, 1961), pp. 175–234.
4 Anonymous, *Last Letters From Stalingrad* (New York: The New American Library, 1961), p. 125. Cf. Edith Wyschogrod, "Sport, Death and the Elemental," in *The Phenomenon of Death* (New York: Harper and Row, 1973), pp. 166–97. She writes, "To engage in sport as a mode of being in the elemental is not merely to *want* to die, but to be *willing* to do so" (p. 197).
5 Cf. A. Alvarez, *The Savage God: A Study of Suicide* (New York: Random House, 1972).
6 Albert Camus, *The Myth of Sisyphus* (New York: Alfred Knopf, 1955), p. 3.
7 Sören Kierkegaard, cited in Alvarez, *Savage God*, p. 114.
8 Camus, *Myth of Sisyphus*, p. 40.
9 William James, "Diary," in *The Writings of William James*, ed. John J. McDermott (Chicago: University of Chicago Press, 1977), p. 8.
10 Sigmund Freud, *Civilization and Its Discontents* (London: Hogarth Press, 1953): "If the evolution of civilization has such a far-reaching similarity with the development of an individual, and if the same methods are employed in both, would not the diagnosis be justified that many systems of civilization—or epochs of it—possibly even the whole of humanity—have become 'neurotic' under the pressure of the civilizing trends?" (p. 141).
11 Norman O. Brown, *Life Against Death* (Middletown: Wesleyan University Press, 1970), p. 105.
12 Brown himself, subsequently, is to disappoint us in this regard, opting for a doctrine of the cycle, which effectively removes the novelty from time passing. Cf. Norman O. Brown, *Closing Time* (New York: Random House, 1973).
13 Cf. Norman O. Brown, *Love's Body* (New York: Vintage Books, 1968): "The world annihilated, the destruction of illusion. The world is the veil we spin to hide the void. The destruction of what never existed. The day breaks, and the shadows flee away" (p. 261).
14 Cf. Jacques Merleau-Ponty and Bruno Morando, *The Rebirth of Cosmology* (New York: Alfred Knopf, 1976), pp. 275–76.
15 Strictly speaking, we should no longer speak of "world," "cosmos," or "universe," all of which connote an order, a singularity, which is not verified by contemporary cosmology. Perhaps we should adopt the position of William James and speak of a pluralistic universe. Cf. William James, *A Pluralistic Universe* (Cambridge: Harvard University Press, 1977).
16 Cf. John Dewey, "The Need of a Theory of Experience," in *The Philosophy of John Dewey*, ed. John J. McDermott, vol. 2 (Chicago: University of Chicago Press, 1981): "Everything depends upon the *quality* of the experience which is had" (p. 508).
17 William James, *Essays in Radical Empiricism* (Cambridge: Harvard University Press, 1976), p. 42. Cf. John J. McDermott, "Life Is in the Transitions," in *The Culture of Experience: Philosophical Essays in the American Grain* (New York: New York University Press, 1976), pp. 99–117.

18 John Dewey, *Democracy and Education*, vol. 9 (1980) of *The Middle Works* (Carbondale: Southern Illinois University Press, 1976–83), p. 56. See also John Dewey, "Education as Growth," in *Philosophy of John Dewey*, vol. 2, p. 492.
19 Dewey, *Democracy and Education*, p. 47.
20 Marcus Aurelius, *Meditations* (Chicago: Henry Regnery Co., 1956), pp. 18–19.
21 John Dewey, "Criteria of Experience," in *Philosophy of John Dewey*, vol. 2, p. 523.
22 Rainer Maria Rilke, "The Ninth Elegy," *Duino Elegies* (New York: W. W. Norton and Co., 1939), p. 73.

11   DO NOT BEQUEATH A SHAMBLE

1 Apocalyptic literature, which portends our impending disaster, is not pleasant to read. Still, if only half of the predictions are correct, our children and their children face an enormously hazardous future. See, e.g., Gordon Rattray Taylor, *The Doomsday Book* (Greenwich: Fawcett Publications, 1970); Edward Goldsmith, *Blueprint for Survival* (New York: New American Library, 1972); Donella H. Meadows et al., *The Limits of Growth* (New York: Universe Books, 1972); Raymond F. Dasman, *Planet in Peril* (New York: Meridian Books, 1972); Lester Brown, *The Twenty-Ninth Day* (New York: W. W. Norton, 1978); Paul Colinvaux, *Why Big Fierce Animals Are Rare and Other Essays* (Princeton: Princeton University Press, 1979); Wendell Berry, *The Unsettling of America, Culture and Agriculture* (New York: Avon Books, 1977); Mary Douglas and Aaron Wildavsky, *Risk and Culture* (Berkeley: University of California Press, 1982); Robert Jay Lifton and Richard Falk, *Indefensible Weapons* (New York: Basic Books, 1982); Tom Regan, ed., *Earthbound: New Introductory Essays in Environmental Ethics* (New York: Random House, 1984). For the position that all will go well, cf. Julian L. Simon and Herman Kahn, *The Resourceful Earth: A Response to "Global 2000"* (Oxford: Basil Blackwell, 1984).
2 John Dewey, *Experience and Nature*, vol. 1 (1981) of *The Later Works* (Carbondale: Southern Illinois University Press, 1981–), p. 43.
3 Rita Kramer, *Maria Montessori, A Biography* (New York: G. P. Putnam's Sons, 1976), pp. 107–57.
4 Cf. E. M. Standing, *Maria Montessori, Her Life and Work* (New York: New American Library, 1962), p. 61; and ibid., pp. 155–57.
5 Cf. John J. McDermott, "Introduction" to Maria Montessori, *Spontaneous Activity in Education* (New York: Schocken Books, 1977 [1965]), pp. xvi–xxiv, for a discussion of the prepared environment in the light of the culturally disadvantaged child.
6 The following passage, with editorial changes, is taken from ibid., p. xii.
7 Montessori, *Spontaneous Activity in Education*, p. 207.
8 Ibid., p. 203.
9 Maria Montessori, *The Montessori Method* (New York: Schocken Books, 1964 [1912]), pp. 212–14.

12   CULTURAL LITERACY

1 James B. Conant, *The Education of American Teachers* (New York: McGraw-Hill, 1963). Although published over twenty years ago, this report retains its significance. The situation is now worse and the reforms suggested have not been implemented. Of the twenty-six recommendations, the most telling is that fledgling teachers be certified after having successfully majored and graduated in a field or discipline in the arts, sciences, and social sciences and having completed successful student teaching. This procedure enables

some prospective teachers to bypass the usual "college of education" curriculum and offers a new source of competent teachers in our schools. Learning how to teach, after all, is significant in direct proportion to whether one knows something worth teaching others. For a recent statement on this issue, see David Stewart, "Schools of Teacher Education Should be Eliminated," *English Journal* 71, no. 8 (December 1982): 10, 12.

2 Unfortunately, it is necessary to clarify the term humanistic. In my use, it has no relation to the contemporary conflict between the Moral Majority and its alleged opponent, secular humanism. To the contrary, humanistic education appeals to the entire history of human activity, including religion and religious experience, as reflectively undergone and aesthetically articulated. Equally germane to this effort are the thoughts of Cicero and those of St. Teresa, the revelation scriptures, and Goethe's *Faust*.

3 The reeducation of teachers so that the humanities become the matrix on and through which education takes place is precisely the ongoing legacy of the work of the National Humanities Faculty, which arranges for outstanding university scholar-teachers to visit secondary schools and assist in developing new approaches to the teaching of the humanities. It is extraordinary to witness the impact of a visiting N.H.F. member, when he or she provides insight as to how to galvanize and enliven an existing curriculum.

4 Cf. William James, *Essays in Radical Empiricism* (Cambridge: Harvard University Press, 1976), p. 42. See also "A World of Pure Experience," in *The Writings of William James,* ed. John J. McDermott (Chicago: University of Chicago Press, 1977): "Experience itself, taken at large, can grow by its edges. That one moment of it proliferates into the next by transitions which, whether conjunctive or disjunctive, continue the experiential tissue, cannot, I contend, be denied" (p. 212). Cited earlier, on pp. 37, 141.

5 Cf. *Evaluation of Liver Function in Clinical Practice* (Indianapolis: Lilly Research Foundation, 1965).

6 Another alternative is to have the students rewrite an extant play in their own words, or, again, to put an extant biography or short story into dramatic form. The latter was done some years ago at Huntington High School in New York. The students rewrote and dramatized Vonnegut's "Harrison Bergeron," with electrifying success.

13   GLASS WITHOUT FEET

1 James Marston Fitch, "Experiential Basis for Aesthetic Decision," in *Environmental Psychology,* ed. Harold M. Proshansky et al. (New York: Holt, Rinehart and Winston, 1970), p. 79.

2 From countless sources, to experience the child experiencing the world, I suggest Henry Roth, *Call It Sleep* (New York: Avon Books, 1962 [1934]).

3 Earlier versions of this relationship can be found in John J. McDermott, "Nature Nostalgia and the City: An American Dilemma," and "Space, Time and Touch: Philosophical Dimensions of Urban Consciousness," in *The Culture of Experience: Philosophical Essays in the American Grain* (New York: New York University Press, 1976), pp. 179–231.

4 Samuel Sewall, "Phaenomena," in *The Puritans,* ed. Perry Miller and Thomas H. Johnson, vol. 1 (New York: Harper Torchbooks, 1963), p. 377.

5 Granting statehood to Hawaii, therefore, ranks as one of our most saving decisions, for Hawaii ties us back to the beginning, to the Orient, and enables us to rejoin the new hegira of East to West, just at the time when the original journey, begun more than one thousand years ago, has come to an end.

6 Ralph Waldo Emerson, "Education," in *Works,* vol. 10 (Boston: Houghton Mifflin, 1903–1904), p. 132.

7 Cf. *The Journals of Ralph Waldo Emerson*, vol. 9 (Boston: Houghton Mifflin, 1909–1914), pp. 277–78. For fuller treatment of this theme, see chap. 2, p. oo.

8 I am aware that beginning with the Astrodome in Houston, and continuing on with the Silverdome and the Kingdome, baseball is now frequently played indoors. Despite customer convenience this is blasphemous and should be stopped. It is as if an Indian rain dance were held inside a wigwam. After all, is not being "rained out" the stuff of life?

9 The absence of personscape in the new urban architecture is depressingly obvious in a recent article by Bob Schwaller, "Pillars, Pedestals and Porticoes," *Texas Business*, November 1983, pp. 57–66. Apparently money and the size of buildings are the dominant theme. A second article, by Michael McCullar, "Scanning the Skylines, Citing the Singular," pp. 68–73, discusses monumentality and the turf of architects. Speaking of the new Southwest Center building in Houston, McCullar writes that it "will reaffirm the apparent fact that because of land values, human egos and an almost primal need for man to be awestruck by his architecture—big buildings are getting more monumental all the time." This is macho, male chauvinist America at its worst. Cities are for people and not for the aggrandizement of architectural egos. We do not live in the sky. We live on the ground, where we walk seeking to be at home.

14   ISOLATION AS STARVATION

1 The Random House Dictionary (unabridged), Webster's International (unabridged), and the multivolume Oxford English Dictionary all stress the meaning of "handicapped" as a penalty to the superior for the purpose of equalization. A secondary meaning is given as an emotional or physical defect.

2 Cited in Alan Abeson and Jeffrey Zettel, "The End of the Quiet Revolution: The Education for All Handicapped Children Act of 1975," *Exceptional Children*, October 1977, pp. 115–28.

3 Frederick Weintraub, "Editorial Comment," ibid., p. 114.

4 Cf. Raymond S. Nickerson, "Human Factors and the Handicapped," *Human Factors* 20, no. 3 (June 1978): 259–72.

5 John Dewey, *Experience and Nature*, vol. 1 (1981) of *The Later Works* (Carbondale: Southern Illinois University Press, 1981–), p. 43. For a more complete text, see chap. 11, pp. 172–73.

6 Ibid., p. 51.

7 Ibid., pp. 51–52.

8 Ibid., p. 52.

9 John Dewey, "The Practical Character of Reality," in *The Philosophy of John Dewey*, ed. John J. McDermott, vol. 1 (Chicago: University of Chicago Press, 1981), p. 222.

10 Ibid., p. 221.

11 John Dewey, *The Quest for Certainty*, vol. 4 (1984) of *The Later Works*, p. 6. The chapter in question is entitled, appropriately, "Escape from Peril."

12 Ibid., p. 14. Still, Dewey's aspiration is for "shared experience" which "is the greatest of human goods" (*Experience and Nature*, p. 157).

13 John Dewey, *Art as Experience* (New York: G. P. Putnam's Sons, 1934), p. 18.

14 Ibid., p. 14.

15 John Dewey, *Reconstruction in Philosophy*, vol. 12 (1982) of *The Middle Works* (Carbondale: Southern Illinois University Press, 1976–1983), p. 134.

16 John Dewey, *My Pedagogic Creed*, vol. 5 (1972) of *The Early Works* (Carbondale: Southern Illinois University Press, 1969–1972), p. 87.

17 John Dewey, "Science and Society," in *Philosophy of John Dewey*, vol. 2, p. 397.

18 John Dewey, *Democracy and Education*, vol. 9 (1980) of *The Middle Works*, p. 56.
19 John Dewey, *Experience and Education* (New York: Macmillan Co., 1938), p. 16.
20 John Dewey, *The Need for a Recovery of Philosophy*, vol. 10 (1980) of *The Middle Works*, p. 6.
21 Dewey, *Democracy and Education*, p. 146.
22 Ibid., p. 151.
23 Nancy Rubin, "Carnegie Council Raised Storms—and Some Dust," *New York Times*, March 2, 1980, sect. 4, p. E9.
24 John Dewey, *The School and Society*, vol. 1 (1976) of *The Middle Works*, p. 5.
25 John Dewey, *Liberalism and Social Action* (New York: G. P. Putnam's Sons, 1935), p. 61.
26 John Dewey, "Philosophies of Freedom," in *Philosophy and Civilization* (New York: Minton, Balch and Co., 1931), p. 281.
27 John Dewey, "Creative Democracy—The Task Before Us," in *Classic American Philosophers*, ed. Max Fisch (New York: Appleton-Century-Crofts, 1951), p. 393. Cf. Dewey's perceptive remark in a similar vein, as found in *Democracy and Education*: "Only gradually and with a widening of the area of vision through a growth of social sympathies does thinking develop to include what lies beyond our *direct* interests: a fact of great significance for education" (p. 155).
28 Dewey, *Experience and Nature*, pp. 67–68. See also Dewey, "Existence as Precarious and Stable," *Philosophy of John Dewey*, p. 300.

APPENDIX

1 Ralph Waldo Emerson, "Nature," in *The Complete Works of Ralph Waldo Emerson*, vol. 1 (Boston: Houghton Mifflin, 1903–1904), p. 3. For a fuller citation, see above, chap. 2, p. 31.
2 Cf. Philip P. Wiener, *Evolution and the Founders of Pragmatism* (Cambridge: Harvard University Press, 1949), p. v. For a detailed consideration of this period, see Ralph Barton Perry, *The Thought and Character of William James*, 2 vols. (Boston: Little, Brown and Co., 1935).
3 For a discussion of the major American philosophers after the classical period, see Andrew J. Reck, *Recent American Philosophy* (New York: Pantheon Books, 1964) and *The New American Philosophers* (Baton Rouge: Louisiana State University Press, 1968).
4 For a brilliant, provocative, and contentious evaluation of the central importance of the Harvard philosophy department during this period, see Bruce Kuklick, *The Rise of American Philosophy—Cambridge, Massachusetts, 1860–1930* (New Haven: Yale University Press, 1977).
5 The fascinating story of how this Peirce project came to be is retold in later interviews with Richard Bernstein, given by Hartshorne and Weiss. See "Recollections of Editing the Peirce Papers," *Transactions of the Charles S. Peirce Society* 6 (1970): 149–88 (ed. Richard Bernstein).

INDEX OF NAMES